Seeing Historic Alabama

Fifteen Guided Tours

NEW EDITION

Virginia Van der Veer Hamilton

&

Jacqueline A. Matte

**The University
of Alabama Press**

Tuscaloosa and London

Copyright © 1996

The University of Alabama Press

Tuscaloosa, Alabama 35487-0380

All rights reserved

Manufactured in the United States of America

Cover and interior designed by

Erin Toppin Bradley

∞

The paper on which this book is printed
meets the minimum requirements of
American National Standard for Information
Science-Permanence of Paper for
Printed Library Materials, ANSI Z39.48-1984.

Library of Congress
Cataloging-in-Publication Data

Hamilton, Virginia Van der Veer.
Matte, Jacqueline A.
Seeing Historic Alabama : fifteen guided tours /
Virginia Van der Veer Hamilton
& Jacqueline A. Matte. — Rev. ed.
        p.   cm.
Includes index.
ISBN 0-8173-0790-7 (pbk. : alk. paper)
1. Historic sites—Alabama—Guidebooks.
2. Historical museums—Alabama—Guidebooks.
3. Alabama—Tours.
I. Matte, Jacqueline Anderson.
II. Title.
F327.H35   1996
917.6104'63—dc20   95-50431

British Library
Cataloguing-in-Publication Data available

On Frontispiece
Edmund Pettus Bridge, Selma

On p. xii
Exhibit at Pike Pioneer Museum, Troy

On Front Cover
CLOCKWISE FROM TOP LEFT

Civil Rights Memorial, Montgomery
*(Courtesy of Alabama Bureau
of Tourism and Travel)*

Black Belt Slave Cabin
(Photograph by Lowell S. Hamilton)

U.S. Space and Rocket Center
*(Courtesy of Alabama Bureau
of Toursim and Travel)*

Kirkwood, Eutaw
*(Courtesy of Alabama Bureau
of Tourism and Travel)*

Contents

Preface

In my twenty-three years of teaching Alabama History to ninth grade students, one of the most useful supplemental books was the first edition of *Seeing Historic Alabama: Fifteen Guided Tours.* I used it for student projects to teach the geography, history, and economics of Alabama. Many of these projects won first place in state competitions. As the years passed, my students collected new materials as additional historic sites were identified and opened for the public. These materials collected from all the counties in the state are filed in our school library for future generations to use. Students worked together cooperatively; they were assigned such tasks as writing letters to chambers of commerce or county seats, making maps, creating budgets for tour expenses, designing travel brochures describing historical significance of sites, and producing videotaped marketing presentations.

This book is such a wonderful teaching tool as well as a sight-seeing guide for families and visitors that, when the opportunity arose for me to help produce an updated second edition, I was eager to do so. My major contribution has been to identify new sites added to the historical scene in Alabama since 1979. These include museums and memorials to major civil rights events, as well as sites added by lay historians to the National Register. Among the new sites included in this edition are: in Birmingham, The Civil Rights Institute, the Sixteenth Street Baptist Church, and Kelly Ingram Park; in Montgomery, the famed Civil Rights Memorial Fountain designed by Maya Lin, the nationally known architect of the Vietnam Wall in Washington, D.C.; in Selma, museums to the famous 1965 voting rights march. Among other outstanding sites are: in Birmingham, the enlarged Birmingham Museum of Art; in Montgomery, the renovated Alabama State Capitol, Alabama Shakespeare Festival, the new Montgomery Museum of Art, and the expanded Hull Street Historic District; in west Alabama, the Tom Bevill Visitor Center for the Tennessee-Tombigbee Waterway; and in Huntsville, the expanded Constitution Hall Historic District. Because of the cooperation of local historians and photographers in the state of Alabama, ninety-six new photographs have been added to supplement the original illustrations. It is our hope, that well into the twenty-first century, this second edition will be useful to residents of Alabama, teachers, students, and visitors from all over the world.

I want to thank my students for their enthusiasm and interest in the history of Alabama; the state, county, and city employees who answered

letters of inquiry; the Mountain Brook
Junior High School librarian, Jeannie
Ennis Harrison, for storing our materials; the librarians at Emmet O'Neal
Library and the Birmingham Public
Library-Archives; and librarians all
over the state who helped students
with research. I especially thank my
husband, Jack, and my children, Mike,
Jim, Frank, and Kathy, in their early
years for listening to my stories of
the history of Alabama while we traveled
around the state.

Jacqueline Anderson Matte

Preface to the 1982 Edition

Traditionally we begin our study of history with the printed word, turning to biography, textbook, historical novel, or scholarly monograph to illumine the past. As our society becomes ever more visually oriented, history books blossom with illustrations and television brings historical dramas into our living rooms.

But also we seek to *sense* history by standing in the presence of its remains. Thus we can measure the physical impact of these relics, take note of their surroundings, and feel the faint presence of those who long ago inhabited these places. Personal encounter impresses the site indelibly upon the mind's eye. We have seen it for ourselves, not filtered through a camera lens. We have experienced it directly without the intervention of historian, biographer, scriptwriter, or novelist. (Ideally, we should rush to the library after such an encounter, eager for the background and insight to interpret what we have seen.)

Generations of Americans, guidebooks in hand, have toured the obligatory shrines of Eastern and Western civilization. American pilgrims by the thousands have trooped to sites hallowed by association with the founding and great epochs of this nation. Yet, oddly enough, most such travelers do not set forth with ardor to experience historic sites within a few miles of their homes.

Why does enthusiasm flag when it comes to historic shrines of one's state, community, and neighborhood? Perhaps because of the human preference for exotic and faraway places above those that seem more commonplace because they are nearby. Perhaps due to a feeling that more significant events in human history took place in older lands. But also, I suspect, because there are few guidebooks to the historic sites of individual American states.

On an automobile trip through England, my husband and I chose out of hundreds of guidebooks the one that led us mile by mile, sometimes inch by inch, through the historic sites of a country roughly the size of Alabama. Yet when I began to prepare a bicentennial history of this state and two Alabama history textbooks, I could find no such satisfactory tool to direct me to sites that would give me a sense of Alabama's past.

I might never have stood before the lonely grave of William Weatherford, the famed "Red Eagle" of the war between Americans and Creeks in 1813–14, had it not been for a chance encounter with a highway department worker who knew every side road in Baldwin County. I might never have found the only covered bridge in Alabama that still retains its original wooden pegs without the help of a woman who wheeled her truck down a dirt road in Lee County and rumbled straight through Salem-Shotwell Covered Bridge, causing it to tremble on its foundations. I might have given up the search for the most perfectly preserved of all the South's old blast furnaces except for the assurance of a toothless man in a service station that if I would keep bearing to the right down a network of Cherokee County's unpaved roads I would come eventually upon Cornwall Furnace.

Alabamians and visitors to this state have no difficulty finding such an obvious site as the state capitol. But how will they know to knock on the downstairs door of nearby Dexter Avenue Baptist Church and ask to see the large folk art mural depicting the life of world-famous Dr. Martin Luther King, Jr., who was once its pastor?

How are they to discover other churches like St. John's-in-the-Prairies at Forkland, St. Andrew's at Gallion, and St. Luke's at Martin's Station, each a small gem of gothic Revival architecture? Or dignified, antebellum houses of worship like the Greek Revival First Baptist and First Presbyterian churches in the hamlet of Newbern? Or simple frame churches like Little Sandy Baptist near Tuscaloosa, Carthage Presbyterian at Moundville, and the old Methodist church at Daphne? Without a guidebook, they are not likely to stumble across the old log churches like Pine Torch in

Bankhead National Forest, Clay Bank near Ozark, Shoal Creek near Edwardsville, or the old Methodist church in McIntosh.

Gaineswood at Demopolis, often compared in originality with Thomas Jefferson's Monticello, is a widely publicized state museum. But other unusual antebellum mansions, such as Faith Manor in Talladega County, with its combination of Georgian and Carolina seaboard influences, and Goode Hall near the Tennessee River, with its one-story wings and late Georgian detail, lie hidden along Alabama's byways.

Tannehill Historical State Park and Pike Pioneer Museum, each with large collections of folk structures and possessions, are generally known. But to see a two-story single-pen log house, one must find the Daniel Murphree Cabin on a mountaintop near Oneonta. To visit Alabama's only surviving double dogtrot house, one must be directed to the Looney House in a quiet cove of St. Clair County.

Visitors to Selma can scarcely miss Pettus Bridge, scene of the historic voting rights march of 1965. But an engineer from Australia who wanted to study Blount County's wooden covered bridges found it necessary to wander up and down back roads to locate them for himself. Tuscumbia and Florence have made it easy to find the birthplaces of Helen Keller and W. C. Handy, but Ashland does not boast of being the boyhood home of Hugo L. Black and The University of Alabama School of Law makes no particular effort to draw visitors to a replica of Justice Black's study, with its original books and furnishings, hidden away in its law library.

Most Alabamians know that Eufaula, Huntsville, and Mobile are treasure troves of antebellum architecture. Yet few realize that Bridgeport, in the northeast corner of the state, and Troy, in the southeast, each contain neighborhoods of handsome Victorian houses still used as homes and as spruce as if they had been built yesterday.

To a greater degree than people in other sections of this country, Southerners are prone to dwell on their nineteenth-century history. But it is important to remind ourselves that another century, in which momentous events also occurred, is drawing to its close. Touring historic Alabama, we can see the marks of the twentieth century on our state: huge dams, lakes, and power plants in the Tennessee Valley, central Alabama, and along our eastern border; nuclear plants; artifacts of this century's wars displayed at Fort Rucker and Fort McClellan; landmarks of the civil rights movement that transformed race relations in the South; the Tennessee-Tombigbee Waterway and the ever-growing Alabama State Docks on Mobile Bay; the giant rockets at Huntsville that propelled the first human beings to the moon.

I probably would never have undertaken nor completed this task without the companionship and aid of my husband, Larry, who accompanied me virtually every mile of the way.

I am also grateful to dozens of anonymous individuals along the roadsides who gladly directed us, "Just go down here about a mile to the old Turner place and turn right on a dirt road and cross the bridge and bear left and . . ."

Virginia Van der Veer Hamilton
Emerita Professor of History
The University of Alabama at Birmingham

Using This Guide

This is a guide to touring historic Alabama by car. Thus the first and most important prerequisite for the user is a detailed state map such as the one prepared and distributed by the Alabama Bureau of Tourism and Travel in Montgomery. These maps may be obtained without charge at official Alabama welcome centers or by writing the Alabama Bureau of Tourism and Travel, 401 Adams Avenue, Montgomery, AL 36103-4309. Travelers are encouraged to do background reading in advance of each tour; therefore, lists of suggested readings are included herein. For a brief general interpretive history of the state, see Virginia Hamilton, *Alabama: A History* (New York: W. W. Norton, 1977).

With the exceptions of Tours 1 and 2 (Tennessee Valley), Tour 5 (Near Interstate 65), and Tour 14 (Baldwin County), all tours begin and end at major cities. Tours 3 (Appalachian Alabama), 4 (Blount County Covered Bridges), 6 (Birmingham), 7 (Northwest Alabama), 8 (West Central Alabama), and 9 (East Central Alabama) begin and end in Birmingham. Tours 10 (Montgomery), 11 (Western Black Belt), 12 (South Central Alabama), and 13 (Eufaula and the Wiregrass) begin and end in Montgomery. Tour 15 covers the area in and around Mobile. For flexibility, points at which travelers could switch from one tour to another are noted. The Tennessee Valley tours may be taken in a west-east direction, rather than east-west, simply by reversing the directions. Likewise, the Near Interstate 65 tour could just as easily be followed south to north. Of course travelers may shorten any tour by keeping to main routes and omitting sidetrips.

This guide lists numerous places open to the public, such as museums and house museums. But it is also a touring guide in the sense that it directs travelers along city streets, back roads, and to small hamlets for the pleasure of glimpsing antebellum homes of architectural interest, locating the deserted scene of a battle between Indians and whites, seeing some other site of historic interest, or simply to get a feel for the past. Many homes mentioned in this book are privately owned. Unless a house is specifically designated as open to the public, it should be considered a private residence. Tourists may enjoy seeing these sites from the roadside but should not seek admission or disturb the occupants.

When possible, hours and days when houses, museums, and other places are open are specified. The term "open daily" indicates that a site or place is open seven days a week. Some telephone numbers have been included for the convenience of those seeking further information. Readers should realize, however, that matters such as these are subject to change.

In smaller communities, the availability of comfortable motels has been noted but it is assumed that readers will know that accommodations are available in medium and larger cities. State parks located near historic sites also are noted. Those wishing further information on lodges or campgrounds should telephone 1-800-ALABAMA or write to the Alabama Bureau of Tourism and Travel, 401 Adams Avenue, Montgomery, AL 36103-4309.

Finally, this guide notes those sites and structures listed on the National Register of Historic Places, the official inventory of the historical, archaeological, and architectural resources of this nation maintained by the U.S. Department of the Interior. Alabama sites and structures designated by the secretary of the interior as National Historic Landmarks because they are deemed nationally significant in an architectural, archaeological, or historical sense also are noted. Because new listings frequently are added to these two registers, some sites mentioned in this guide may have attained National Register or National Historic Landmark status since publication of this book.

TOUR 1
Eastern Tennessee Valley

Bridgeport

Russell Cave

Scottsboro

Guntersville

Huntsville

Mooresville

Decatur

prehistoric campsite

Victorian homes

TVA steam plant and dam

TVA lakes

moon rockets

space vehicles

antebellum homes and village

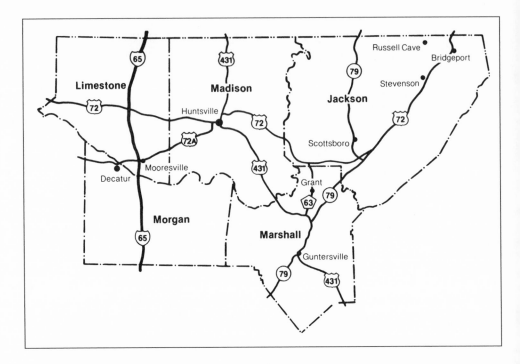

Tennessee Valley

Touring Alabama's Tennessee River valley, one can see evidence of human history ranging from 9,000 B.C. to the space age of today and tomorrow. In the northeast corner of Alabama, human beings sought shelter in caves and cave openings some 100 centuries ago. Russell Cave is the earliest site of human occupation thus far discovered in the southeastern United States. At the Alabama Space and Rocket Center in Huntsville, scientists tested the original space shuttle that successfully completed its maiden voyage into orbit and back to earth in April 1981.

Prior to 1930, the Tennessee Valley was one of Alabama's most impoverished regions as well as one of the nation's poverty areas. Today this is Alabama's fastest growing section in per capita wealth and industrialization. The catalyst has been the Tennessee Valley Authority.

Before TVA, the Tennessee River, which flows east to west across northern Alabama, was subject to floods that capsized vessels, washed away topsoil, and devastated entire towns. The western end of the river's course through Alabama was almost impassable due to a series of rapids where the Tennessee dropped 100 feet. These rapids, named for freshwater mussels, became known as Muscle Shoals. (The word *mussel* was spelled incorrectly.) During the Civil War, Union leaders found it impossible to send troop transports up the Tennessee to Chattanooga because of this great natural barrier. In the 1830s, a canal was built around the shoals, and later a railroad brought goods past this stretch of the river.

In 1933, President Franklin D. Roosevelt asked Congress to create the Tennessee Valley Authority to construct dams, control floods, improve navigation, generate electric power, produce fertilizer, and teach local residents to conserve soil and timber. Political leaders and engineers from many other nations have visited TVA and have used it as a model for developments in their own countries. Its great dams stopped flooding and created what are known as "the Great Lakes of the South." One dam, the Wilson Dam, created a lake where the treacherous shoals once impeded the flow of river traffic.

TVA also supplies electricity to millions of customers through municipal agencies and cooperatives in several states. By the late 1930s, many farm families were able to have refrigerators, electric stoves, electric lights, and radios for the first time. As use of electricity grew, TVA began building large coal-fired steam plants such as the Widow's Creek plant near Stevenson to augment its earlier hydroelectric plants. In 1966 TVA started to construct one of the world's largest nuclear plants, which now is in operation at **Brown's Ferry** near Decatur. The Brown's Ferry Energy Connection, the visitor's center, is open to the public Monday through Saturday, 10 a.m. to 4 p.m. Free admission. Telephone:

(205) 729-3300. Another TVA nuclear plant, Bellefonte, has been started. Its future will be determined according to need.

Electricity has brought many industries to the banks of the Tennessee, the most dramatic of which is the space industry. At Huntsville Dr. Wernher von Braun and fellow German-born scientists developed the early rockets that boosted America's first astronauts to the moon.

Commercial navigation on the Tennessee now extends 650 miles from Knoxville, Tennessee, across Alabama to the Ohio River. Principal products being shipped on the barges that can be seen on the river are coal and coke, grain, petroleum products, chemicals, forest products, iron and steel products, and stone, sand, and gravel. Approximately 36,000 pleasure boats also travel the Tennessee and its lakes in pursuit of bass, walleye, sauger, crappie, and catfish, pulling waterskiers, or just sightseeing.

Tours: TVA dams and locks at Guntersville, Town Creek, and Florence–Muscle Shoals are open to visitors. TVA public safety officers escort visitors on plant tours. Around 13 million persons tour the TVA system each year. No admission charge. TVA dams and steam plants (except nuclear plants) are open to the public during daylight hours seven days a week. Tour arrangements for groups interested in technical aspects of dam and

3

steam plant operation can be made by contacting the TVA Visitor Staff, Knoxville, TN 37902.

suggestions for background reading

Akens, David S. *Historical Origins of the George C. Marshall Space Flight Center.* Huntsville: National Aeronautics and Space Administration, 1960.

Betts, Edward Chambers. *Historic Huntsville, Alabama, 1804–1870.* Birmingham: Southern University Press, 1966.

Brantley, William H. *Three Capitals: A Book About the First Three Capitals of Alabama, St. Stephens, Huntsville, and Cahawba.* Boston: Merrymount Press, 1947.

Carter, Dan T. *Scottsboro: A Tragedy of the American South.* Baton Rouge: Louisiana State University Press, 1969; revised ed. 1979.

Clayton, Lawrence A., Vernon James Knight, Jr., and Edward C. Moore, eds. *The De Soto Chronicles: The Expedition of Hernando de Soto to North America in 1539–1543.* 2 vols. Tuscaloosa: University of Alabama Press, 1993.

Clopton, Virginia Clay. *A Belle of the Fifties.* New York: Doubleday Page, 1904.

Deal, Babs. *It's Always Three O'Clock.* New York: McKay, 1961. Reprint. Tuscaloosa: University of Alabama Press, 1990. (Fiction)

Deal, Borden. *Dunbar's Cove.* New York: Scribners, 1957. (Fiction)

Droze, Wilmon H. *High Dams and Slack Waters: TVA Rebuilds a River.* Baton Rouge: Louisiana State University Press, 1965.

Royall, Anne. *Letters from Alabama on Various Subjects.* Edited by Lucille Griffith. University: University of Alabama Press, 1969.

Walters, Helen B. *Wernher von Braun: Rocket Engineer.* New York: Macmillan, 1964.

Bridgeport

Start tour at Bridgeport on U.S. 72 in extreme northeast Alabama, or, reversing the order, start from Decatur on Alternate U.S. 72.

According to legend, the Spanish explorer Hernando de Soto and his expedition entered Alabama in June 1540 near present Bridgeport. At the Indian village of Chiaha on what some believe is now Burns Island in the Tennessee River, the expedition had rested for several weeks before entering Alabama. The Bridgeport Ferry is one of the few remaining in the state. Highway 72 between Bridgeport and Scottsboro traverses approximately the same route along which De Soto and his men passed over 450 years ago.

White settlers came to Bridgeport as early as 1814. During the Civil War, General William T. Sherman established a supply depot here preparatory to his "march to the sea." During the latter part of the nineteenth century, Bridgeport was the focus of a land boom led by eastern financiers headed by Henry Morgenthau. A $90,000 hotel and lavish houses, some erroneously said to have been designed by architect Stanford White, were built before the boom collapsed during the panic of 1893. The hotel was dismantled and rebuilt as a dormitory on the campus of the University of the South at Sewanee, Tennessee, but was destroyed by fire in 1918. **Battery Hill**, on a bluff overlooking the river, was used as a fortified location by both Confederate and Union troops. **Battery Hill Residential District** (c. 1890) contains ten elaborate frame houses built during the boom period, including **Denton Home** (c. 1893). This district also offers a splendid view of the Tennessee River. **Kilpatrick Row Residential District** (c. 1890), also built for the speculative boom, comprises seven two-story duplexes, a neighborhood of homes unique in Alabama.

From Bridgeport, follow signs to Russell Cave National Monument.

Entrance to Russell Cave

Russell Cave

Russell Cave has been scientifically dated as the oldest known site of human occupation in the southeastern United States. Archaeologists from the Smithsonian Institution and the National Geographic Society, using the radiocarbon method to determine the age of ancient charcoal found within the cave, determined that human beings first sought shelter in this cavern more than 9,000 years ago.

Nomadic bands of Indians, hunting in the vicinity, stumbled upon this cave long before the rise of the first true civilizations of Egypt and the Near East. They lived here only during the autumn and winter seasons when they needed shelter from the elements. Successive bands of hunters with their families took shelter in this cave until A.D. 1000. Archaeological digs have uncovered charcoal from their fires, the bones of animals they ate, the tools they fashioned from animal bones, spear and arrow points, broken pot-

tery, and several burials. Human beings moved from caves and open campsites to permanent villages along the Tennessee River about 1,000 years after the birth of Christ.

In addition to the cave itself, the Russell Cave National Monument includes a small but excellent museum depicting the life of these cave dwellers and displaying their artifacts. Demonstrations are presented on aspects of the life of the ancient Indians, including use of the *atlatl* (throwing stick), grinding of corn, cracking of walnuts, flaking of flint to prepare stone tools, cutting of leather thongs, and cooking by heat transfer.

Russell Cave, a National Historic Landmark operated by the National Park Service, is a must for all interested in the history of this region. Open daily 8 a.m. to 5 p.m. except Christmas Day. No admission charge.

At **Doran's Cove** near the entrance to Russell Cave are remains of buildings erected by Major James Doran, an early settler, including square-log barn, one-story stone house (c. 1815)

5

with sixteen-inch walls and rifle holes, and one-story log springhouse.

Return to Route 72. Head west toward Scottsboro.

On the outskirts of Stevenson, watch for a sign indicating Widow's Creek Steam Plant. For a close-up view of a TVA coal-fired steam plant, follow this road two miles. No visitor facilities.

Stevenson

The junction of two vital supply railroads to Chattanooga, Stevenson was occupied by Union troops in July 1862. Eastern redoubts built by these troops are located at the **Fort Harker site** one-half mile south of the Stevenson Depot. This site is on the National Register. A one-story log cabin, moved from Bennett's Cove in 1975, has been restored in Stevenson City Park for use by the Boy Scouts. **Stevenson Depot** and **Hotel** (c. 1872), on Main Street, also on the National Register and the **Depot Museum** bring back memories of the area's past with displays of Indian heritage, railroading history, Civil War artifacts and tools from early American farms. Open Monday through Saturday, 9 a.m. to 5 p.m. Free admission.

The downtown area of Main Street contains a number of Victorian-era commercial buildings and is on the National Register. Marking one end of the district is the **Rudder Home**, used during the Civil War as a field hospital. At the other end is the **Cowan Home**, once a Union Army field head-quarters. In summer 1863, Rosecrans plotted strategy for his Union Army from a nearby structure known as **The Little Brick**. This site, now in ruins, has also been named to the National Register. Since the early 1900s, Sanders Russell had a racetrack and stables here for training harness racers. Russell won more than 1,100 trotting horse races, including the Hambletonian when he was sixty-two years old. He is listed in the Alabama Sports Hall of Fame in the Birmingham-Jefferson Civic Center. Ask directions locally to Russell Pike and the harness race training track.

Proceeding south on U.S. 72, watch for TVA's Bellefonte Nuclear Plant, under construction on the left at Hollywood, and continue to Scottsboro.

Scottsboro

When Scottsboro became the seat of Jackson County in 1868, circuit court opened on the first Monday in March and the first Monday in September. Court days always drew large crowds from the county. Soon men began horse trading. As the custom grew, people began to come on the first Monday of every month to trade horses and mules. Among articles that have been traded on "First Monday" have been guns, fishing rods, sausage mills, pigs, crickets, plowstocks, horse collars, frying pans, axes, grindstones, sorghum syrup, goats, coins, arrowheads, old magazines and books, local arts and crafts, and plain junk. Traders come as early as 10 a.m. on Saturday to set up shops around the square. Wares are displayed in car trunks and trucks, on card tables and sidewalks. Anyone can swap or trade on "First Monday" or sell a dog or old and used articles, but no one can take a stock of goods and enter into direct competition with local merchants without a city license. "First Monday" is not a promotion of any kind; it is not scheduled, sponsored, planned, or organized. Perhaps this is the reason for its success.

Scottsboro/Jackson County Heritage Center, municipal living history museum and social center, housed in the Neoclassical Revival **Brown-Proctor House**, (c. 1880s) on the National Register, depicts 1860s Jackson County life. Open Tuesday through Friday, 1 to 4 p.m.; other times by appointment. Admission charged. Telephone (205) 259-2122.

Jackson County Courthouse (c. 1912) was the scene of the first trial of the "Scottsboro Boys" in 1931. Nine black youths were arrested at **Paint Rock**, charged with having raped two white women aboard a freight train. Eight of the nine (the ninth was thirteen years old) were quickly convicted and sentenced to death. The Alabama Supreme Court affirmed seven of the convictions but the United States Supreme Court overruled this verdict on the ground that the defendants had not been adequately represented by counsel. Tried and retried during the 1930s, the case attracted worldwide attention. During World War II the Alabama Pardon and Parole Board quietly began to parole the Scottsboro prisoners. One escaped to Michigan before he could be paroled. The last defendant was paroled in 1950.

Leaving Scottsboro, follow Alabama 79 and U.S. 431 south to Guntersville.

Guntersville

According to legend, the De Soto expedition passed near present Guntersville in 1540 following the Tennessee River westward. U.S. 431 south crosses Lake Guntersville, passing near a submerged site perhaps where the Indian village of Tali was located in the sixteenth century. Here De Soto replenished his supplies and abducted a number of Indians to serve as porters.

Cherokees lived in this vicinity until their expulsion from Alabama in the 1830s. In 1820 the Foreign Mission Board of the Presbyterian Church established the first school for Indians in this area. (This site is marked on Alabama 79 south of Guntersville.) **Creek Path**, an ancient trail leading north toward present Kentucky, Indiana, and Illinois, passed near several Indian villages in this vicinity. (This site is marked on U.S. 79 at Brown Creek south of Guntersville.) Indian burial mounds still exist on an island in Lake Guntersville and in Marshall County Park on a bluff overlooking Guntersville. Among the Cherokees sent west from this area in 1837 was the great-grandmother of Will Rogers, the famed American humorist. Rogers had always planned to visit Guntersville, but in 1935 he died in an airplane crash in Alaska before this long-planned visit could take place.

Originally known as Gunter's Landing for a Scotsman, John Gunter, who settled in this area a year after the American Revolution ended, Guntersville has been a river port for two centuries. The coming of steamboats in the early 1800s made this a boom town. The creation of the Tennessee Valley Authority in the 1930s transformed Guntersville from a small trading center into a thriving recreational and industrial city.

Guntersville Dam required five years to construct and employed a peak labor force of 3,500. As the reservoir began filling in 1939, it created a huge lake over stretches of the Tennessee River that previously had been as shallow as three feet during dry periods. Guntersville developed into the southernmost port on the new waterway. Its major commodity is midwestern grain that is barged in to serve the poultry and livestock industry of this region. Lake Guntersville, the largest body of water wholly within Alabama, contains 68,000 acres of water and almost 1,000 miles of shoreline.

Those interested in visiting **Guntersville Dam and Locks** should follow U.S. 431 north toward Huntsville, watching for a sign on the left about ten miles from Guntersville. This facility has a visitors' center and an observation deck from which visitors may view the process of lifting and lowering boats and barges like a giant elevator. No admission charge.

Guntersville Historic District (c. mid-nineteenth century) contains fourteen commercial and residential structures, including the oldest section of the town's business district. Lake Guntersville Aero, Inc. Replica Fighter Museum, at Guntersville Airport, houses the largest collection of replica flying machines from the World War I era. Admission charged. Open daily 9 a.m. to 4 p.m.; closed some holidays. Telephone (205) 582-4309.

Accommodations: Lake Guntersville State Park, offering spectacular vistas of Lake Guntersville, spreads from the top of Little Mountain to the lakeshore and contains campgrounds, cottages, and a lodge. A wildlife preserve, the park now has an eagle population that has become established. Telephone (205) 571-5440. Guntersville has comfortable motels.

Leaving Guntersville, take U.S. 431 north to Marshall County 63. Turn north and proceed five miles to Grant.

Grant

Offering a glimpse of Alabama's hills and coves, the picturesque drive along Marshall County 63 toward Grant leads to Kennamer's Cove, a favorite hiding place for north Alabamians who sided with the Union during the Civil War. Inhabitants of this valley below Gunter Mountain sympathized with these so-called mossbacks and did not betray their hiding place. Many hill people, descendants of soldiers who had fought in the American Revolution, were firm believers in the Union and fought for its survival.

To assist children whose parents scratched a bare living from infertile patches of soil in these hills, a remarkable school was founded in 1924. Named the **Kate Duncan Smith School for Mountain Children**, the institution was built in part by mountain people in their old barn-raising tradition. Still in operation, the school is funded and maintained by the Daughters of the American Revolution.

KDS School is the only high school in the nation owned and operated by the D.A.R. The site on Gunter Mountain was selected from twenty-seven communities that asked for a school when the D.A.R. announced plans to build its school in some mountainous section of Alabama populated with descendants of revolutionary war patriots and isolated from educational advantages. On the day this site was chosen, mountain men, women, and children, four abreast, lined the road leading to the crest of the mountain to welcome the D.A.R. committee. Volunteers built the first four-room unit from mountain stone. When the school had no funds to build a library in 1935, the mountain people built one of logs and handmade oak shingles, as their forefathers had built houses a century earlier.

KDS School, which started with two teachers, four rooms, and fewer than 100 students now has 38 buildings, a 240-acre campus, and more than 1,000 students. In addition to subjects also taught at public schools, the school emphasizes home economics, business education, and industrial skills. The D.A.R. operates the school in cooperation with Marshall County, which provides salaries for many of the teachers, transportation for students, and fuel. Visitors are welcome during school hours Monday through Friday.

Near Grant (inquire for directions locally) is **Cathedral Caverns Park**, featuring a cave with one of the largest known cave openings in the world. Primitive campgrounds are available in the park.

*Continue past KDS campus on Marshall County 63 to U.S. 72. Head west toward Huntsville. This route passes through **Paint Rock**, a hamlet that made national headlines in 1931 when the nine "Scottsboro Boys" were arrested here. (See Scottsboro.)*

Space Shuttle Orbiter Enterprise

Huntsville

While on an exploratory trip in 1805, John Hunt, from east Tennessee, came to the site of present-day Huntsville. Impressed by the beauty and fertility of this area, he built a log cabin near a big spring, cleared the wilderness, and planted crops. Others soon joined him.

Eventually this rich river valley attracted wealthier men like Leroy Pope of Georgia, who named the settlement Twickenham after the London suburb that was the home of his favorite English poet, Alexander Pope. But as the War of 1812 neared, anti-British feelings caused settlers to change the name of their town to Huntsville, honoring its original settler. (Tradition also holds that they did not like the name of Twickenham and had trouble spelling it.) Huntsville was chartered in 1811. During the Creek War, Andrew Jackson became so impressed with the potential of this area that he bought large tracts of land near here.

While Alabama's first capitol was being constructed at Cahaba, Huntsville served as temporary capital. In 1819, the state's first constitution was written here by a constitutional convention. The first state legislature met in Huntsville, and Alabama's first governor, William Wyatt Bibb, was inaugurated here. Although Huntsville residents hoped to make their town Alabama's permanent capital, they lost this prize because most Alabamians felt that Cahaba was more centrally located.

During the antebellum period, the Huntsville vicinity was an important center of cotton growing and textile manufacturing. A railroad was built to help transport these products to markets, but Union troops who captured Huntsville in 1862 severed the Memphis and Charleston Railroad, the South's only major east-west railroad.

From the time of Reconstruction until the end of World War II, Huntsville was a small, quiet southern city. But in 1950 this quiet town became one of the major centers of America's space program when Dr. Wernher von Braun, a German-born scientist, and members of his team were assigned to Redstone Arsenal. Von Braun and his associates developed the first Redstone rocket, launched at Cape Kennedy, Florida, in 1953. In 1958 the first United States satellite, Explorer I, was boosted into orbit around the earth by a Jupiter-C rocket developed at Redstone.

As Americans became excited about exploring outer space, a part of Redstone Arsenal was separated from the army and named the George C. Marshall Space Flight Center. The major accomplishment of the von Braun team was the huge Saturn V rocket that propelled the Apollo spacecraft to the moon in 1969. The Marshall Center developed the moon buggy in which astronauts explored the moon's surface, and also worked on the original space shuttle.

Accommodations: Monte Sano State Park, on Monte Sano Mountain above Huntsville, contains rustic cabins and primitive campsites. (205) 534-3757. Huntsville has comfortable motels.

Big Spring Park (below Courthouse Square in downtown Huntsville) contains the natural spring that first attracted settlers to this site. From this blowing spring, 24 million gallons of water flow each day. Near Big Spring was **Fearn Canal** (c. 1820), first navigable waterway from Huntsville to the Tennessee River. Barges carrying 50 passengers and up to 100 sacks of cotton, weighing about 300 pounds apiece, once plied this waterway.

Just above Big Spring is the **First National Bank Building** (c. 1836), now the First Alabama Bank, originally the Huntsville branch of the State Bank of Alabama. During the 1850s this structure, with an Ionic portico designed by the architect George Steele, was known as the "Marble Palace." In its back rooms were detention cells for slaves impounded for their masters' debts. Federal troops who occupied Huntsville during the Civil War spared this handsome building. It is the oldest building in Alabama in continuous use as a bank.

Constitution Hall Village, near the bank, commemorates the place and events of Alabama's 1819 constitutional convention. It includes reconstructions of **Constitution Hall**, a two-story frame structure in which Alabama's first constitution was written; the law office of Clement Comer Clay, former governor of Alabama (1835–37); and other structures depicting life in early Huntsville. Ninety-minute tours are conducted Monday through Saturday from 9 a.m.; last tour 4 p.m. Open March through December. Admission charge. Located one block south of the courthouse square at corner of Franklin Street and Gates Ave. Phone (205) 535-6565 or 1-800-678-1819.

Self-guided tours of **Twickenham and Old Town Historic districts** may be obtained at the Tourist Information Center located at the Von

11

Braun Civic Center downtown. Special tours are available through the Huntsville Heritage Tours, Inc. This area, located just east of Big Spring, is a museum of architecture spanning sixteen decades of American building styles, including Federal, Greek Revival, Italianate, and Gothic Revival, and it is on the National Register. Among its interesting structures are the totally remodeled **James G. Birney Law Office** (c. 1820), 307 Franklin Street, where Birney practiced law for five years before moving to Kentucky and becoming the Abolitionist party candidate for president in 1840; **Morgan-Neal Home**, 558 Franklin Street, birthplace of Confederate raider John Hunt Morgan; **Sparkman Home**, 619 Adams Street, home of Alabama's long-time Senator John J. Sparkman (1946–79); **Moore Home** (c. 1857), 603 Adams Street, where a reception was held in the rear courtyard in 1892 honoring Lily Flagg, world-champion butterfat-producing cow; **Pope-Patton Spragins Home** (c. 1814), 403 Echols Avenue, a Federal house with Classical Revival portico added later and designed by George Steele (Leroy Pope, who built this home and developed Huntsville, once owned Big Spring; therefore this house is still furnished free water by terms of Pope's deed of Big Spring to the City of Huntsville); **Bibb Home** (c. 1830), 300 Williams Street, Greek Revival brick home built by Thomas Bibb, second governor of

Constitution Hall Village, Huntsville

Alabama, copied from Belle Mina, the Bibbs' country home nearby; **Weeden House** (c. 1819), 302 Gates Avenue, on the National Register, Federal-style brick home of John McKinley, associate justice of the Supreme Court (1837–52) and lifelong home of nationally famous woman artist and poet (Maria) Howard Weeden (1847–1905), open 1 to 4 p.m. Tuesday through Sunday, March through December, admission charged. **First Presbyterian Church** (1860), 307 Gates Avenue, Gothic Revival mother church of this denomination in Alabama; and **Episcopal Church of the Nativity** (c. 1847), 212 Eustis Avenue, on the National Register, a Gothic Revival church said to have been spared from becoming a stable for horses of Union troops when soldiers read the inscription "Reverence My Sanctuary" engraved over the entrance.

Old Town Historic District (c. 1820–1930) is adjacent to Twickenham Historic District, bounded by Clinton and Walker avenues, Dement and Lincoln streets. This district comprises some 250 homes of varied architectural styles. Outstanding is the **Humphreys-Rodgers Home** (c. 1850), 502 Clinton Avenue, townhouse with two-story porch and Italianate bracketed cornices built by David C. Humphreys, a leader of the peace movement in Alabama near the end of the Civil War.

Other Huntsville homes on the National Register are **Hundley House** (c. 1899–1900), 401 Madison Avenue, one of the last surviving ornate Victorian homes near downtown Huntsville; **Oaklawn** (c. 1840s), 2709 Meridian Street North, Greek Revival with unusual projecting front wings; **Oak Place** (c. 1840), 808 Maysville Road, Greek Revival house built by the noted antebellum architect George Steele for his own use; and **Clemens House** (c. 1830s), 219 Clinton Avenue West, now a city utilities office but once the home of Jeremiah Clemens, an antisecessionist.

Also of interest are **Steamboat Gothic House** (c. 1890), Lowe Avenue and South Greene Street, Victorian with two-story "bridge" from the porch, now the clubhouse of the Madison County Federation of Women's Clubs, and **Wernher von Braun Home** (c. 1960), 1516 Big Cove Road, brick and redwood split-level former home of the director of NASA's Marshall Space Flight Center.

Huntsville Depot (c. 1860), 320 Church Street, on the National Register, is the oldest railroad passenger terminal in Alabama and has been restored by the city of Huntsville as a museum. Graffiti on the walls of its upper stories testify to the building's role as a prison for captured Confederate militia, a billet for Union troops, and a hospital for Civil War casualties. The depot was used as a passenger station by the Memphis and Charleston Railroad and later by the Southern Railway System until 1968, when Southern's Memphis-to-New York streamliner "The Tennessean," made its final run. Visitors may tour its baggage area, platform shed, and railroad shop, as well as board a passenger train and observe the mighty exhaust and whistle of its steam locomotive. An exciting audiovisual presentation covers the history of Huntsville, and exhibits focus on growth through transportation, commerce, and industry. Watch as the ingenuity of robotics brings to life a stationmaster, a telegrapher, and an engineer. Old-time steam excursions occasionally are offered by the North Alabama Railroad Club. For information, write P.O. Box 4163, Huntsville, AL 35802. Open Wednesday through Sunday; summer, Tuesday through Sunday; closed January and February. Admission. **Depot Trolley**

13

offers a 30-minute circular tour of downtown Huntsville. Depart from the depot museum and disembark at any of the downtown attractions while reboarding for free. Operates Wednesday through Sunday, 11 to 12:30 and 1:30 to 4:00; summer, Tuesday through Sunday, 10 to 12:30 and 1:30 to 4:30. Admission. Telephone (205) 539 – 1860.

Those interested in black history may wish to visit **Saint Bartley Primitive Baptist Church**, 3020 Belafonte Avenue Northwest, whose congregation, organized in 1820, was one of the earliest independent black congregations in Alabama.

Huntsville Museum of Art, adjacent to the Von Braun Civic Center at the corner of Clinton and Monroe streets, displays works by national, regional, and local artists in addition to frequent traveling exhibits and special programs. Included in its permanent collection are hand-colored lithographs of North American Indians and natural flora and fauna of the region. Open Tuesday through Sunday. No admission charge. For information, telephone (205) 535-4350.

On the campus of **The University of Alabama in Huntsville** is **Union Chapel** (c. 1840), a one-story frame church moved from Hazel Green and restored as an art museum. The university was founded in 1950, the same year that Dr. Wernher von Braun and a group of German-born scientists ar-

Burritt Museum

rived in Huntsville. Dr. von Braun, an early supporter of UAH, secured funding for its Research Institute, built in response to the aerospace and missile needs of the U.S. Army and NASA installations at Redstone Arsenal. In the early years, UAH's curriculum leaned heavily toward the sciences and engineering but, with the cutbacks in the space program at the onset of the 1970s, UAH began to develop a broader-based curriculum. It now offers baccalaureate degrees in thirty-nine disciplines, master's degrees in twenty-two areas, and doctorates in ten areas. More than 8,300 students are taught by some 294 full-time faculty.

Burritt Museum and Park (c. 1936), on Monte Sano Mountain, includes a two-story mansion willed to Huntsville for use as an art and history museum. On the grounds a group of pioneer log and frame cabins complete with period furnishings, a smokehouse, barn, blacksmith shop, and small church vividly depict the lifestyle of early Madison County settlers. On display in the museum are rocks and minerals, Confederate rel-

14

ics, archaeological artifacts, early medical instruments, dolls, and paintings by (Maria) Howard Weeden. The drive is worthwhile for the view of Huntsville alone. The main building is open Tuesday through Sunday, 1 to 5 p.m., March through December. Donation requested. Follow U.S. 431 east to top of mountain and follow signs. Telephone (205) 536-2882.

Madison County Nature Trail, six miles off U.S. 431/231 north, atop Green Mountain, is open daily. No admission charge. Historic structures along this two-mile trail include **Cambron Covered Bridge**, a pioneer homestead, and a log schoolroom. Picnic facilities are available. Follow signs leading to the trail from Haysland Square off U.S. 431/231 north.

Proceed three miles north of Huntsville on U.S. 431/231 to Normal.

Normal

Alabama Agricultural and Mechanical University (c. 1875), in Normal, was chartered as the Colored Normal School by the Alabama legislature in 1873. Its first president, William Hooper Councill, who served thirty-five years, opened this school with two teachers and sixty-one students. The school also was supported in its early years by the Peabody fund and federal funds. It has grown into one of Alabama's large public universities. Its **Domestic Science Building** (c. 1911),

Neoclassical in style, is on the National Register.

A marker designates the site of the first President's House, a stone structure originally known as Green Bottom Inn, which burned in 1930. It was located near a racetrack on which Andrew Jackson's horses frequently raced. The most famous horse to race at this track was Gray Gander, owned by Green Bottom's innkeeper and reputed to be the fastest horse of his day.

Leaving Normal, return to Alternate U.S. 72 west and follow to U.S. Space and Rocket Center.

U.S. Space and Rocket Center

The world's largest space and rocket museum is listed on the National Register of Historic Places because its exhibits include a **Saturn V space vehicle**, a sister ship to the Apollos that went to the moon. This "moon rocket" is displayed in Rocket Park. Lying on its side, it stretches the length of a football field. Visitors may view all major parts easily because the three

Apollo Saturn V moon rocket

15

Space and Rocket Center

rocket stages are separated. However, visitors can see only a few of the five million pieces that had to function in order to get man to the moon. The Saturn V was designed and developed at NASA's Marshall Space Flight Center for the purpose of sending man to the moon. Thirteen Saturn V vehicles were launched, all performing successfully. This type of rocket has boosted six moon flights, two unmanned test flights, and one flight that lifted the Skylab space station into earth orbit. The vehicle on display in Huntsville was used for dynamic testing and facility checkout. Officially it belongs to the National Air and Space Museum of the Smithsonian Institution in Washington, D.C., but has been loaned to the Space and Rocket Center for permanent display.

Also on the National Register is the historic **Redstone Test Stand**, which may be seen during a bus tour of nearby Marshall Space Flight Center. This stand was used during the 1950s for many of America's earliest rocket tests.

The Space and Rocket Center offers glimpses of future technological hardware and vehicles as well as many ex-

hibits associated with America's space program. On display are a **Mercury capsule**, one of the first manned ships to fly in space; a **quarantine van** used to house the first astronauts after their flight to the moon; and a **moon buggy** in which astronauts explored the surface of the moon. This is not a dusty museum but a "hands-on" place where visitors are encouraged to get involved in the excitement of space travel. Visitors may fire a rocket engine, ride a gyro chair, see their heartbeats on a TV-like screen, or handle fifty or more other space gadgets. On display is a representation of the space shuttle, which offers visitors a simulated trip into space. Visitors also may admire the sleek SR-71/A-12 Blackbird, which clocked in at Mach 3, and thrill to a sight and sound sensation in the spacedome Theater, where Omnimax movies are projected on a 67-foot "domed" screen for spectacular viewing and special effects.

The U.S. Space and Rocket Center/ NASA Visitor Center is open daily from 9 a.m. to 6 p.m., September through May, and 8 a.m. to 7 p.m., June through August. It is owned and operated by the state of Alabama. To qualify for group rates, visitors should make reservations for groups of 15 or more persons. Admission to the U.S. Space and Rocket Center includes a bus tour of NASA's nearby Marshall Space Flight Center. Telephone (205) 837-3400 or 1-800-63-SPACE.

George C. Marshall Space Flight Center

NASA bus tours are conducted daily except Christmas Day. These tours (less than two hours long) originate at the NASA Visitor Information Center on the ground of the U.S. Space and Rocket Center. Buses take visitors through the birthplace of America's space program. Here a team of scientists and engineers under the late Dr. Wernher von Braun developed the early rockets that launched America's first satellites and carried the first astronauts into space. The center's series of huge Saturn rockets later took man to the moon and hefted the giant space station Skylab, also developed at Marshall, into orbit around the earth. Here also was developed the Lunar Rover, a space buggy in which America's astronauts explored the moon surface.

The center was also involved in developing and testing the world's first true space ship, the space shuttle, which successfully completed its maiden voyage in 1981.

Visitors may view the test stand where the Huntsville team tested the Redstone rocket that carried Alan Shepard and Gus Grissom into space. Nearby is the towering stand used to test the giant Saturn V moon rocket. More recently, this stand housed the space shuttle when it was tested for its ability to function under the stressful conditions of an actual flight into space. Tours also visit the huge neutral buoyancy simulator where astronauts and engineers work in an environment closely resembling the weightlessness of space. Astronauts and scientists may be seen training for future space flights. Visitors also may climb aboard an engineering version of Skylab and visit a mockup of the space shuttle's flight deck. An overview of test and training parts for Space Station Freedom also highlights the NASA tour.

Continue west on Alternate U.S. 72; watch for Bedingfield Store at entrance to Mooresville one mile east of Interstate 65.

Mooresville

Incorporated in 1818, Mooresville has been remarkably unchanged by the passage of more than 150 years. Like Lowndesboro in the Black Belt, this is primarily a residential community that retains much of its nineteenth-century atmosphere. North Alabama's best preserved antebellum village, Mooresville is on the National

Stagecoach Inn at Mooresville (1930s photograph)

Register. To turn off busy Alternate U.S. 72 onto the lanes of Mooresville is to journey back in time. The best way to see Mooresville is on foot. Visitors may park at the general store and stroll through the whole community in a pleasant half-hour walk without encountering a single automobile. Houses are privately owned and not open to the public.

Go inside the **post office** (c. 1840) and look at the original wooden call boxes where today's residents still get their mail. Pause at the **Stagecoach Inn** (c. 1825), an early stop for stagecoaches. If the **Old Brick Church** (c. 1822) is open, look at the slave gallery and original lighting fixtures of this simple Federal building, which is listed on the National Register. The two-story frame **Church of Christ** (c. 1854) was one of the earliest churches of that denomination in Alabama. Union General James A. Garfield, who was to become twentieth president of the United States, preached in this church during the Civil War. At the corner of Piney and Market streets is the site of a tailoring shop (c. 1824) where Andrew Johnson, seventeenth president of the United States, worked briefly as an apprentice before returning to his own tailor shop in Tennessee. He resided in the nearby Sloss House, recently restored.

Directly across from Mooresville, Limestone County 71 leads to **Belle Mina** (c. 1826), the two-story brick mansion built by Alabama's second governor, Thomas Bibb (1820–21), now on the National Register. Privately owned, Belle Mina is not open to the public but may be seen from the road. Its six great Doric columns were constructed from poplar logs surrounded by brick and then plastered. Note that the span between the two center columns is wider than between the others, thus making for a more handsome entrance. Bricks for Belle Mina were made on this property by skilled slave brickmasons.

Near this mansion is **Woodside** (c. 1845), two-story frame mansion built by Governor Thomas Bibb for one of his daughters. Nearby **Belle Mina village** (c. late 1800s) contains ten structures.

Return to Alternate U.S. 72 and continue west to Decatur.

Decatur

Decatur was created in 1820 by an order of President James Monroe that a site near a great river be reserved for a town named for Commodore Stephen Decatur, naval hero of the War of 1812. The present site of Decatur, where a ferry owned by Dr. Henry Rhodes then crossed the Tennessee River, was chartered in 1826 for development by a land company. In 1834 Decatur became an important railroad center when Tuscumbia Railroad reached here, connecting the town with Tuscumbia and permitting shipments around the treacherous Muscle Shoals of the Tennessee River. During the Civil War, Decatur was a frequent target for troops of both sides. Only four of its major buildings remained when the war ended.

Decatur came to international attention during the 1930s when the trials of the "Scottsboro Boys," nine black youths accused of raping two white women aboard a freight train (see *Scottsboro*), were moved from Jackson County to Morgan County. When the jury demanded a death sentence in the trial of one of the defendants, a courageous judge, James Edwin Horton, Jr., granted a new trial because he was convinced that the evidence did not support this verdict. (Judge Horton's home may be seen in the small community of Greenbrier in Limestone County.) Eventually five of the black youths were convicted but charges were dropped against four others. The Alabama Pardon and Parole Board quietly began to parole the Scottsboro prisoners during World War II. In 1950 the last defendant was freed from Kilby Prison.

TVA affected Decatur as dramatically as it did Huntsville, Athens, and the Tri-Cities (Decatur, Florence, and Sheffield). No longer was Decatur threatened by dangerous flooding. New industries, attracted by low-cost electricity and river transportation and stimulated during the 1940s by World

Old Decatur Historic District

War II, brought jobs and prosperity to the town. In the 1960s Decatur began a face-lifting program called Operation New Decatur, which has resulted in a new city hall, courthouse, library, and other handsome public structures. The top floor of City Hall in the new Civic Center contains an observation deck.

Accommodations: There are comfortable motels in Decatur.

Old Decatur Historic District includes a number of residences that replaced those destroyed during the Civil War. It is one of the most intact Victorian-era neighborhoods in Alabama. These well-built frame structures, dating from 1870 to 1910, reflect the taste and lifestyle of the middle class in nineteenth-century Decatur. None of these houses is open to the public except at Christmas, but those wishing to observe a variety of architectural styles of this era are invited to write for or pick up a copy of the walking tour guide at the Decatur Chamber of Commerce, Walnut Street and Sixth Avenue.

Included in this tour is **Bank Street**

19

Bank Street

(c. 1880s and 1890s), dating to the era when Decatur was a rough, rowdy riverboat settlement. Holes supposedly caused by bullets during a shootout may be seen in the metal top of a structure on the corner of Bank and LaFayette streets. Narrow LaFayette Street between Bank and Railroad streets was known as Dead Man's Alley because of the number of men who died in fights outside the saloons that lined the street. Second stories were often homes of merchants not prosperous enough to own residences.

At the foot of Bank Street is the **State Bank Building** (c. 1833), built as the Tennessee Valley branch of the State Bank of Alabama. According to tradition, President Martin Van Buren attended the dedication of this building. As a climax to the dedication ceremonies, the builder of the bank freed the slaves who had labored so long to build this Classical Revival structure. This two-story brick building, on the National Register, was used as a private bank after the state bank folded about 1840. (Alabama abandoned its state banking system during the 1840s and 1850s.) Note that the bank has five solid stone Doric columns, making it necessary to have two entrances to balance its facade. The original vault is on the first floor. Another legend is that a tunnel led from the bank to the Tennessee River whereby money was transported to avoid robbers. The old bank, which served as a hospital during the Civil War, has been restored as a museum. Visitors may tour the bank, including the cashier's apartment on the second floor.

Hines-McEntire Home (c. 1824), 120 Sycamore Street, a two-story brick structure built by slaves, was used as headquarters for Union and Confederate officers during the Civil War. In this house General Albert Sidney Johnston is said to have planned the Confederate strategy that led to the Battle of Shiloh. Generals Ulysses S. Grant and William T. Sherman also are said to have conferred here on Union strategy following the fall of Vicksburg in 1863.

Albany Historic District in Decatur comprises eight blocks of approximately thirty Victorian and Neoclassical Revival houses constructed during the late nineteenth and early twentieth centuries by a land company.

State Bank Building

Also of interest in Decatur is the site of **Morgan County Courthouse**, where the famous Scottsboro case of the 1930s was tried, and **Quad Site**, east of Keller Memorial Bridge on the old north bank of the Tennessee River, where numerous artifacts of Indian inhabitation have been found, indicating that this was once a hunting ground for various tribes.

Wheeler National Wildlife Refuge, two miles south of Decatur on Alabama 67, contains a waterfowl observation building with a two-story viewing platform where visitors may observe such waterfowl as Canadian geese, mallards, wood ducks, and black ducks feeding in nearby ponds and fields of this 35,000-acre refuge. The refuge also features a wildlife interpretive center containing exhibits of wildlife, including waterfowl and bats. Open Tuesday through Sunday, 10 a.m. to 5 p.m. No admission charge. Telephone (205) 350-2028.

Constitution Hall Village, Huntsville (p. 11)

TOUR 2
Western Tennessee Valley

From Decatur

Wheeler

Courtland

Town Creek

Wheeler Dam

Florence

Natchez Trace

Sheffield

Muscle Shoals

Tuscumbia

Return to Decatur

antebellum homes

hydroelectric dams and locks

old trail

Helen Keller birthplace

museums

prehistoric Indian mound

*From Decatur, proceed west on Alternate
U.S. 72 toward Wheeler and Courtland.*

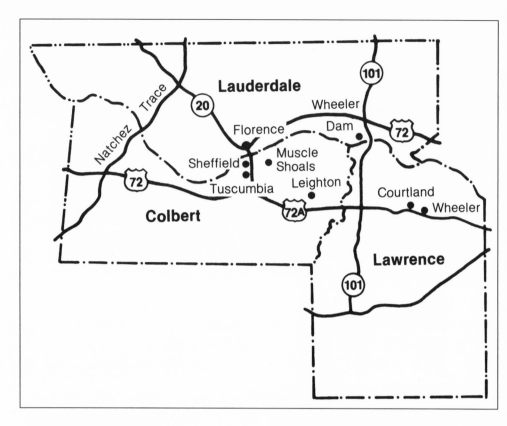

Wheeler

Joseph Wheeler Plantation (c. early 1800s), on the National Register, comprises a log dogtrot house (c. 1818), log and clapboard house (c. 1827), and frame house (c. 1875), all of which belonged to General Joseph Wheeler, Confederate cavalry leader, major-general in the Spanish-American War, and member of Congress. The frame house contains old portraits, documents, and uniforms worn by General Wheeler in the Civil and Spanish-American wars. Now owned by the Alabama Historic Commission, the site is staffed by a resident curator. Call in advance to make an appoint-

ment for a tour. Admission fee. For more information, telephone (205) 637-8513.

During the Civil War, Wheeler and his cavalrymen helped defend north Alabama from Union raiders. Robert E. Lee considered Wheeler and J. E. B. Stuart the South's outstanding cavalry leaders. Wheeler was noted for fast-moving, hard-hitting raids. He earned his nickname, "Fighting Joe," while taking part in some 200 engagements and 800 skirmishes of that war. Reputedly General Wheeler, while serving the United States in the Spanish-American War, forgot which war he was fighting and ordered his troops to "charge the damnyankees!"

While a member of Congress in 1898, Wheeler introduced a bill to permit Alabama Power Company to operate a hydroelectric power plant at Muscle Shoals. Because of his early interest in development of the Tennessee River, one of its major dams and a lake bear his name.

Leaving Wheeler, continue west on Alternate U.S. 72 toward Courtland and Town Creek.

suggestions
for background reading

Dyer, John P. *"Fightin' Joe" Wheeler*. Baton Rouge: Louisiana State University Press, 1941.

Handy, W. C. *Father of the Blues: An Autobiography*. New York: Macmillan Co., 1964.

Hickok, Lorena. *The Story of Helen Keller*. New York: Grosset and Dunlap, 1958.

Hubbard, Preston J. *Origins of the TVA: The Muscle Shoals Controversy, 1920–1931*. Nashville: Vanderbilt University Press, 1957.

Keller, Helen. *The Story of My Life*. New York: Doubleday and Co., 1954.

Lash, Joseph. *Helen and Teacher: The Story of Helen Keller and Anne Sullivan Macy*. Lawrence, N.Y.: Delacorte Press, 1980.

Winn, Joshua Nicholas, III. *Muscle Shoals Canal-Life with the Canalers*. Huntsville: Strode, 1979.

Courtland

Established in 1818, Courtland was once the site of a land office, where early Alabama land sales took place, as well as a federal court building. Many of its homes were destroyed during the Civil War.

Courtland Historic District includes **Simpson House** (c. 1820), a two-story frame house used as a Confederate hospital during the Civil War, and **Courtland Presbyterian Church** (c. 1858–60), an early brick Victorian structure.

At Town Creek, turn north on Alabama 101. Three miles north of Town Creek on Route 101, then right one mile on a gravel road, is **Saunders (Goode) Hall** (c. 1824), on the National Register, an unusual two-story brick mansion with one-story wings and late Georgian detail.

Continue on Alabama 101 to Wheeler Dam.

Wheeler Locks and Dam

Wheeler Dam (c. 1933–36), the second dam constructed by the Tennessee Valley Authority, was named for General Joseph Wheeler. Along with Wilson Dam and Pickwick Landing Dam, Wheeler Dam eliminated the mussel shoals that once hampered navigation on the Tennessee River.

Wheeler Dam powerhouse has a visitors' lobby open daily 9 a.m. to 5 p.m. Visitors are invited to view the dam from here and to take a guided tour of its eleven electric generating units, which have produced as much as 1.5 billion kilowatts of electricity a year, about as much as was used in 1933 in the entire region where TVA power is now sold. No admission fee.

Across the lake from the powerhouse are **Wheeler Locks**, through which barges and pleasure boats pass

Wheeler Dam

as they traverse the Tennessee River. The main lock, 600 feet long and 110 feet wide, requires only ten minutes to fill or empty its chamber of 25 million gallons capacity. This and an auxiliary lock raise or lower boats 45 feet. Visitors are invited to witness this interesting process from an observation deck that is open daily. No admission charge.

Accommodations: Continue on route 101 to U.S. 72. Turn east five miles to Wheeler State Park, which includes camping facilities and a large lodge. Florence also has a number of comfortable motels.

From Wheeler Dam, follow U.S. 72 west to Florence.

Florence

Florence was established in 1818 by a group of land developers, including General John Coffee, surveyor general of the Alabama Territory; John McKinley, later a Supreme Court justice; and James Jackson, a wealthy planter and horse breeder. General Andrew Jackson was among the first

to buy lots in Florence. Its name was chosen in honor of the Italian city, in recognition of the work of a young Italian surveyor who laid out the town.

With the help of Secretary of War John Calhoun and President James Monroe, citizens of Florence persuaded the federal government to assist in financing the construction of a canal around the tortuous shoals known as Muscle Shoals, where the river was impassable by barge. The canal, completed in 1836, proved inoperable after a year but eventually was supplanted by the Tuscumbia, Courtland and Decatur Railroad. Construction of Wilson Locks and Dam during World War I led to creation of Wilson Lake, which now covers the treacherous shoals.

Rocket passing through TVA lock

26

During the Civil War, Florence was invaded several times by Federal troops and was threatened by Union gunboats on the river. However, Florence was not as heavily damaged as Decatur, Athens, and Huntsville. At Gravelley Springs, fifteen miles west of Florence, Union general James H. Wilson started his 1865 raid into south Alabama that climaxed at Selma.

Promoters of navigation on the Tennessee River in this area renewed their efforts after the Civil War. Such citizen appeals led finally to construction of **Wilson Dam** (c. 1917–26), started during World War I to provide synthetic nitrogen for ammunition. Later Wilson Dam became the first hydro-electric facility of the Tennessee Valley Authority. Today agriculture and industry combine to create a climate of prosperity in Lauderdale County.

Florence was the home city of four Alabama governors, Hugh McVay (1837), Robert M. Patton (1865–67), Edward A. O'Neal (1882–86), and his son, Emmet O'Neal (1911–15). A fifth governor, George Houston (1874–78), was reared on his father's plantation about fifteen miles west of Florence. Another famous son of Florence was the black composer W. C. Handy, internationally known as "the father of the blues."

Accommodations: In addition to nearby Wheeler State Park, there are several comfortable motels in the Florence area.

Wawmanona Indian Mound (prehistoric), at Court Street and the Tennessee River, is a forty-three-foot-high mound, largest in the Tennessee Valley. Such mounds were not always used for burials, as often is thought, but instead as foundations for temples, other important buildings, or the homes of chiefs.

Long before the coming of Christopher Columbus to this hemisphere, Mound Builders, as they are now known, were constructing huge earthen mounds along the Mississippi and other rivers of middle America (see Moundville). The **Indian Mound Museum**, operated by the city of Florence, contains artifacts of these ancient people, including sharp flint axes, hatchets, arrowheads, hoes, and other tools. Open Tuesday through Saturday, 10 a.m. to 4 p.m. Small admission charge.

Pope's Tavern (Lambeth House) (c. 1811), 203 Hermitage Drive, a one-and-one-half-story brick building, has been a stage stop and tavern, private dwelling, and Confederate hospital; it is now a museum. Built by slave labor in the early years of Florence, it was intended originally as a stagecoach inn. Wounded soldiers, both Confederate and Union, were treated here following a skirmish in Florence and after the later battles at Elk River and Franklin, Tennessee. The foundation of Pope's Tavern is 12-x-12-inch handmade brick and 3-x-10-inch blue pop-

Courtview (Rogers Hall)

lar sills. Its double outside walls are made of 4-inch handmade brick. The windows were fashioned from some of the early glass produced in this country. The tavern houses the Susan K. Vaughn Museum, which contains numerous artifacts of pioneer times. Open Tuesday through Saturday, 10 a.m. to 4 p.m. Small admission charge.

Sannoner Historic District (c. 1825–1925), on the National Register, was named for Ferdinand Sannoner, the Italian surveyor who laid out Florence. This district contains numerous examples of early- and mid-nineteenth-century architecture, including **Courtview (Rogers Hall)** (c. 1855), at the north end of Court Street, a three-story brick Greek Revival mansion that was once the residence of Governor Emmet O'Neal and is now part of the University of North Alabama; **Hickory Place** (c. 1832), 461 North Pine, brick Federal-style house; and **Irvin Place** (c. 1843), 459 North Court Street, two-story brick.

Karsner-Kennedy House (c. 1825), 303 North Pine Street, one-

and-one-half-story brick Federal-style structure (on the National Register); **Kennedy-Douglass House** (c. 1917), 217 East Tuscaloosa Street, two-story brick, now an arts center and museum (open Monday through Friday, 9 a.m. to 4 p.m., no admission charge); and **T. B. Larrimore House** (c. 1870), on the Mars Hill Bible School campus, two-story frame Victorian structure (on the National Register), are among other sites of interest in Florence.

Walnut Street and Wood Street Historical districts (c. 1890–1930) include homes reflecting changing stylistic influences in these fashionable residential districts. Walnut Street is on the National Register.

W. C. Handy home and museum

Rosenbaum House, 601 Riverview Drive, is the only house in Alabama designed by Frank Lloyd Wright as well as the oldest Wright house in the United States that is occupied by its original owners. Built in 1939–40, this house is one of the best examples of Wright's Usonian style, a design for modest-sized houses of open, spacious design, built on a concrete slab with no attic or basement, carports rather than garages, some built-in furniture, and access to the outdoors from most rooms. Open for tours by appointment 10 a.m. to 5 p.m. Admission charge. Group rates. Telephone (205) 774–5274.

W. C. Handy House (c. 1845) **and Museum**, 620 West College Street, was the birthplace of the famed black composer of blues and jazz, W. C. Handy. Born in this log cabin in 1873, Handy began his musical career when he brought home a guitar as a young boy. His father, a Methodist minister, was shocked and told his son to trade the "sinful" instrument for a dictionary. But young Handy, determined to become a musician, obtained a cornet and joined a local band and later a minstrel show. Touring the country during the hard times of the 1890s, he was inspired to write the song that brought him fame, "St. Louis Blues." When he moved to Memphis, Handy wrote "Memphis Blues." By the time of his death in New York City in 1958, Handy was an internationally known

Wesleyan Hall, Florence

composer and the head of his own music publishing house. The museum, open Tuesday through Saturday, 10 a.m. to 4 p.m., contains musical instruments, sheet music, and other memorabilia of Handy's career. Small admission charge.

The University of North Alabama traces its origins to LaGrange College, founded in Colbert County by Methodists of the Tennessee Conference in 1830 to provide a liberal education for young people of this area. In 1854 the faculty, trustees, and students of LaGrange College split into two factions, one of which moved to Florence and took the name of Florence Wesleyan University. In 1872 the institution was deeded to the state of Alabama, becoming the oldest state-supported teachers' college south of the Ohio River. **Wesleyan Hall** (c.

1855), a three-story brick structure, is one of the few surviving Gothic Revival public buildings in the Tennessee Valley. It is on the National Register.

Sweetwater Plantation (Patton Home) (c. 1835), on Florence Boulevard (U.S. 72 east), a two-story brick residence of late Georgian architecture (on the National Register), was the home of Robert M. Patton, governor of Alabama prior to Reconstruction. A former Whig and an opponent of secession, Patton supported the Confederacy during the war. One of three former opponents of secession who sought the governor's seat following Appomattox, Patton was inaugurated in December 1865 as Alabama's first postwar governor.

Portion of the Natchez Trace

Five miles west of Florence on the old Jackson Road near the modern Mansion View subdivision are the ruins of **Forks of Cypress** (c. 1822), once Alabama's finest example of a temple-type mansion, located on a hilltop. This handsome home was built by an Irishman, James Jackson, who settled in Alabama before it became a state and who helped organize the land company that developed Florence. A lover of racehorses, Jackson built stables and a regulation racetrack on the grounds of his mansion. In 1835 he sent a buyer to England to purchase Glencoe, a great racehorse of that day once owned by King George IV. All but one of the mansion's twenty-four Ionic columns remain, although a fire destroyed the rest of the mansion in 1972. These columns were made of crossed blocks of wood, overlaid with stucco made from sand, horsehair, charcoal, and molasses. The former coachman's house, a log cabin with open dogtrot, can still be seen on the grounds.

Departing Florence, take Alabama 20 west to Natchez Trace Parkway. Turn south on the parkway toward Mississippi.

Natchez Trace

The word *trace* means a beaten path, trail, or line of footprints left by the repeated passage of people. This old trace was originally an Indian trail that ran from Natchez, Mississippi, to the Choctaw villages near present Jackson, Mississippi, then on to the Chickasaw villages in northern Alabama. French traders, missionaries, and soldiers often traveled over the old Indian route. Around 1785, men from Ohio, Kentucky, and other parts of the frontier began to float products such as flour, pork, tobacco, hemp, and iron down the Mississippi River to Natchez and New Orleans. The only way for these "Kaintuck" boatmen to get home was to walk or ride the 450-mile trail from Natchez to Nashville. Portions of this old rough road may be seen along the parkway.

From 1800 to 1820, this was the most heavily traveled road in the old Southwest. Boatmen, soldiers, postmen, missionaries, Indians, and pioneers moved along the road, plagued by swamps, floods, insects, accidents, sickness, unfriendly Indians, and robbers.

Many stopped at crude inns (called *stands*) such as that at Buzzard Roost, on Buzzard Roost Creek off U.S. 72, west of Cherokee, operated by Levi Colbert, brother of the chief of the Chickasaws. This site is on the National Register.

The 450-mile modern parkway roughly follows the route of the original Natchez Trace through Alabama, Mississippi, and Tennessee. At Threet's Crossroads, **Liberty Baptist Church** (c. 1852), home of one of the longest-existing congregations in the area, contains a hand-carved pulpit. Note also **Austin's Place** (c. 1854), a farm including a blacksmith shop used during the Civil War.

At U.S. 72, turn east. Two and one-half miles west of Cherokee is Barton Hall, one mile off U.S. 72.

Barton Hall, a National Historic Landmark, is a two-story Greek Revival frame mansion with a third-story belvedere (structure on its roof), Doric front and side porches, a Doric loggia, and one of the most magnificent double stairways in Alabama.

Six miles north of Cherokee is **Old Natchez Trace Historic District** (c. early 1800s), with seven structures remaining from pioneer days. This district and the old trace are on the National Register.

Eight miles south of Cherokee is a unique burial ground, **Coon Dog Cemetery**, where Alabama hunters bury faithful hounds whose bays no longer echo in the Tennessee Valley. To be eligible for burial here, a dog must have an unquestionable reputation as an outstanding hunter. Each has its own tombstone. The cemetery is located in picturesque Deer Park.

*Return to U.S. 72 and continue east toward Tuscumbia. Fifteen miles west of Tuscumbia is the **Stanfield-Worley Bluff Shelter**, where archaeologists have excavated evidence of occupation by humans from 7690 to 450 B.C. Turn north on U.S. 43 to Sheffield.*

Wilson Dam

Sheffield

A trading post as early as 1815, Sheffield was developed in 1816 by a group of land speculators, including generals Andrew Jackson and John Coffee. However, this development was soon abandoned in favor of Florence on the opposite bank of the river. In 1884, the Sheffield Development Company started a new industrial town on this site in hope of prospering from the coal, iron, asphalt, and water power resources of the region. Sheffield did not develop on the scale of the "magic city" of Birmingham, although five blast furnaces operated in this boom town before 1900.

With the coming of TVA, Sheffield, like Florence and Tuscumbia, experienced substantial growth in industry, population, and prosperity.

North Alabama Railroad Museum, located in the Southern Railway Station, houses a collection of railroad memorabilia emphasizing the Great Steam Era. Displays include steam lo-

comotive No. 77, built in 1920, plus a boxcar, baggage car, and caboose. Guided tours Wednesday and Saturday mornings. Free admission.

Follow signs locally to Muscle Shoals.

Muscle Shoals

Named for the famous rapids that once hampered navigation on the Tennessee River, Muscle Shoals today is the center of a multimillion-dollar music recording business. Many widely known singers come to record in the studios of Muscle Shoals.

Wilson Dam, a National Historic Landmark, is just east of U.S. 43 at the river's edge. Begun in 1918, this massive hydroelectric facility was completed in 1926. Visitors are welcome to drive through the parklike TVA grounds that surround the **National Fertilizer Development Center** and Wilson Dam. The fertilizer plant is open to the public Monday through Friday, 8 a.m. to 4 p.m. Teams of TVA specialists go to underdeveloped countries to advise on the use of fertilizers to increase food production. Guided tours of chemical labs, a waste-heat greenhouse, and a biological recycling project are available, as well as a movie that explains the process of converting nitrogen into fertilizer. No admission charge.

Wilson Locks, across the river, can raise or lower barges 100 feet in a single operation. The 100-foot single lift lock is the highest of its kind in the world. Visitors are welcome to view this interesting operation from an observation deck. Open daily. No admission fee.

Follow signs locally or take U.S. 72 west to Tuscumbia.

Tuscumbia

Once the site of a Chickasaw town, Tuscumbia bears an Indian name meaning "warrior who kills." White settlers aided by Cherokee Indians raided and burned this Chickasaw town in 1787. By 1821 whites had built their own town here, originally named Big Spring for the spring in Spring Park, which has a daily flow of 55 million gallons. President Jimmy Carter opened his 1980 campaign for reelection in this park.

The first railroad west of the Alleghenies, running forty-five miles from Tuscumbia to Decatur, was constructed during the antebellum period to circumvent the dangerous shoals of the Tennessee River. During the Civil War this railroad changed hands several times. Tuscumbia was the site of several skirmishes between Union raiders and Confederate cavalry led by General Nathan Bedford Forrest.

Colbert County Courthouse District (c. 1840–1912), on the National Register, features **Commercial Row** between Water and Main streets on West Fifth Avenue, which includes several structures built in the 1840s as well as residences and churches, among them **Abernathy Home** (c. early 1800s), 204 North Main Street, brick with hand-hewn beams, **First Presbyterian Church** (c. 1824), corner of Fourth and Broad streets, handmade brick with former slave gallery around three sides of the sanctuary; **St. John's Episcopal Church** (c. 1852), small frame Gothic Revival with square towers; and **Tuscumbia Depot** (c. 1888), 200 West Fifth Street, two-story brick Victorian, now a community center.

Five miles southeast of Tuscumbia, off Alabama 43, is **Belle Mont (Thornton Plantation)** (c. 1830), two-story brick with rear courtyard. It is an outstanding example of the Palladian or Jeffersonian Classicism style.

Ivy Green (1820), 300 West North Common Street, a two-story frame cottage, was the birthplace in 1880 of world-famous Helen Keller, who surmounted the handicap of being both deaf and blind. A bright and normal child at birth, Helen lost her sight and

Ivy Green, Tuscumbia

hearing as the result of an illness in early childhood. Frustrated by her inability to communicate with others, Helen became a difficult and fractious child.

When she was seven years old, Helen came under the tutelage of Anne Sullivan, a young woman who had been trained to teach the blind. At first Miss Sullivan could not break through the wall of darkness and silence in which Helen lived. Then one day she took Helen to a well in the yard, placed her hand over the pump spout, and, as she pumped and water gushed forth, spelled the syllables for water into Helen's hand.

Suddenly Helen understood. She realized that the sign language for "w-a-t-e-r" meant the cool liquid flowing over her hand.

After that dramatic moment, Helen learned rapidly, using both sign language and Braille. With Miss Sullivan's help, she became the first deaf-blind person to earn a college degree. Later she traveled over the world to visit schools for the deaf and blind and to inspire others by her courageous example. Eight presidents invited her to the White House. Her success led to publication of many textbooks in Braille and training of more teachers for the deaf and blind.

Visitors to Ivy Green can see hundreds of mementos of Miss Keller's life, including the old well, Miss Keller's Braille typewriter, her library of Braille

Well at Ivy Green

books, and copies of books that she wrote, including her autobiography, which has been translated into fifty languages. Open daily 8:30 a.m. to 4:00 p.m.; Sunday, 1 to 4 p.m. Small admission fee.

The Miracle Worker, by William Gibson, a dramatization of the story of Helen Keller and Anne Sullivan, is presented on the grounds of Ivy Green on Friday and Saturday evenings for two weekends in June and four weekends in July. Small admission fee.

Across the street from Helen Keller's home, the **Tennessee Valley Arts Center**, on Water Street and North Commons, presents a new exhibit each month. Open Monday through Friday, 9 a.m. to 5 p.m.; Sunday, 2 to 4 p.m. Small admission fee.

34

Leaving Tuscumbia, follow Alternate U.S. 72 east to Decatur or join Tour 7. Off Alternate 72 are four historic sites.

Leighton Vicinity

LaGrange Bluff Shelter (prehistoric) on Alabama 157 near Leighton, on the National Register, has been excavated, revealing evidence of human habitation approximately 10,000 B.C. **Old Brick Presbyterian Church** (c. 1828), north of Leighton, is a handmade brick structure with original pews and horsehair plaster on its interior walls.

Southwest of Leighton near the **Spring Valley** community is the site of **LaGrange College**, founded by Methodists in 1830. LaGrange College and Spring Hill College in Mobile were the two earliest colleges in Alabama. For twenty-five years, LaGrange produced ministers and educated lay people from this mountaintop location. Eventually a portion of its faculty, trustees, and students voted to move to Florence to establish Florence Wesleyan University, a forerunner of the University of North Alabama. Part of the faculty who remained organized the LaGrange College and Military Academy in 1858. Because this institution helped to train cadets for the Confederacy, it was destroyed by Union forces in 1863. The site, owned by the Alabama Historical Commission, occupies LaGrange Mountain and is identified by a granite marker.

Another National Register site in this vicinity is **The Oaks (Ricks Mansion)** (c. 1832), on Ricks Lane off Alabama 157 at the base of LaGrange Mountain. This property, which includes a log cabin (c. 1816) as well as the Georgian-influenced plantation house, illustrates the rapid change from frontier to plantation economy in areas of fertile soil such as the Tennessee Valley.

Exhibit at W. C. Handy House (p. 29)

TOUR 3

Appalachian Alabama

From Birmingham

Springville

St. Clair Springs

Ashville

Fort Payne

Valley Head

Mentone

Gaylesville

Cedar Bluff

Centre

Gadsden

Return to Birmingham

Victorian homes and structures

pioneer structures

caves

Civil War sites

Weiss Lake

antebellum blast furnace

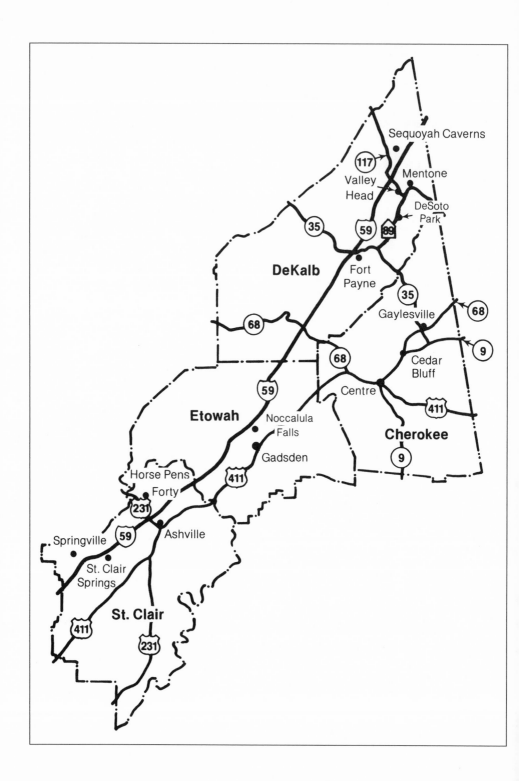

Cherokee Indians, driven out of Pennsylvania by rival Indian groups, migrated to the Carolinas, Georgia, and northeastern Alabama. The word "Cherokee" means "people of the cave country."

When white settlers began to encroach on their lands in the early nineteenth century, many Cherokees took up the ways of whites, accepting Christianity and becoming farmers. Some became prosperous cotton planters and owned black slaves. Sequoyah, a crippled Cherokee silversmith who lived part of his life in northeastern Alabama, devised a syllabary, or written language, so that his people could express themselves, write to one another, and carry on business in their own language. After working twelve years on this project, Sequoyah presented his syllabary to Cherokee chiefs in 1821 at various sites in northeastern Alabama.

Sequoyah's syllabary contains eighty-six symbols, one for each syllable used by the Cherokees in their spoken language. When their chiefs were convinced that this was not some form of trickery or witchcraft, the Cherokees quickly learned this new skill. They published their own newspaper, hymnbook, and laws, translated the Bible into Cherokee, and wrote letters to their relatives in the West. As years passed, however, Cherokees learned only English in school and forgot how to write and speak their native language. Recently,

Sequoyah's Syllabary

at schools in North Carolina and Oklahoma, young Cherokees have renewed their interest in learning their own language with the help of Sequoyah's syllabary. Sequoyah is the only individual ever known to have devised an entire alphabet.

Despite the fact that Cherokees were peaceful farmers who lived much like whites, they were pressured to cede their lands in northern Georgia and Alabama when gold was discovered in their Georgia territory. In the Treaty of New Echota in 1835, Cherokee leaders reluctantly agreed to give up their ancestral lands. Yet many refused to move. Eventually United States troops rounded them up in stockades, like Fort Payne, and forced them to march westward to new lands in Oklahoma. This tragic march, during which 4,000 died, is known as the "Trail of Tears." Many historic sites associated with the Cherokees, including caves, may be visited in this area of Alabama.

White farm people took over the area ceded by the Cherokees. During the Civil War, many of these predominantly nonslaveowning whites supported the Union and opposed secession. The great majority, however, eventually served in the Confederate army. One of the most dramatic episodes of the Civil War, a four-day running engagement between Union and Confederate cavalry, ended near Cedar Bluff in Cherokee County. Here Confederate general Nathan B. Forrest, with 600 men, forced the surrender of Union colonel A. D. Streight and his force of 1,500.

Following the war, Fort Payne, Gadsden, and Battelle (now a ghost town) were boom towns of a "New South" whose leaders attempted to balance agriculture with industry. Today these hills and coves where Cherokees once hunted and farmed are inhabited by farmers and by workers in factories and industries. In the Mentone area, Lookout Mountain, part of the Appalachian range, remains a favorite haven from the heat of Alabama summers.

suggestions for background reading

Carter, Samuel, III. *Cherokee Sunset: A Nation Betrayed.* Garden City, N.Y.: Doubleday, 1976.

Corkran, David H. *The Cherokee Frontier: Conflict and Survival, 1740–1762.* Norman: University of Oklahoma Press, 1962.

Cotterill, Robert S. *Southern Indians: Story of the Civilized Tribes before Removal.* Norman: University of Oklahoma Press, 1956.

Foreman, Grant. *Five Civilized Tribes.* Norman: University of Oklahoma Press, 1934.

Henry, Robert Selph, ed. *As They Saw Forrest: Some Reflections and Comments of Contemporaries.* Jackson, Tenn.: McCowat-Mercer Press, 1956.

Howard, Elizabeth S. *The Vagabond Dreamer.* Huntsville: Strode Publishers, 1976. (Locale: Fort Payne-Mentone)

Hudson, Charles. *The Southeastern Indians.* Knoxville: University of Tennessee Press, 1976.

Wyeth, John A. *That Devil Forrest.* Revised ed. New York: Harper's, 1959.

From Birmingham, take Interstate 59 north toward Chattanooga. Exit at Springville.

Springville and St. Clair Springs

Leave Interstate 59 briefly for a glimpse of two late-nineteenth-century communities. **Springville Historic District** along U.S. 11 contains thirty predominantly Victorian commercial and residential structures in a community little changed in physical appearance since the 1930s.

Across the interstate from Springville on Alabama 23 is **St. Clair Springs Historic District**, once a popular health resort and summer retreat from yellow fever and malaria epidemics. The district, which is on the National Register, includes approximately twenty houses originally built as summer cottages.

Return to Interstate 59 north. Take the Ashville exit from Interstate 59 and follow U.S. 231 south into Ashville.

Ashville

This small community, centered around a courthouse square, contains a number of residential and commercial structures representing various stages in the development of this old town. **St. Clair County Courthouse** (c. 1844) is a Neoclassical Revival enlargement of an older courthouse. This is one of two courthouses in St. Clair County; the other is located in Pell City. Ashville's library contains archival material on pioneer settlers. The Greek Revival **Inzer House** (c. 1852), on Hartford Avenue, is on the National Register.

Follow signs in Ashville about ten miles to **Looney House** (c. 1820), possibly one of the oldest two-story log dogtrot houses in Alabama and undoubtedly one of the most impressive pioneer homes of its type in the state. Built by John Looney and his son Henry, who served in Andrew Jackson's volunteer army during the Creek War of 1813–14, the house stands as steady as the day it was built with a few crude tools and native materials. It contains four large rooms, two downstairs and two upstairs. Each downstairs room has a fireplace large enough to burn five-foot logs. Note that it has dogtrots both up and down. The foundation is made of huge stones quarried from the hillside. Sills are of cedar. Pine logs were dovetailed to fit perfectly. Exposed rafters are held together with hand-carved pegs; there

Looney House, Ashville

are no metal nails in the entire structure. The twin chimneys are of hand-pressed brick made from clay found on nearby land. Looney House, an excellent example of pioneer architecture, is on the National Register. Open Saturday and Sunday, noon to 5 p.m. Small admission fee. Each year the St. Clair Historical Society sponsors a fall festival during which the house and grounds are alive with people enjoying such attractions as candledipping, soapmaking, quilting, basketweaving, and fiddling. For the date of the fall festival, write Ashville Public Library.

From Ashville, follow U.S. 231 north to St. Clair County 35. Watch for signs to Horse Pens Forty.

Horse Pens Forty

This forty-acre mountaintop park, an ideal spot for picnicking, contains numerous natural rock formations, including a large stone corral used by Indians during the Creek War of 1813–14 and later by Confederates as a secure place for their horses. It offers pleasant views of the surrounding countryside. Small admission fee.

Noccalula Falls

The city of Gadsden has developed a park and pioneer village near Noccalula Falls where, legend has it, an Indian girl leaped to her death because she was not allowed to marry the man she loved. The pioneer park includes **Gilliland Covered Bridge (Old Reese City Bridge)**, a forty-foot structure moved here and restored, as well as a dogtrot house (moved from Tennessee), a gristmill, loom house, cook house, wash shed, blacksmith shop, smokehouse, barn, schoolhouse, and hog pen. Open daily 8 a.m. to sunset year round; peak season March through October. Small admission

Noccalula Falls, Gadsden

charge for pioneer village. Telephone (205) 549-4663. A campground is available.

Return to Interstate 59 and continue northeast to Fort Payne.

Fort Payne

Under pressure from the federal government, Cherokees reluctantly ceded their lands in northeastern Alabama in 1835. But when many Indian families still refused to move west of the Mississippi, United States troops rounded them up in stockades to await a forced march that became known as the "Trail of Tears." The major stockade in northeastern Alabama was Fort Payne, named for Captain John Payne, who was in charge of removing the Cherokees from this region.

Fort Payne was located near a Cherokee village known as Wills Town, where Sequoyah worked as a silversmith and blacksmith while devising a syllabary, or written language, for his people.

From 1888 to 1891, Fort Payne boomed as a group of investors from New England attempted to establish an industrial center between Lookout and Sand mountains that they hoped would grow as rapidly as Birmingham. The Fort Payne Coal and Iron Company raised $1 million to purchase 32,000 acres in this vicinity to mine iron and coal. Furnaces and rolling mills sprang up. Hundreds of visitors and potential investors came to see "the Chicago of the South" and to stay at the DeKalb Hotel, which had 180 rooms and occupied an entire city block. Those who decided to settle here built substantial Victorian homes, offices, churches, and schools. However, Fort Payne did not develop into a new Birmingham; the boom collapsed quickly and many settlers returned to New England. By 1900 the town had shrunk to a small village, and in 1918 its great hotel was destroyed by fire.

Fort Payne Commercial Historic District and **Fort Payne Residential District** contain many structures built during the boom period, including: the **Opera House** (c. 1889), 512 Gault Avenue North, on the National Register, which is open to visitors when plays are being presented and on other special occasions; **French Flats** (c. 1889), 405 Alabama Avenue North, once a two-story frame boarding house and now an office; **Fort Payne**

Fort Payne Depot

Depot (c. 1891), on the National Register, at Northeast Fifth Street, built of gray sandstone with pink granite trim and Victorian-style dwellings with distinctive New England vertical character on Forrest Avenue, Alabama Avenue, and Fifth Street North, sometimes called "Yankee houses." Note especially the **Davenport Home**, 700 Forrest Avenue North, two-story Colonial Revival built by A. C. Spaulding, president of the Fort Payne Coal and Iron Company, which promoted the boom. Spaulding imported Tiffany glass from New England for the upper panels of windows in this house.

On the outskirts of Fort Payne is **Manitou Cave**, 1000 Manitou Avenue South, probably inhabited by bands of prehistoric Indians and, in historic times, by Cherokees. Cherokees may have named the cave *manitou*, meaning "Great Spirit." During the Civil War the Confederate government took over Manitou Cave and mined its saltpeter deposits for use in making gunpowder (see *De Soto Caverns*). In the

Fort Payne Opera House

1890s the cave was used by Fort Payne residents as a ballroom lighted with hundreds of tallow candles. It is no longer in use.

After its boom era, Fort Payne became a hosiery-producing center. The **W. B. Davis Hosiery Mills**, located in a boom-era industrial building, manufactured eleven million socks for servicemen during World War II. The Davis mill and the mill houses on Gault Avenue North are on the National Register.

Accommodations: There are comfortable motels in Fort Payne. Follow Alabama 35 east from Fort Payne and follow signs to De Soto State Park, which has facilities for camping, cabins, and a motel.

Leaving Fort Payne, follow Interstate 59 north to Valley Head exit. Follow signs to Sequoyah Caverns.

Sequoyah Caverns

These underground caves are reputed to have been used as a hiding place by Cherokees who hoped to escape being sent west on the "Trail of Tears." Old salt troughs, cooking pottery, and other artifacts were found in its entrance room by early explorers. Names, initials, and dates going back to 1824 may still be seen on its walls and formations. On one large column is inscribed "Sam Houston, 1830." Early white settlers held square dances and old time "singings" in the caverns

and explored them by torchlight. The caverns are now part of a park, open to the public for picnicking and camping. An old log cabin has been restored here. Near the caverns roam a herd of white fallow deer and several buffalo (bison). Open daily 8:30 a.m. to 5 p.m., March through November; weekends only, December through February. Admission charge. Telephone (205) 635-6423.

Leaving the caverns, return to Interstate 59 and turn south to Valley Head.

Valley Head

Near this small town is the abandoned site of Battelle, another late-nineteenth-century boom town. Only ruins remain. In Valley Head is **Winston Place** (c. 1835), a two-story mansion built around a log cabin that was erected by an early settler. Winston Place, on the National Register, was the home of William Overton Winston, who brought the Alabama Great Southern Railroad into this area and who opposed secession in 1861. The present verandah, one of the most lavish in Alabama, was not part of the mansion as originally conceived but was added later to furnish ample space for outdoor living.

A giant red oak once stood on the grounds of Winston Place and marked one of the sites where Sequoyah is said to have taught his alphabet to Cherokees of this vicinity. During the Civil

44

War, 30,000 Union troops camped on the Winston plantation. Their commander, General Jefferson Davis (no relation to the Confederate president), made his headquarters at Winston Place.

Leaving Valley Head, follow Alabama 117 east to Mentone atop Lookout Mountain.

Mentone

Lookout Mountain is part of the Appalachian range. On its western brow is Mentone, once a fashionable and popular vacation resort, which was named for Menton, a resort in France. Throngs of "summer people" came to Valley Head by train and rode by horse-drawn carriages and later by automobiles to the hotels and summer homes atop this ridge during the late nineteenth and early twentieth centuries. Two old hotels and many summer cottages remain. **Mentone Springs Hotel** (c. 1884), a fifty-seven-room structure, on the National Register, was once a popular resort. **Windward Inn**, on the brow west of the town, was operated as a rustic inn until the 1970s. Numerous camps are located in the Mentone vicinity. Two interesting churches are **St. Joseph's on the Mountain**, a rustic Episcopal church in the center of Mentone, and **Howard's Chapel** near De Soto Park, one end of which is formed by a huge boulder. Buried at Howard's Chapel is Colonel Milford W. Howard, Populist congressman and a developer of Fort Payne and Mentone.

*Leaving Mentone, follow DeKalb County 89 to **De Soto Falls** and De Soto State Park.*

The falls of Little River, one of the country's last unpolluted streams, are named for Hernando de Soto, whose expedition, according to some speculations, passed near this vicinity in 1540. The park, developed during the 1930s with the help of the Civilian Conservation Corps, contains cottages, a motel, and campgrounds. Its older cabins and the stone section of its lodge were built by CCC workers.

Leaving De Soto State Park, follow DeKalb County 89 south to Alabama 35. Follow signs to Little River Canyon.

Little River Canyon

The largest natural gorge in Alabama and one of the deepest east of the Rocky Mountains, Little River Canyon is eighteen miles long, three-fourths of a mile wide at one point, and 700 feet deep. Cherokees once lived in the canyon. It is said that Union troops, hurrying to join General William T. Sherman in capturing Atlanta, tried in vain to climb its sheer walls. Those interested in seeing the entire gorge can drive to the canyon mouth by automobile. (Turn right just before the bridge over Little River. The road is slow and winding but easily passable. A campground is located at the canyon mouth.)

Howard's Chapel

A portion of the canyon also may be seen from the bridge and picnic area on Alabama 35. Follow this road south to Gaylesville.

Gaylesville

On October 30, 1864, some 19,000 Union troops were ordered by General William T. Sherman to begin their "march to the sea" through Georgia from this hamlet. A marker denotes the start of the famous march. On Alabama 68 in Gaylesville, note **Webb-**

De Soto Falls

Chestnutt House (c. 1849), a two-story hand-hewn log and frame house with three cantilevered balconies. Originally a dogtrot house, this was once a doctor's office and clinic.

Follow Alabama 68 south to Cedar Bluff.

Cedar Bluff and Cornwall Furnace

*Two miles east of Cedar Bluff on Alabama 9, follow signs to **Cornwall Furnace.***

This fifty-foot stone furnace, built in 1864 to supply pig iron to the Confederacy to make arms at Selma, is the best-preserved pig iron furnace in the Southeast. Although its works were destroyed by Union forces under General Sherman, the stack and arch of this furnace escaped harm. At one time it produced six tons a day of pig iron from local brown hematite ore. The furnace closed in 1875 after its founder, Samuel Noble, moved his operations to Anniston. Well worth the effort to see, the furnace is on the National Register. Pleasant picnic grounds are nearby on the shore of Weiss Lake.

Return to Cedar Bluff and follow Alabama 9 toward Centre.

On May 3, 1863, Confederate cavalry leader Nathan B. Forrest, with a force of 600, forced the surrender of Colonel A. D. Streight and 1,500 mule-mounted Union troops near Cedar Bluff, thus ending "the great cavalry chase" that had started four days earlier. Only when he surrendered did

46

Cornwall Furnace

Gadsden

Once a pioneer farm village named Double Springs, this town was named Gadsden in the 1850s by admirers of Colonel James Gadsden, who negotiated the Gadsden Purchase from Mexico in 1853 and who had once visited this area as General Andrew Jackson's chief of staff to negotiate treaties with the Indians. During the Civil War, General Nathan B. Forrest and his cavalry, chasing a much larger Union force under Colonel A. D. Streight, came to a halt at Black Creek where the Federals had burned a bridge. Emma Sansom, a sixteen-year-old girl, volunteered to guide Forrest to a ford in the creek despite gunfire from Union troops on the opposite bank. Emma showed Forrest a place where his men and horses could cross and continue their chase, which ended near Cedar Bluff. Alabama's legislature later awarded the girl a gold medal and a section of land in tribute to her bravery.

Streight learn that Forrest's force was less than half the size of his own. Streight was angered to discover that he had been fooled by Forrest. Streight's men were sent to Atlanta as prisoners of war over the railroad from Atlanta to Chattanooga, which they had planned to destroy.

Alabama 9 crosses Weiss Lake, a 30,000-acre lake bordered by 447 miles of shoreline. This Alabama Power facility is a popular fishing area. A free tour of the power plant and dam may be arranged in advance through the community relations section of the Alabama Power Company in Birmingham. Telephone (205) 250-3739.

After the Civil War, Gadsden developed into an industrial center, using nearby resources of iron, manganese, coal, and limestone. Many industries, the largest of which are Republic Steel Corporation and Goodyear Rubber Company, are located here.

Accommodations: There are several comfortable motels in Gadsden.

Centre

Turkey Town site, now Centre Junior High School, was a famed Indian council site named for the noted Chief Turkey. Here Cherokees, Chickasaws, and Creeks signed a treaty with Andrew Jackson in 1816 following the Creek War.

Follow U.S. 411 west from Centre to Gadsden.

At Broad and First streets, at the edge of the Coosa River, is the **Emma**

47

Emma Sansom Statue, Gadsden

place (c. 1830), 309 Tuscaloosa Avenue, was the first home in Double Springs. Made of logs fastened with wooden pegs, it has been extensively remodeled. The structure has served as a school, post office, and community meeting house.

Leaving Gadsden, return on Interstate 59 south to Birmingham.

Sansom Memorial Statue, erected in 1907 by the United Daughters of the Confederacy. A life-size marble figure of Emma Sansom stands atop the monument. On the base is a bas-relief showing Emma seated behind General Forrest on his horse, pointing the way to the ford on Black Creek. Nearby is a memorial to John Wisdom, called the "Paul Revere of the Confederacy" because he rode all night to warn Rome, Georgia, that Union raiders were headed that way.

Two National Register structures in Gadsden are **Alabama City (Nichols Memorial) Library** (c. 1902), 1 Cabot Avenue, one of the earliest free public libraries in Alabama, and the **Federal Building and Courthouse** (c. 1910), 600 Broad Street, a three-story marble and wood structure. **Hughes Home-**

TOUR 4

Blount County Covered Bridges

From Birmingham

Oneonta

Return to Birmingham

covered bridges

pioneer structures

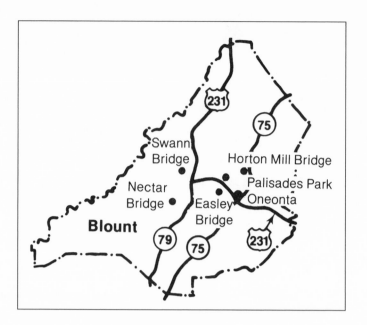

Covered bridges were first built in the United States in the late 1700s. The covering protected the wooden structural elements from rain and heat and prevented horses from being frightened by the rushing waters beneath. Such bridges often served as havens for weary travelers. They also are known as "kissing bridges."

America's first covered bridges originated in Pennsylvania where the first recorded frame timber bridge was built across the Schuykill River at Yellow Creek in 1787. The bridges were generally made of pine and constructed with such tools as the broad axe, adze, crosscut saw, chisel, and mallet. Very little iron was used.

Once hundreds of covered bridges crossed almost every river and creek in Alabama. Many were toll bridges, providing additional revenue for an area.

Today only fifteen of Alabama's covered bridges remain (see Appendix 3).

Blount County, with three early-twentieth-century covered bridges still standing, lays valid claim to the title of "covered bridge capital of Alabama." Swann is one of the longest such bridges in the South. Blount County owns all its covered bridges, including Horton Mill, deeded to the county in 1995 by the Alabama Historical Commission. All of these bridges are on the National Register.

Builders of these Blount County bridges used a Town-type truss promoted by a New Englander, Ithiel Town, who was granted a patent on his truss. Town's bridges were built in a lattice style with planks forming a webbing. Only vertical forces were used on the abutments. A genuine American invention, the Town truss made for a durable bridge that could withstand heavy weights.

The most remarkable thing about Blount County's bridges is the fact that they are still in daily use. It is a pleasant surprise to a motorist to round a curve in a country road and find a sturdy, old wooden bridge waiting to transport cars, bicyclists, and pedestrians across a stream.

Daniel Murphree cabin

Leaving Birmingham, proceed north on Alabama 79 thirty-five miles to Cleveland. Turn left on Alabama 160 and go four miles to the site of the Nectar Bridge that burned in 1993. Turn left between the church and the cemetery to the bridge site.

With a total span of 385 feet (longer than a football field), Nectar Covered Bridge (c. 1934) was the longest bridge of its kind left standing in Alabama, fourth longest in the United States, and twelfth longest in the world. It spanned the Locust Fork of the Black Warrior River 38 feet above water.

suggestions for background reading

Prince, A. G. *Alabama's Covered Bridges—Past and Present.* Birmingham: Privately printed, 1972.
Sangster, Tom, and Bess S. Sangster. *Alabama's Covered Bridges.* Montgomery: Coffeetable Publications, 1980.

Swann Covered Bridge

Return to Alabama 79 in Cleveland. Turn north onto this road, go about one mile to the next paved road, turn left, and proceed about a mile.

Another long bridge, Swann Covered Bridge (c. 1933) stretches 324 feet across the Locust Fork of the Black Warrior River.

Easley Covered Bridge

Returning from Swann Covered Bridge, cross Alabama 79 and proceed straight ahead for several blocks to U.S. 231. Turn right onto U.S. 231 and follow this route through Cleveland. Just beyond Rosa, turn right at Pine Grove Church and proceed 1.5 miles to Easley Covered Bridge.

The smallest covered bridge in Blount County, Easley Covered Bridge (c. 1927) spans a small creek whose banks are covered with mountain laurel, yellow jasmine, and honeysuckle, which bloom in the spring.

Return to U.S. 231. Turn east toward Oneonta. At Oneonta city limits, turn left (at sign) and go about four miles (when in doubt on this road, bear right) to Palisades Park near the fire tower, which is in sight on the way up this mountain drive.

51

Horton Mill covered bridge

Palisades Park

An eighty-acre country park atop Ebell Mountain, Palisades includes a number of long overlooks along its hiking trails. A special feature of this park is the Blount County Historical Society's restoration project of farm buildings. (Fine place for a picnic.)

The **Daniel Murphree Cabin** (c. 1816) was constructed by an early settler of Murphree's Valley near Hood's Crossroads. It is an unusual single-pen structure with tall walls and a half story in the loft. A log barn of the same period and a log smokehouse or corn crib have been reassembled in the park. The park is open daily 9 a.m. to 5 p.m. with a later closing time in summer. No admission charge.

Leaving Palisades Park, continue to Oneonta on U.S. 231.

Blount County Memorial Museum, in Oneonta's Courthouse Square, is open weekdays and from noon to 3 p.m. on Sundays. Telephone (205) 589-2263. It contains arrowheads, sandstone, covered bridge art, maps, and a Thomas Alva Edison display.

Leaving Oneonta, take Alabama 75 north about five miles to Horton Mill Covered Bridge, just off this highway to the left.

Horton Mill Covered Bridge

Horton Mill Covered Bridge (c. 1935), which spans a gorge with vertical rock cliffs, is the highest covered bridge above water in the United States, standing 70 feet above the Calvert prong of the Locust Fork of the Black Warrior river. At 220 feet in length, it is one of the longest covered bridges in the South. There is a recreation area and nature trail near the bridge. No admission charge.

Leaving Oneonta, return to Birmingham via Alabama 75 south or via U.S. 231 south and Interstate 59.

TOUR 5
Near
Interstate
65

Part One
North of Birmingham

ARDMORE
space rocket

ATHENS
nuclear plant

SOMERVILLE
courthouse

CULLMAN
covered bridge
gristmill
German homes

Part Two
*Between Birmingham
and Montgomery*

VERBENA
Victorian homes

MOUNTAIN CREEK
Civil War cemetery

BUENA VISTA
early industrial center

Part Three
*Between Montgomery
and Mobile*

BUTLER COUNTY
Bartram Trail

MONROEVILLE
home of novelist Harper Lee

PERDUE HILL
historic sites

CLAIBORNE
antebellum homes

POARCH
Creek settlement

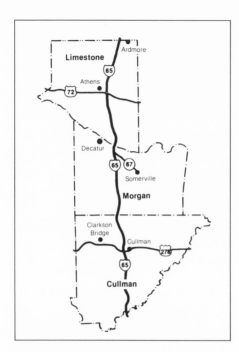

Part One

North of Birmingham

Ardmore

The **Alabama Welcome Center** near here is marked by a huge **Saturn 1B space vehicle**, transferred to this location from its former home at NASA's Marshall Space Flight Center (see *Huntsville*) over a forty-mile route. The trip over country roads at a five-mile-per-hour pace was the longest distance that a rocket this size had ever been carried.

The Saturn 1B was designed and developed at the Marshall Center. It was used as the manned launch vehicle in Apollo, Skylab, and Apollo-Soyuz earth orbital missions. The Sat-urn 1B also served as a backup launch vehicle until all programs using Saturn class rockets were completed.

Continue south on Interstate 65 to Athens.

Athens

Founded in 1818, Athens became a center for antebellum planters of the Tennessee Valley, as did Greensboro, Eutaw, and Marion in the Black Belt. In 1862 Athens became one of the first Alabama towns to be occupied by Union troops. Their commander, Russian-born Colonel John Turchin, permitted his men to burn homes and to steal. Later Turchin was court-martialed for violating the rules of war, but the charges against him were dropped.

In 1934, Athens became the first municipality in Alabama to purchase electrical current from the Tennessee Valley Authority. Like other cities in

Saturn 1B at Ardmore Welcome Center

54

Founders' Hall, Athens

the Tennessee Valley, Athens has prospered because of TVA. In 1966, TVA began construction of the world's second largest nuclear plant, Brown's Ferry, about ten miles southwest of Athens. This immense project brought jobs, newcomers, and controversy over the use of nuclear power.

Athens College was chartered in 1842. Originally a girls' college, it later became coeducational. **Founders' Hall** (c. 1842), Greek Revival, suffered architecturally when its third story was added in 1905. **Beaty-Mason House** (c. 1826), 211 Beaty Street South, Federal style, enlarged and converted to Greek Revival in 1845, was built by the founder of Athens, Robert Beaty. Federal troops used it as officers' quarters. It later became the residence of presidents of Athens College. In the rear, a one-time slave cabin (c. 1826) has been converted to a guest house.

Donnell House (c. 1840s), 601 South Clinton Street, with two-story central portico, is on the National Register. It has a central hall with rear cross hall and front and rear stairways. Built by Robert Donnell, a north Alabama religious leader, it has been restored and is open for tours by ap-

pointment. Telephone (205) 232-5471 or (205) 232-0743. **Houston House** (c. 1843–45), 101 Houston Street, two-story frame, was once the home of George Houston, who represented Alabama in Congress for twenty years (1841–61) and, although a Unionist, led the Alabama delegation in presenting notification of this state's secession. Known as "the bald eagle of the mountains," Houston led Democrats in regaining political control of Alabama from Radical Republicans when he was elected governor in 1874. On election night Athens blazed with lights and its courthouse filled with excited citizens, eager to acclaim the governor-elect. Houston House is now Houston Memorial Library.

Pryor House (c. 1836), 405 Jefferson Street, was the home of Luke Pryor, state legislator and U.S. senator (1879–84). A Greek Revival structure enlarged and remodeled to Italianate, it features a glass-enclosed cupola in which its owner is said to have sat with a telescope to watch his slaves work in the fields.

Donnell House, Athens

Also of interest are the **James With-er Sloss House** (c. 1845), corner of Beaty and Hobbs streets, built by one of the founders of Birmingham and now converted to apartments; Federal-style **Lovvorn House** (c. 1830), 301 East Washington; **Richardson House** (c. 1832), 401 South Clinton, Federal with Greek Revival portico; and **Jones-Hatchett House** (1855), 517 South Clinton, Greek Revival.

Another National Register site in Limestone County is **Sulphur Trestle Fort** (c. 1864), seven miles north of Athens near Limestone County 127 in the vicinity of Elkmont. This seventy-yard-square redoubt was manned during the Civil War by two Union companies of black troops. The fort and the trestle that once crossed Sulphur Creek were burned by Confederate general Nathan B. Forrest in a raid to disrupt the Union supply lines. Nearby **Bridgeforth Home** (c. 1830), two-story brick with central Greek Revival portico, served as a hospital after this battle.

From Athens, follow U.S. 72 west six miles. Turn south at the sign for **Brown's Ferry**. *Although not open to the public, the world's second largest nuclear plant is visible from this road. Return to Athens and take Interstate 65 south to Decatur (see Tour 1).*

Those wishing to see the Tennessee Valley region of Alabama may take Tour 1 (in reverse order) at the Mooresville-Huntsville exit of Interstate 65 or join Tour 2 at Decatur.

From Decatur, take Alabama 67 east twelve miles to Somerville.

Somerville Courthouse

Somerville

Those interested in Alabama court-houses may wish to see the oldest standing courthouse in the state. **Somerville Courthouse** (c. 1837), on the National Register, a two-story brick building with cupola, is now used as a satellite station for the sheriff's department. **Somerville Historic District** (c. mid to late 1800s) contains seventeen structures, including hotels and stores. **Somerville School** (c. 1920) is a typical one-story frame schoolhouse of its era.

Return to Interstate 65 south. At the second Cullman exit from Interstate 65, take U.S. 278 west nine miles to Clarkson Covered Bridge (watch for sign).

Clarkson Covered Bridge

One of fifteen covered bridges still standing in Alabama (see *Blount*

County), Clarkson Bridge (also known as Legg Bridge) was built in 1904, destroyed by a flood in 1921, and rebuilt in 1922. In 1976 it was restored by the Cullman County Commission as a bicentennial project. Its builder used a Town-type truss. Listed on the National Register, Clarkson Covered Bridge stretches 270 feet across Crooked Creek and is located in a park that also contains a gristmill, dogtrot log cabin, and picnic area. Near here in 1863 occurred the Battle of Hog's Mountain between Confederate cavalrymen led by General Nathan B. Forrest and Union cavalry under Colonel A. D. Streight, part of the famed cavalry chase that ended in surrender by the Union troops in Cherokee County. Another engagement between these two forces, the Battle of Day's Gap, took place eight miles north of Cullman on present U.S. 31 near **Hurricane Creek** Park.

Follow U.S. 278 east from Clarkson Covered Bridge to Cullman.

suggestion for further reading

Jones, Margaret Jean. *Combing Cullman County.* Cullman: Modernistic Printers, 1972.

Cullman

Colonel Johann Cullman, a German refugee, obtained several hundred thousand acres in Blount County from the Louisville and Nashville Railroad in 1873. He intended to establish a colony of German immigrants here who would make their living by growing grapes and making wine. Cullman advertised his land in the Northern press thus: "Tracts, 40 acres and up. $2.00–$6.00 per acre. Agricultural, timber, iron, coal, and minerals. Climate healthful. No malaria, no swamps, no grasshoppers, no hurricanes, no blizzards."

Unfortunately there was also little fertile land in Cullman's tract. Germans who settled here quickly found that the soil and climate were not suitable for growing grapes. Out of necessity, these industrious people learned to raise corn, sweet potatoes, chickens, and strawberries and to operate and work in small industries.

For many years citizens of Cullman spoke German, read German-language newspapers, and attended religious services conducted in their native tongue. During World Wars I and II, however, hostility to Germany made the German language unpopular in this country, and its use gradually ceased in Cullman. In recent years Cullman citizens have renewed their pride in their German origins and have begun to hold festivals commemorating the town's original settlers.

Cullman Historic District (c. late 1800s) includes six blocks of Victorian and Neoclassical Revival structures. **Cullman House**, 211 Second Avenue Northeast, now the home of the Cullman Chamber of Commerce,

Cullman House

Cullman County Museum, and Cullman County Historical Society, is a replica of the two-story frame Swiss Victorian house built by Colonel Cullman. Mementos of the original settlers, including clothing, farm implements, and a traditional German beer wagon, are displayed here. Open Monday through Wednesday and Friday, 9 a.m. to noon and 1 to 4 p.m.; Thursday, 9 a.m. to noon; Sunday, 1:30 to 4:30 p.m. Admission charge.

Cullman once had two colleges supported by Catholic religious orders. **Sacred Heart College** (c. 1902), 200 Convent Road, was begun by independent sisters as an academy for Catholic girls. It became a two-year college in 1940 and coeducational Cullman College in 1970. **St. Bernard Abbey and College** (c. 1892), one

mile east of Cullman on U.S. 278, was founded by Benedictine monks from Pennsylvania who moved to Cullman to serve its German-speaking farmers. This college closed in 1979; the Benedictines now operate St. Bernard College Prep. Nearby **Ave Maria Grotto**, containing 125 miniature stone models of religious shrines, which were the lifetime work of one of these monks, still is open to visitors daily. Small admission fee.

Other points of historic interest include: **Louisville and Nashville Bridges and Railroad Cut** (c. 1910–14), a thirty-foot, eight-block cut that lowered the railroad tracks below street level and that bisects the downtown area; **Cullman Ice Factory** (1894), 414 First Avenue Southeast, typical of business establishments where Germans lived above or adjacent to their businesses; **Stifelmeyer's** (c. 1888), 202 First Avenue Southeast, another typical German business structure; **old downtown business district**, on either side of railroad tracks along First Avenue Southwest and First Avenue Southeast, containing other typical German buildings; **Weiss Cottage** (c. 1873), First Avenue Southeast at Fourth Street South, Cullman's oldest home, once a snuff factory and also known as the "Goat House" because one owner kept goats in the cellar. **Cullman Depot** (c. 1913), 109 Arnold Street, is on the National Register. **Sacred Heart**

Catholic Church (c. 1900), whose tall twin spires dominate the Cullman skyline, was built by German immigrants as a Benedictine parish church.

Southeast Cullman Historic District includes a wide variety of residential architectural styles from the 1870s to the present, including Queen Anne, Eastlake, Georgian Revival, Colonial Revival, Classical Revival, Bungalows, and more modern styles. The area includes **St. John's United Church** (c. 1924), 512 Second Avenue Southeast, which replaced an earlier structure attended by the founders of Cullman, including Colonel Cullman; **Folsom Home** (c. 1913), 702 Fifth Avenue Southeast, two-story frame home of former Alabama governor James E. ("Big Jim") Folsom (1947–51 and 1955–59); **Anna Lola Price Home** (c.1938–39), 700 Fifth Street Southeast, home of the first woman in Alabama appointed to a high court position (judge of the Alabama Court of Appeals and Court of Criminal Appeals).

Leaving Cullman, return to Interstate 65. To see three more covered bridges, take Alabama 160 east at the Rickwood Caverns exit of Interstate 65 to Nectar. See Tour 4 for further directions to site. To see Birmingham should take Tour 6. Travelers wishing to see the coal mining country of northwest Alabama, the Appalachian area of northeast Alabama, The University of Alabama, Moundville, or Horseshoe Bend National Military Park may join Tours 3, 7, 8, or 9 at Birmingham. Or proceed south on Interstate 65 from this point to tour historic points between Birmingham and Montgomery.

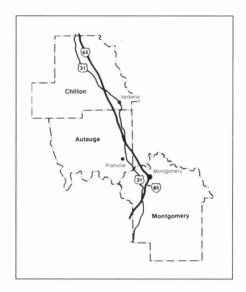

Part Two

Between Birmingham and Montgomery

From Birmingham, take Interstate 65 south to the Verbena exit.

Verbena

Verbena was a resort town begun by city dwellers fleeing epidemics of yellow fever. Its predominantly Victorian **historic district**, including homes and churches, is on the National Register.

Continue south on U.S. 31 to Mountain Creek. Turn east at park sign on Alabama 143. Proceed one mile.

Confederate Memorial Park

Confederate Memorial Park (c. 1902) was founded as a home for Confederate soldiers and their widows. The site of Alabama's last home for Confederate veterans, which closed in the 1930s, is adjacent to two of the few cemeteries in the nation where only Confederate Civil War veterans are buried. The Alabama Historical Commission, which owns this park, has developed nature trails, walkways, and a picnic area. The **Confederate Memorial Museum** in this park displays Civil War artifacts, Confederate uniforms, equipment, and flags as well as documents and photographs associated with the Confederate Soldiers Home. Open daily 9 a.m. to 5 p.m. No admission charge.

Return to U.S. 31 and continue south to Prattville.

Prattville

Founded in 1838 by an enterprising New Englander, Daniel Pratt, this was one of Alabama's earliest industrial communities. Pratt moved west from Georgia in 1833 to found a branch of his cotton gin business near the fertile Black Belt. By the early 1840s, his gins were known throughout the South and his factory was the largest producer of gins in the world. The Pratt works turned out a dozen gins a week by 1847 and employed both skilled slaves and white workers. In 1847 Pratt built a cotton mill in his village. His osnaburg (a cheap form of woven cotton) soon outsold similar cloth from New England factories. By the start of the Civil War, Pratt had become a millionaire from the profits of his gin factory, cotton mill, and other enterprises. He long had advocated the establishment of other industrial villages in the South, but developments of this type were halted by the Civil War. Pratt established the Red Mountain Coal and Iron Company in Birmingham in the early 1870s and his son-in-law, Henry F. DeBardeleben, became one of that city's chief developers. Pratt died at his home in Prattville in 1873 and is buried in a family cemetery that overlooks his enterprises.

Pratt Historic District contains the original manufacturing village laid out by Daniel Pratt following the pattern of a traditional New England mill town. **Pratt Gin Company** (c. 1838) comprises two original buildings of the factory erected on Autauga Creek by Pratt. **Gurney Manufacturing Company** (c. 1888) adjoins.

Another widely known resident of Prattville was the poet Sidney Lanier, who once rented a room in **Lanier House**, corner of South Chestnut and Third streets. Lady Bird Johnson, wife of President Lyndon Johnson, lived during part of her childhood in the home of her grandfather, Luther Pattillo, in the small community of Billingsley just off U.S. 82 north of Prattville.

From Prattville follow U.S. 82 south toward

Montgomery. Just before the Alabama River ridge, turn west on Autauga County 4 for two miles.

Buena Vista

Rich land along the Alabama River bottoms was sought eagerly by early migrants to the Black Belt. Many of those fortunate enough to purchase such land (for $50 to $100 an acre or more) at land sales in Milledgeville, Georgia, and later at Cahaba reaped fortunes from bountiful cotton crops.

An early example of the home of a prosperous planter is **Buena Vista** (c. 1821), a two-and-one-half-story frame house with four Ionic columns and brick portico. On the National Register, Buena Vista sits in splendid isolation much as it did more than 150 years ago.

Return to U.S. 82 and turn south to Montgomery.

Montgomery historic sites are described in Tour 10. Those wishing to see the plantation homes and Greek Revival mansions of Alabama's Black Belt may join Tour 11 at Montgomery.

Those wishing to see Tuskegee Institute, Auburn University, Eufaula, and other sites in south central Alabama and the Wiregrass may join Tour 12 or 13 from Montgomery. Or proceed on Interstate 65 south for historic sites between Montgomery and Mobile.

Part Three

Between Montgomery and Mobile

Take first Greenville exit off Interstate 65 south onto Alabama 263 north. Turn north on Alabama 185 three miles from exit.

Bartram Trail and Old Federal Road

The naturalist William Bartram traveled through what is now Butler County in 1776 following old Indian trails and some of the prehistoric communication lines of the South. Creeks called this old trail "the wolf trail" or "the great trading path."

In 1805 Congress provided funds for opening the Federal Road, a horse path following these Indian trails along the crests of ridges. In 1813 General F. L. Claiborne and his Missis-

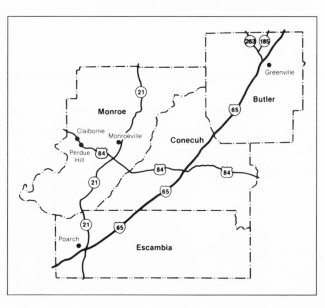

sippi volunteers widened the road on their way to fight Creeks at the Battle of the Holy Ground and bridged several streams to accommodate two-wheeled carts.

Many famous men other than Bartram traveled this road. Sam Dale passed this way in 1815 when he rode 600 miles in eight days to bring word to General Andrew Jackson at New Orleans that the War of 1812 was ended. General Thomas S. Woodward, an early Alabama historian, and Colonel William Barrett Travis, a hero who died at the Alamo, also passed along Federal Road.

The Butler County Historical Landmarks Foundation has marked a four-and-one-half-mile portion of the Bartram Trail and old Federal Road along Alabama 185 and Butler County 54. Except for the fact that the old road has been widened and paved, this stretch of Alabama, which is still sparsely populated, looks much as it did when Bartram passed this way 200 years ago.

Historic sites include **Oak Grove Methodist Church** (c. 1872); **Fort Dale site** (c. 1818), an early fort for protection against Indians; **Fort Dale Cemetery** (c. 1818), burial site of many pioneers; an **old log barn** (c. 1825); **The Palings site** (c. 1818), where an old stagecoach inn once stood; **Gary's Stockade site** (c. 1817), where a log fort served as a refuge from Indians; and **Ogly Massacre site** (c.

1818), where six persons were killed by Creek warriors. Ask directions locally to these sites.

Accommodations: Sherling Lake, off Alabama 263, a pleasant county park, offers camping sites. Comfortable motels at Greenville.

Return to Interstate 65 south.

Leave Interstate 65 below Evergreen on U.S. 84. Follow U.S. 84 west to Alabama 21. Turn north to Monroeville.

Monroeville

This quiet southern town was the childhood home of two famous American novelists. Harper Lee, a native of Monroeville, made that community the setting for her Pulitzer Prize–winning novel, *To Kill a Mockingbird.* Truman Capote recounted his childhood experiences in Monroeville in his memoir, *A Christmas Memory.* The old **Monroe County Courthouse** (c. 1903), on the National Register, a three-story brick structure with octagonal dome and central oval section, figured in both books. The courtroom on the second floor of the old court-

Monroe County Courthouse

62

house has been converted to a small community museum. Open Monday through Friday, 8 a.m. to 4 p.m.; Saturday, 9 a.m. to 1 p.m.; special tours by appointment.

Leaving Monroeville, follow U.S. 84 west fifteen miles to Perdue Hill.

suggestions for background reading

Capote, Truman. *A Christmas Memory.* New York: Random House, 1956. (Fiction)

Cruickshank, Helen G., ed. *John and William Bartram's America.* Garden City: Doubleday and Co., 1961.

Jackson, Harvey H., III. *Rivers of History: Life on the Coosa, Tallapoosa, Cahaba, and Alabama.* Tuscaloosa: University of Alabama Press, 1995.

Lee, Harper. *To Kill a Mockingbird.* New York: Popular Library, 1960. (Fiction)

Sutton, Ann, and Myron Sutton. *Exploring with the Bartrams.* Chicago: Rand-McNally, 1963.

Perdue Hill

Perdue Hill Historic District includes **Perdue Hill Masonic Lodge** (c. 1819), one of the oldest lodges in Alabama. This two-story frame building, with seven-bay facade and later portico, was moved from Claiborne where it once served as a county courthouse. General Lafayette was entertained in this building in 1825. Note also **Perdue Hill Presbyterian Church** (c. 1860), with unusual open bell tower; **Broughton Home** (c. 1853), across from the lodge, once a private academy; **Old Bullard Place** (c. 1858), two-story frame with two-story gal-

lery; and **Old Gilliard Home** (c. 1853), one-story frame with unusually wide double doors in front and back halls. Ask directions locally to these homes.

Just west of Perdue Hill on U.S. 84 is Claiborne.

Claiborne

A stop on the old Federal Road and one of the largest inland cotton markets in antebellum Alabama, Claiborne today is virtually a ghost town, with only a few crumbling buildings and a marker to tell of its storied past. A boulder with a plaque commemorates the site of Piache, an ancient Indian town visited by De Soto in 1540. Another Spaniard, Don Tristan de Luna, started a settlement here at a later Indian village, Nanipacana, in 1560. This attempt failed because of Indian hostility and lack of food.

During the Creek War of 1813–14, General F. L. Claiborne, leading a force of Mississippi volunteers, established a supply fort here on his way to defeat the Creeks at the Battle of the Holy Ground. A famous canoe fight, in which "Big Sam" Dale with two other whites and a black slave vanquished nine Creek warriors in hand-to-hand combat between the occupants of two canoes, took place on the Alabama River near Claiborne.

Lafayette, touring the backwoods of

a nation he had helped to found, was entertained at Claiborne in 1825. At the height of the cotton kingdom, several thousand residents lived in Claiborne. But as cotton trade dwindled after the Civil War, Claiborne, too, began to disappear.

Claiborne Historic District, much of it now overgrown by weeds and trees, includes **Fort Claiborne site** (c. 1813); **Travis Home** (c. mid-1800s), one-story frame containing a portion of the original house built by William Barrett Travis, who practiced law at Perdue Hill and later became a hero of the Alamo; and **Limestone Creek Indian Mound** (prehistoric) 100 feet long and 18 feet high. Ask directions locally to these sites and to **Deer-Dellet Home** (c. 1835), two-and-one-half-story frame Greek Revival, at the end of a long row of trees nearby.

For a splendid view of the Alabama River, continue west on U.S. 84 across an old steel bridge. Fossil beds of the Alabama River in this vicinity have yielded numerous ancient fossils.

Take U.S. 84 east to Alabama 21. Turn south to Poarch.

Poarch

In the vicinity of this small community live more than 800 descendants of the original Creek nation. Members of the Poarch Band of Creeks are descended from Creeks who remained friendly during the Creek War of 1813–14. For his loyalty, Lynn McGhee, an Indian guide, received a tract of land in rural Escambia County about fifty miles east of Mobile. Here the Creeks lived an isolated existence for nearly 150 years. Whites in neighboring communities excluded them from their schools and discriminated against them in other ways.

In 1947 Calvin McGhee, a descendant of Lynn McGhee, organized an effort by the Creeks to improve their community and relationship with government organizations. The Poarch Band filed a claim with the Indian Claims Commission for payment for lands ceded by the Treaty of Fort Jackson in 1814. After these Indian claims were settled in 1972, the Poarch Band began to improve the social, economic, and educational status of its nearly 2,100 members.

An eighteen-member tribal council represents the community in local, state, and national matters. Areas of particular concern include education, job training, health, nutrition, and Indian cultural awareness. The band was federally recognized by the Bureau of Indian Affairs in 1984 as an Indian tribe.

The **Tribal Multipurpose Center** (formerly the Poarch Consolidated Indian School) houses most of the Creek community's programs and activities, including council offices, youth programs, senior citizens' activities, a library, and archives. The former school building has become an important symbol of Indian progress as well as a focus of community activities.

For the past two decades, the Poarch Band has staged an annual **Thanksgiving Day Homecoming** during which Creeks who do not live in this vicinity return to Poarch to visit family and friends. These gatherings are celebrated with dancing, feasting, contests, games, and a solemn ceremony of thanksgiving for a year of bounty and good health. Traditional crafts are displayed and sold. For date and further information, write Poarch Creek Indians, HCR 69A Box 85B, Atmore, AL 36502, or telephone (334) 368-9136.

Accommodations: Little River State Park, fourteen miles north of Poarch on Alabama 21, offers primitive campgrounds and a few cottages. Atmore offers comfortable motels.

Return to Interstate 65 south and proceed to Baldwin County (see Tour 14) or to Mobile (see Tour 15), or return on Interstate 65 north to Birmingham for Tour 6.

Sloss Furnaces, Birmingham (p. 73)

TOUR 6

Birmingham

museums

statues

tours

historic districts

civil rights sites

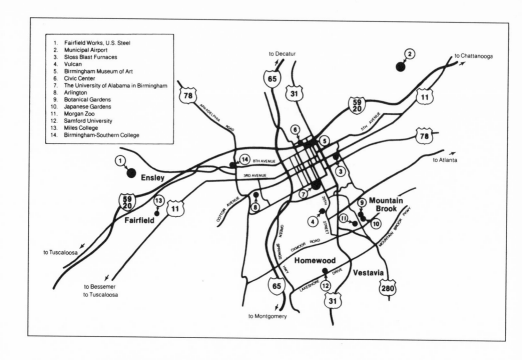

1. Fairfield Works, U.S. Steel
2. Municipal Airport
3. Sloss Blast Furnaces
4. Vulcan
5. Birmingham Museum of Art
6. Civic Center
7. The University of Alabama in Birmingham
8. Arlington
9. Botanical Gardens
10. Japanese Gardens
11. Morgan Zoo
12. Samford University
13. Miles College
14. Birmingham-Southern College

After the Civil War many Southerners believed that the Confederacy had lost because the South lacked industrial strength. They proposed building a "New South" in which agriculture would be balanced by industry. Industrial workers would provide a market for food and for cotton produced on farms while new industries would supply the South with manufactured goods.

Six years after the end of the war, a group of enterprising men broke ground for what they envisioned as a "great workshop town" located in Jones Valley near rich deposits of coal, iron, and limestone, the three essential ingredients for making steel. Railroad investors arranged to have two major lines cross at this point. Optimistic promoters named their new town for the English industrial city of Birmingham.

Between 1880 and 1890, Birmingham's population boomed from 3,000 to 26,000 as furnaces and rolling mills sprang up. In 1899 the Tennessee Coal and Iron Company built the district's first open-hearth steel plant. Within a few years this plant was turning out most of the railroad rails in the United States.

By the start of the twentieth century Birmingham was the leading industrial center of the New South. However, most of its small iron companies had been forced by price competition to merge into three large absentee-owned corporations. In 1907 the largest of these corporations, the Tennessee Coal and Iron Company, was purchased by United States Steel Corporation.

Because it was largely a one-industry town, Birmingham was paralyzed by the Great Depression of the 1930s. With one third of its people dependent for food upon the inadequate private welfare of that day, Birmingham was often described as "the hardest hit city in the nation." Not until World War II did Birmingham's industry revive. In the late 1940s Birmingham made further economic gains when the Supreme Court and the Interstate Commerce Commission moved to outlaw an artificially high pricing system, which had priced Birmingham ingot steel higher than that of Pittsburgh, and to equalize freight rates.

During the 1950s and early 1960s Birmingham, the most tightly segregated large city in the nation, became a focal point in the civil rights struggle. That struggle climaxed in Birmingham in the spring of 1963 when Dr. Martin Luther King, Jr., led hundreds of blacks, some of them schoolchildren, in demonstrations against segregation and in behalf of job opportunities. Birmingham Police Commissioner Eugene "Bull" Connor met these marchers with firehoses, police dogs, and tear gas, and pictures of the scene aroused nationwide support for blacks. Birmingham's white business leaders then came to terms with leaders of the black community, desegregating the downtown area, promising better jobs, and releasing jailed demonstrators.

Public facilities in Birmingham today are integrated. Blacks and whites have equal access to parks, schools, libraries, restaurants, and hotels, and many blacks hold responsible jobs in offices and stores. In 1979 Birmingham elected its first black mayor, Dr. Richard Arrington, Jr., and in 1981 designated January 15, Dr. King's birthday, an official city holiday, now a national holiday.

The **Birmingham Civil Rights Institute**, opened in 1992, is a state-of-the-art facility housing exhibits that depict historical events from post–World War I racial separation to present day racial progress. The trip begins with a film of Birmingham's early history. As the screen lifts to reveal "colored" and "white" drinking fountains, visitors enter the era of segregation. Lifelike figures and detailed exhibits recall the city's mining indus-

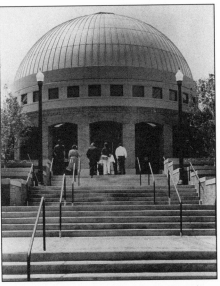

Birmingham Civil Rights Institute

69

Birmingham Civil Rights Institute exhibit:
Rosa Parks

Birmingham Civil Rights Institute exhibit:
Freedom Riders' bus

try, a streetcar, a shotgun house, a movie theater, and other slices of everyday life in a segregated city. Visitors can choose selections from favorite musicians on a video jukebox, then eavesdrop on conversations of people discussing race in the 1950s. Dramatic moments of the civil rights movement are replayed in four mini-theaters. Visitors then join a procession of figures, celebrating the victories achieved through the civil rights struggle. The journey ends with an exhibit gallery depicting contemporary human rights issues around the world. The Institute is the centerpiece of the city's historic civil rights district, which includes the historic **Sixteenth Street Baptist Church**, bombed in 1963, and **Kelly Ingram Park**, site of demonstrations and confrontations. Both can be

viewed from windows inside the Institute. Sixteenth Street Baptist Church (1911), 1530 Sixth Avenue North, a modified Romanesque-style church designed by a prominent black architect and built by a black contractor and craftsmen, was the scene of the tragic Sunday school bombing in 1963 in which four children were killed by an explosion near the sanctuary. A stained-glass window, donated by the

Sixteenth Street Baptist Church, Birmingham

70

Sixteenth Street Baptist Church Wales Window

suggestions for background reading

Armes, Ethel. *The Story of Coal and Iron in Alabama.* Cambridge, Mass.: Harvard University Press, 1910. Reprint. Birmingham: Book-Keepers Press, 1972.

Atkins, Leah. *Birmingham: An Illustrated History.* Woodland Hills, Calif.: Windsor Publishing Co., 1981.

Calloway-Thomas, Carolyn, and John Louis Lucaites, eds. *Martin Luther King, Jr., and the Sermonic Power of Public Discourse.* Tuscaloosa: University of Alabama Press, 1993.

Coleman, John Shields. *Josiah Morris, 1818–1891: Montgomery Banker Whose Faith Built Birmingham.* New York: Newcomen Society, 1948.

Crane, Mary P. *The Life of James R. Powell and Early History of Alabama.* Brooklyn: Brounworth and Co., 1930.

Franklin, Jimmie Lewis. *Back to Birmingham: Richard Arrington, Jr., and His Times.* Tuscaloosa: University of Alabama Press, 1989.

Harris, Carl V. *Political Power in Birmingham, 1871–1921.* Knoxville: University of Tennessee Press, 1977.

people of Wales, commemorates the tragedy with the image of a crucified black Christ. **Kelly Ingram Park**, across from this church, was the scene of massive civil rights demonstrations in the 1960s.

Two other historically significant areas are located within walking distance of the Institute: the revitalized **Fourth Avenue Business District** and the renovated **Carver Theatre**, home of the Jazz Hall of Fame featuring jazz greats, such as Nat King Cole, Duke Ellington, Lionel Hampton and Erskine Hawkins, with ties to Alabama, and the music that made them famous. The **Alabama Jazz Hall of Fame**, 1631 Fourth Avenue North is open Tuesday through Saturday, 10 a.m. to 6 p.m.; Sunday 1 to 5 p.m. No admission charge.

Kelly Ingram Park

Hassinger, Bernice Shield. *Henderson Steel: Birmingham's First Steel*. Birmingham: Jefferson County Historical Commission, 1978.

Lewis, W. David. *Sloss Furnaces and the Rise of the Birmingham District: An Industrial Epic*. Tuscaloosa: University of Alabama Press, 1994.

McMillan, Malcolm C. *Yesterday's Birmingham*. Miami: E. A. Seemann Publishing Co., 1975.

Nunnelley, William A. *Bull Connor*. Tuscaloosa: University of Alabama Press, 1990.

Pioneer Club. *Early Days in Birmingham*. Birmingham: Southern University Press, 1968.

Satterfield, Carolyn Green, comp. *Historic Sites of Jefferson County, Alabama*. Birmingham: Birmingham Printing Co., 1976.

Sikora, Frank. *Until Justice Rolls Down: The Birmingham Church Bombing Case*. Tuscaloosa: University of Alabama Press, 1991.

Sterne, Emma Gelders. *The Calico Ball*. New York: Dodd, Mead and Co., 1934. Reprint ed., Birmingham: Privately printed, 1971. (Fiction)

Warren, Dorothea. *The Practical Dreamer: A Story of John T. Milner: His Family and Forebears*. Birmingham: Southern Family Press, 1959.

White, Marjorie L., ed. *Downtown Birmingham: Architectural and Historical Walking Tour Guide*. Birmingham: Birmingham Historical Society and First National Bank, 1978.

White, Marjorie L. *The Birmingham District: An Industrial History and Guide*. Birmingham: Birmingham Historical Society, 1981.

Downtown and Environs

A guidebook, *Downtown Birmingham: Architectural and Historical Walking Tour Guide*, is available from the Birmingham Historical Society, 1 Sloss Quarters, telephone (205) 251-1880, or in area bookstores. For children, *Birmingham Heritage Hike Guide*, outlining a downtown walking tour with games and commentary, is available at the Birmingham Historical Society or through the Greater Birmingham Convention and Visitors Information Center, 2200 9th Avenue North, (205) 252-9825. Much of the following information comes from the guidebook *Downtown Birmingham*.

"Heaviest Corner on Earth," First Avenue and 20th Street North, is a rare concentration of four steel-frame skyscrapers constructed between 1902 and 1912. When these four individually distinguished buildings were completed, they dramatically changed the vertical scale of the existing Victorian city. Impressed citizens proudly proclaimed this the "heaviest corner on earth." The buildings are **Woodward Building** (1902–03), **Brown-Marx Building** (1906–08), **John Hand Building** (1912), and **Empire Building** (1909). While the Brown-Marx and Woodward buildings are more restrained with plain textures and the straightforward expression of function and structure of the Commercial style of architecture, the Empire and John Hand buildings, designed in Neoclassical style, are faced with white terra cotta and employ bold classical motifs. In the panels above the paired arches on the 16th floor of the Empire Building, Roman busts depict the building's architect and contractor. Large "E's" along the cornice stand for the Empire Improvement Company, which financed this tower.

Morris Avenue, named for Josiah Morris, one of Birmingham's founders, was the city's first wholesale district,

Sloss Furnaces

Steiner Building

growing up along the railroad tracks that gave birth to the city. Its warehouses were built to house small family enterprises that sold fruits, groceries, coffee, tea, meal, and flour, and ran sawmills, stockyards, and carriage works. The old cobblestones and gaslights along the street were restored after Morris Avenue was designated a National Historic District in 1973.

Steiner Building (1890), First Avenue and 21st Street North, on the National Register, originally housed an important early commercial and investment banking concern. The red brick building, characterized by large semicircular arches and the use of rough cut stone for arches and lintels and for highlighting certain details, is the most striking example of Richardson Romanesque style still standing in Birmingham.

Sloss Blast Furnaces (c. 1882, 1900s, 1920s, 1930s), First Avenue North at 32nd Street, were two of the largest blast furnaces in this area. Beginning in 1882 pig iron was produced continuously here for almost ninety years. The furnaces were shut down in 1970 because of the high cost of pollution-control devices. The oldest portions of these furnaces are the earliest blast furnaces of this type in the United States. This immense structure, on the National Register and a National Historic Landmark, is open to the public Tuesday through Saturday, 10 a.m. to 4 p.m.; Sunday, noon to 5 p.m. Free admission.

Powell School (1887), 2331 Sixth Avenue North, also on the National Register, is the only early school remaining in the downtown area. The three-story red brick schoolhouse, designed in Victorian Gothic style, was

73

Birmingham Museum of Art

named for Colonel James R. Powell, one of Birmingham's founders and its first elected mayor, who donated his full salary to the new school.

The Alabama Theatre (c. 1927), 1811 Third Avenue North, on the National Register, exemplifies the extravagant and lavish movie theaters of the 1920s. Designed to suggest a Spanish palace, the facade is heavy with Moorish details. The grand lobby is decorated with marble columns, gold leaf, and chandeliers, while the auditorium, built to seat about 3,000 people, is crowned with an elliptical dome.

Alabama Penny Savings Bank Building (c. 1913), 310 18th Street North, also on the National Register, was the first black-owned bank in Alabama and in 1907 was the second larg-

est black-owned bank in the nation, loaning money to finance many black homes and churches. But in 1915 the bank encountered financial problems and folded. The Knights of Phythias, a black service organization, has owned the building since 1915.

Oak Hill Cemetery (c. 1871), 1120 19th Street North, on the National Register, contains the graves of many of Birmingham's early residents, including eight mayors, two governors, numerous Confederate and Union soldiers, many ex-slaves, paupers, and even the madame who nursed cholera victims during the 1873 epidemic. Unusual grave markers in the city's oldest cemetery include stone cradles, handsome statues, obelisks, and mausoleums, as well as simple stones inscribed with biblical verses and poetry or engraved with miniature portraits.

Birmingham Museum of Art, 2000 Eighth Avenue North, contains extensive holdings in pre-Columbian and American Indian art. Pre-Columbian material includes an especially fine group of Inca gold; American Indian art includes objects from Moundville.

Arlington

The museum also houses the Rives Collection of archaeological material, major sculptures, and artifacts from the ancient Near East, twelve examples of Frederic Remington's famous bronzes on the Old West, the largest and most complete collection of Oriental art in the South, exceptional collections of English and American silver, one of the largest groups of important and early Wedgewood in the world, contemporary works by local and regional artists, works from the Kress Collection of Italian Renaissance paintings, and the recently acquired Hitt Collection of 18th-century French paintings and decorative arts. Open Tuesday through Saturday, 10 a.m. to 5 p.m.; Sunday, noon to 5 p.m. No admission charge.

Alabama Sports Hall of Fame, located in the Birmingham-Jefferson Civic Center Coliseum, contains plaques and exhibits honoring outstanding figures in the world of sports, including baseball players Willie Mays, Leroy "Satchel" Paige, and Henry "Hank" Aaron; world heavyweight boxing champion Joe Louis; and football coach Paul "Bear" Bryant. Open Monday through Saturday, 9 a.m. to 5 p.m.; Sunday, 1 to 5 p.m. Admission charge.

Arlington (c. 1842), 331 Cotton Avenue Southwest, on the National Register, is older than the city of Birmingham. The house was a private residence and a fashionable boarding house before being purchased by the city of Birmingham as a museum. Open Tuesday through Saturday, 10 a.m. to 4 p.m.; Sunday, 1 to 4 p.m. Admission charge.

Southside

Follow 20th Street South to 8th Ave. Turn west.

You will be in the heart of the campus of **The University of Alabama at Birmingham** (a part of The University of Alabama System, which also includes The University of Alabama, located in Tuscaloosa, and The University of Alabama in Huntsville; these three institutions are autonomous units that have their own presidents, while the system is headed by a chancellor).

The **Medical Center**, at the eastern end of this urban campus, comprises the School of Medicine, School of Dentistry, and School of Public and Allied Health, which includes a School of Nursing, School of Optometry, the Regional Technical Institute, and The University of Alabama Hospitals.

University College, at the western end of the campus, is the other major division of UAB. Established as a degree-granting division of the university in 1966, University College is within convenient commuting distance of thousands of students.

Group tours of the UAB campus may be arranged through the Office of Public Relations. One of the sites of historical interest on the UAB campus is **Reynolds Historical Library**, housed in the Lister Hill Library of the Health Sciences on Eighth Avenue west of 18th Street and of interest to serious students of the history of medicine. Included in this collection are ivory anatomical mannequins, original manuscripts, Arabic books and manuscripts, and hundreds of rare medical, dental, and scientific books, some printed before the year 1500. Literary figures represented in first editions include Walt Whitman, Rudyard Kipling, Ralph Waldo Emerson, Lord Byron, and Robert Browning. Open Monday through Friday, 8 a.m. to 12 noon, 1 p.m. to 5 p.m.

Near the UAB campus is **Southern Research Institute**, 2000 Ninth Avenue South. This research facility is involved in scientific projects that include experimentation with drugs for use in the treatment of cancer and other diseases, as well as development of medical devices and research on air pollution control equipment and high temperature materials. A ninety-minute tour is given Fridays at 2:30 p.m.; group tours are available by appointment on other days. Reservations required. Call (205) 581-2317. No admission charge.

Highland Avenue–Rhodes Park Historic District (1880s–1930), in the vicinity of Highland Avenue–28th Street–Tenth Avenue–30th Street, includes the last concentrated grouping of elegant homes on Birmingham's first planned upper-income boulevard (2700–2908 Highland Avenue). Curving Highland Avenue, with its late Victorian and early-twentieth-century mansions, was considered the most imposing new residential avenue in the South at its height in the early 1900s. The district also contains notable houses on Rhodes Circle and an impressive concentration of more modest structures exemplifying popular early-twentieth-century styles. Note particularly the **Enslen House** (1906–08), 2737 Highland Avenue, on the National Register, two-story brick with two-inch marble facing and paired Doric columns.

Lakeview School (c. 1901), 2800 Clairmont Avenue, the second oldest school in Birmingham, also is on the National Register. Nearby **Chestnut Hill District** (c. early 1900s), an in-town residential neighborhood of early-twentieth-century styles, is experiencing a renaissance as younger families move back into the city.

Forest Park Historic District (c. 1906–1930s), includes more than 250 homes in a variety of styles, many of which were and continue to be residences of city leaders. **Woodward House** (c. 1919), 4101 Altamont Road, now the residence of the president of The University of Alabama at Birmingham, a two-story brick mansion in Italian villa style with servants' quarters and guest houses, is open on special occasions.

Red Mountain cut

Nearby **Swann House** (c. 1929), 3536 Redmont Road, a five-story sandstone mansion in the style of an English manor, was built by an early industrial leader, Theodore Swann.

Red Mountain

The area in which Birmingham is located was once covered by ancient seas. As 500 million years passed, the seas and land surfaces changed in response to horizontal and vertical forces generated in the earth's crust. Earth forces caused the rocks of the crust to fold and eventually break. All these events are recorded in the rocks exposed in Red Mountain Cut.

"Red paint" rock was first discovered by Indians who used it to decorate their bodies for warfare and ceremonies. In the early 1800s two Tennessee frontiersmen noted the red ore rocks on this mountain. Later discoveries of coal and limestone, within a radius of five to fifteen miles, provided the basis for development of an iron- and steel-producing center after the Civil War.

In the early 1900s about sixty mines were producing "red ore" for the blast furnaces and ovens of the Birmingham district. Today no red ore mines are operating in Alabama because it is cheaper to bring in foreign ores of higher grade. An estimated five billion tons of red ore still are unmined in Alabama.

Red Mountain Museum, 1421 22nd Street South, located on Red Mountain overlooking Birmingham, houses exhibits on archaeology, anthropology, geology, astronomy, paleontology, and related fields. Among its holdings are a mosasaur, a fourteen-foot aquatic lizard that lived 85 million years ago; a solar telescope that allows visitors to observe the surface of the sun through the safety of television monitors; and dioramas of "man in the new world," depicting four major cultural periods of human beings in North America. Adjacent to the museum is a geologic walkway where visitors may observe 190 million years of Earth's history exposed by highway excavation. The cut exposed three beds of iron ore, the largest of which is

Vulcan

Botanical Gardens, exterior

twenty feet thick. Open Monday through Friday, 9 a.m. to 3 p.m.; Saturday, 10 a.m. to 4 p.m.; Sunday, 1 to 4 p.m. No admission charge.

Nearby, **The Discovery Place**, 1320 22nd Street South, is a children's museum designed so that children may learn scientific concepts through a "hands-on" process, allowing them to touch and manipulate the exhibits, which highlight energy, health, communications, machinery, natural plants and fish, and city services. Open Monday through Friday, 9 a.m. to 3 p.m.; Saturday, 10 a.m. to 4 p.m.; Sunday, 1 to 4 p.m. Admission charge.

Vulcan, on Red Mountain overlooking the city, the largest cast-iron statue in the world, is 55 feet high and weighs 120,000 pounds. (By way of comparison, Vulcan is about one-third as tall as the Statue of Liberty.) Six tons

of iron were needed to cast the head alone. The statue was executed by Guiseppe Moretti (see *Sylacauga*) as Birmingham's display at the St. Louis Exposition of 1904. The Roman god of the forge was considered an appropriate symbol for a "magic city" of iron and steel. When the exposition closed, the statue was shipped back to Birmingham where it remained on the state fairgrounds for three decades. In 1936 civic and industrial leaders decided to place Vulcan on a 120-foot pedestal atop Red Mountain. The building of this tower was a project of the Works Progress Administration of the New Deal.

To reach Vulcan Park, follow 20th Street South just past the crest of Red Mountain. Turn at sign. Open daily 8:00 a.m. to 10:30 p.m. Admission charge.

Shades Valley

Take U.S. 280 south over Red Mountain. Follow signs for Sylacauga. Take first Mountain Brook exit.

Botanical Gardens, Japanese Gardens, and **Zoo,** although not of historic significance, are of interest to many visitors. The Botanical Gardens adjoin. Open daily. No admission fee. Birmingham Zoo, across from these gardens, is one of the largest in the Southeast. Open daily 9 a.m. to 5 p.m.; June through August, 9 a.m. to 7 p.m. Admission charge.

Mountain Brook

Leaving the zoo, turn south toward Mountain Brook Village and continue to Mountain Brook Parkway. Turn east and wander at will among the curving roadways of this handsome residential district for a glimpse of residential styles from the 1920s to the present.

Mountain Brook, primarily a residential city, was planned by Robert Jemison, Jr., Birmingham's most important realtor and developer, shortly before the stock market crash of 1929. Expanded in succeeding decades, Mountain Brook, with hundreds of expensive homes in a natural setting of wooded hills and valleys, is one of the South's most attractive high-income residential areas.

The Old Mill, on Mountain Brook Parkway, a replica of an old water-powered gristmill, has been converted into a residence. **Beaumont House**, 4151 Montevallo Road, has on its grounds a replica of a one-room log cabin (c. 1850) that was once the commissary for Irondale Furnace. Ask directions to nearby **Irondale Furnace site** in Cherokee Bend. A foot trail

leads to the ruins of this furnace built in 1864 to supply iron for the Confederacy. The furnace was partially destroyed by Union raiders in 1865.

Follow Mountain Brook Parkway west until it becomes Lakeshore Drive.

Samford University, 800 Lakeshore Drive, was founded as Howard College in Marion in 1841 and moved to Birmingham in 1887. After the present campus was built in the late 1950s and 1960s, the college changed its name to Samford University to honor a major benefactor, Frank Park Samford. Cumberland School of Law, formerly located in Lebanon, Tennessee, is now part of this university, as are the Howard College of Arts and Sciences and schools of Business, Divinity, Education, Music, Nursing, and Pharmacy. Samford is affiliated with the Alabama Baptist State Convention. **Rushton Memorial Carillon**, in the steeple of Davis Library, contains sixty bells, each bearing a Latin, biblical, or poetic inscription. These bells were cast at the official bellfoundry of the Crown of Holland, considered the home of carillons because the world's first great bells were cast there in the seventeenth century. The largest of these bells, called the Bourdon Bell, weighs 5,192 pounds. The carillon is played daily on the hour. For information on special concerts, telephone the Music School of Samford University, (205) 870-2851.

On Shades Mountain above Samford stands the **Temple of Sibyl** (c. 1924), a marble and concrete circular temple with dome, moved from its original location on the nearby grounds of a unique round house patterned after the Temple of the Vestal Virgins in Rome. This house, built by Birmingham mayor George B. Ward, has been demolished. The temple, open to the public, affords a good view of Samford University and Shades Valley.

Western Area

Miles College, in Vinesville, was the principal four-year college for black students of Birmingham prior to desegregation of Alabama's institutions of higher learning. Many black teachers in Birmingham public schools received their higher education here. Chartered in 1908, Miles is under the direction of the Christian Methodist Episcopal Church.

Birmingham-Southern College, 900 Arkadelphia Road, a Methodist institution, was the result of a consolidation in 1918 of Birmingham College and old Southern University in Greensboro. Among its unusual buildings are a modern theater and **Meyer Planetarium**. The planetarium is open Monday through Friday, 8 a.m. to noon, by appointment. Small admission charge.

To see Birmingham's iron and steel industry continue southwest on Interstate 59 toward Ensley and Fairfield.

Fairfield Works of United States Steel Corporation, near Interstate 59, includes four blast furnaces that produce iron, Q-Bop furnaces for making steel, a sheet finishing mill, a coke plant (indicated by plumes of steam coming off quenched coke), and in the background a tin mill where tin plate is made.

Nearby **Fairfield** (1909), originally named Corey, was a planned community for those who worked in the steel plants. Enoch T. Ensley, an early industrialist, founded the neighboring community of **Ensley** (1887).

Nixon Building (c. 1922), 1728 20th Street, Ensley, located where two streetcar lines once crossed, contained a dance hall that was a popular gathering place for Birmingham's black community before World War II. The famed jazz composer Erskine Hawkins, a Birmingham native, immortalized this site in his song "Tuxedo Junction."

For Bessemer, see Tour 8 below.

Eastern Area

Cahaba Village (in **Trussville**) and **Palmerdale** were planned communities under the New Deal projects of the 1930s. The concept behind these federal subsistence homestead projects was that industrial workers should be able to purchase low-cost homes and small plots of land for raising vegetables and fruits. Most of the original houses and some community buildings remain.

TOUR 7
Northwest
Alabama

From Birmingham

Jasper

Natural Bridge

Bankhead National Forest

Return to Birmingham

strip mining

coal mining villages

Bankhead family homes

wilderness area

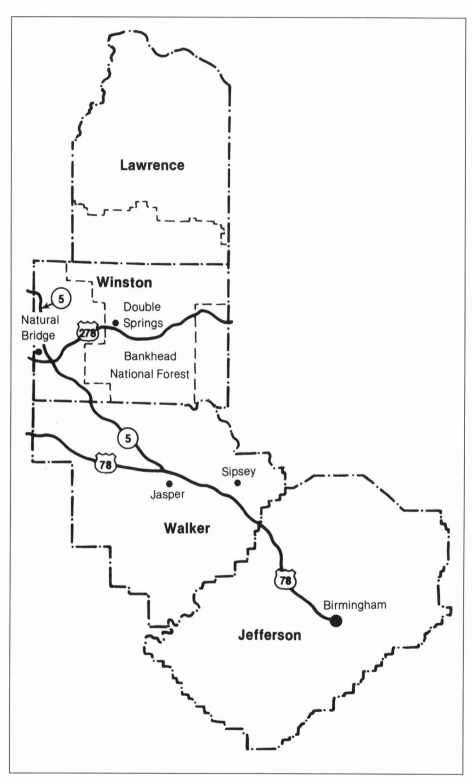

Coal Mine Country

For about 100 million years, a huge, shallow sea covered the entire eastern United States, including the part we now call Alabama. About 350 to 500 million years ago, these waters eventually receded, leaving vast swamps in their wake. Strange plants and huge insects, including giant cockroaches and dragonflies two feet long, adapted to life on dry land. When these plants and insects died, their remains formed deposits that we know today as coal.

Alabama's pioneers mined coal from riverbeds by anchoring flatboats near a seam and loosening the coal with crowbars. Divers went down to grasp the coal and load it into boats. At first such coal was called "stonecoal" to distinguish it from charcoal. When one of Alabama's first coal operators sent a boatload to Mobile for sale, he sent a boy with each bucketful to show the homeowner how it could be lighted and burned.

Early farmers had no use for mineral land. One sold a rocky ten-acre parcel of land near Russellville for fifty dollars. Later that tract became one of the richest possessions of Sloss Sheffield Coal and Iron Company. Unfortunately most pioneers had no concept of the potential wealth beneath their infertile soil.

Among the twenty-five states that produce coal, Alabama ranks eighth. Bituminous (soft) coal, used in power plants and blast furnaces, is found in twenty-two counties in central and northern Alabama. Alabama's biggest coal-producing counties are Walker, Jefferson, and Tuscaloosa. Underground mining largely has given way to strip mining, a faster and more economical method of extracting coal but one that leaves ugly scars on the land unless coal companies move swiftly to repair this damage.

Geologists estimate that about 18.4 billion tons of coal still lie beneath the soil of Alabama, making up part of our nation's coal reserve, enough to last for hundreds of years. However, not all of this coal is clean burning (air pollution laws regulate use of coal in many states) and not all of it is easily mined.

To visit a simulated coal mine, contact Alabama Mining Museum located in old Dora in the 1935 gym built by the WPA. No admission charge but arrangements for individual or group tours must be made in advance. Telephone (205) 648-2442.

suggestions for background reading

Bankhead, Tallulah. *Tallulah: My Autobiography.* New York: Harper, 1952.

Bass, Jack. *Judge Frank M. Johnson, Jr., and the South's Fight over Civil Rights.* New York: Doubleday, 1993.

Elliott, Carl, comp. *Annals of Northwest Alabama.* Jasper: Privately printed, 1958–80.

Gill, Brendan. *Tallulah.* New York: Holt, Rinehart and Winston, 1972.

Hoole, W. Stanley. *Alabama Tories: The First Alabama Cavalry, U.S.A., 1862–1865.* Tuscaloosa: Confederate Publishing Co., 1960.

Powell, E. A. *Fifty-Five Years in West Alabama.* Works Progress Administration Series, Vol. 2. Birmingham: Birmingham Library Board, 1937.

Raines, Howell. *Whisky Man.* New York: Viking, 1977. (Fiction)

Stallworth, Anne N. *This Time Next Year.* New York: Vanguard, 1971. (Fiction)

Thompson, Wesley. *"The Free State of Winston": A History of Winston County, Alabama.* Winfield, Ala.: Pareil Press, 1968.

Yarbrough, Tinsley E. *Judge Frank Johnson and Human Rights in Alabama.* University: University of Alabama Press, 1981.

Sipsey

From Birmingham, take U.S. 78 northwest toward Jasper. About seven miles east of Jasper, watch for the sign to Sipsey. Turn north and proceed five miles on Walker County 22. A large strip mining operation is visible from this road.

Sipsey coal mine community (c. 1912), on the Warrior River at the juncture of the Sipsey and Mulberry forks, was a model coal mine village of the early twentieth century. Originally the village consisted of 200 sturdy four-room houses for workers and their families, renting for $6 a month, each with its own outhouse. Often two families shared a house, each family having two rooms. DeBardeleben Coal Company, which owned the village, also provided elementary schools, a commissary, dairy, medical clinic, and church (used alternately by Methodists and Baptists). For recreation, Sipsey offered an open-air movie theater, dances, scout troops, and baseball games with rival mining communities.

In 1950 the company-owned houses at Sipsey were sold to private individuals.

Departing Sipsey, return to U.S. 78 and continue west to Jasper.

Jasper

Heart of the coal mining country, Jasper was settled in 1815 as a post for trading with the Chickasaw and Choctaw Indians. The town was named for Sergeant Jasper, a soldier in the American Revolution. Nearby is the Gorgas Power Plant of Alabama Power Company, which generates electricity, using coal from the rich Warrior Coal Field. On the campus of **Bevill State Community College** (formerly Walker College) is an old locomotive like those used in the 1920s to transport coal out of this region. Now coal also is transported by trucks and barges.

Among sites of historic interest in Jasper are: **Long Home** (c. 1903), 701 19th Street, two-story frame with eleven Doric columns supporting a porch on three sides; **William B. Bankhead Home** (c. 1925), 800 Seventh Street, home of the speaker of the U.S. House of Representatives (1936–40) and father of famed actress Tallulah Bankhead; **John H. Bankhead, Sr., House** or **Sunset** (c. late 1800s), 1400 Seventh Avenue, two-story frame with columned verandah, formerly owned by John H. Bankhead, Sr., U.S. representative and senator for

"Sunset," Bankhead home, Jasper

thirty-three years and patriarch of one of Alabama's most prominent political families. His son, Senator John H. Bankhead, Jr. (1930–45), also lived here. Young Tallulah, who was reared in this house after the death of her mother, played childhood make-believe roles here, attired in costumes from trunks in the attic.

Departing Jasper, follow Alabama 5 northwest to U.S. 278. Turn west to Natural Bridge.

Natural Bridge

This unusual rock formation was created by the effect of a stream and springs upon a large deposit of sandstone formed over 200 million years ago. Gradually eroded by water, all that remains of the sandstone are two giant arches. The larger is 148 feet long, 60 feet high, and 33 feet wide. By way of comparison, this bridge is almost twice as long as the famed Natural Bridge of Virginia, but the Virginia bridge is three times as high as Alabama's. Alabama men who sympa-

thized with the Union during the Civil War often used this well-known landmark as a meeting place on their way to join northern forces. An impressive natural wonder, Natural Bridge is unspoiled by artificial lighting or piped-in music. Trails in the park area lead past many hardwood trees, including poplar and mulberry.

Alabama has several other natural bridges, including one near Hodges and another in Bankhead National Forest.

Accommodations: Campgrounds in the park. Comfortable motel nearby and others at Haleyville. Picnic facilities.

Departing Natural Bridge, take U.S. 278 east to Double Springs.

Winston County

Many north Alabama farmers, owning few slaves or none, had serious doubts about the wisdom of seceding from the Union over the issue of slavery. At first these loyalists sought neutrality in the Civil War. After the Confederacy passed a conscription act

Natural Bridge

in 1862, neutralists and dissenters hid in caves and coves rather than join the Rebel army. Many met at Natural Bridge to plan their escape to Federal lines. The First Alabama Union Cavalry, composed of these loyalists, marched with Sherman through Georgia and the Carolinas. Statistics show that 2,578 white Alabamians joined the Union army. Hundreds of other Union sympathizers formed bands of deserters and acted as scouts for Union troops. Confederate General Gideon J. Pillow estimated in 1862 that 8,000 to 10,000 so-called Tories and deserters hid in the Alabama mountains. Historians today do not agree as to the extent of dissent from the Confederacy in Alabama. One has stated that peace sentiment was strong enough to have forced Alabama to a negotiated settlement if peace had not come in 1865. Another contends that disloyalty to the Confederacy was minimal and confined largely to Winston County.

Meeting at Looney's Tavern in Winston County, Unionist sympathizers adopted a resolution commending Christopher C. Sheats, their young representative at Alabama's secession convention, for voting against leaving the Union. The 3,000 persons who gathered here on July 4, 1861, to protest secession considered the question of whether a county could secede from a state. Although they took no formal action, the Winston loyalists earned

their county an abiding nickname, "The Free State of Winston." **Looney's Tavern site** is located on Winston County 41 north of Addison.

Winston County's most widely known native son is federal circuit judge Frank M. Johnson, Jr., who handed down major decisions favoring civil rights during the 1960s and decisions attempting to upgrade Alabama's prisons and mental hospitals during the 1970s.

Bankhead National Forest

At **Bankhead Ranger Station** in Double Springs, pick up maps and information about the forest.

Alabama once was covered by thick forests. In northwestern Alabama most trees were hardwoods such as oak and hickory. Following the Civil War, lumbering and fires destroyed most of the hardwoods in the Tennessee Valley, thereby increasing erosion and adding to the problem of flooding. With the help of expert foresters from the Tennessee Valley Authority and the U.S. Forest Service, much of the Tennessee Valley has been reforested today.

Alabama has four national forests, protected and managed by the Forest Service of the U.S. Department of Agriculture. These public lands are purchased, owned, and supported by and for taxpayers. Commercial lumbering is permitted in these forests under su-

Pine Torch Church

pervision of the Forest Service.

Bankhead National Forest shelters the Sipsey Wilderness, a natural wildlife area where streams cascade over rock faces into deep canyons. The Bee Branch scenic area in this wilderness contains one of the last stands of hardwoods that have never been cut and the largest yellow poplar in Alabama. The Forest Service attempts to preserve wilderness areas in their natural state for campers and hikers to enjoy.

An interesting historic site in Bankhead National Forest is **Pine Torch Church** (c. 1820), one of Alabama's few remaining log churches.

After exploring Bankhead National Forest, return to Alabama 5. Return to Birmingham or continue north on U.S. 43 to Tuscumbia and join Tour 2.

Moundville Archaeological Park (p. 101) *Above*: Temple Mound; *Below*: Time phase diorama

TOUR 8
West Central Alabama

From Birmingham

Bessemer

Tannehill Historical State Park

Tuscaloosa

Moundville

Centreville

Brierfield Ironworks Park

Montevallo

Return to Birmingham

pioneer homes
and blast furnaces

Alabama's third capital

The University of Alabama

prehistoric Indian mounds

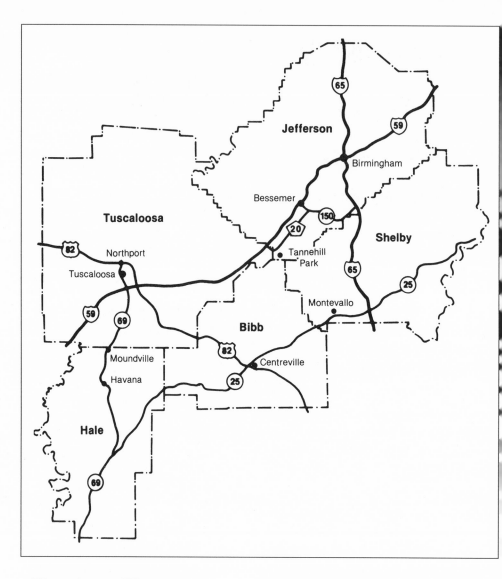

Pioneer Homes

Alabama's first white settlers used its plentiful forests to make their shelters. With the aid of neighbors, simple houses usually were built in a single day. Nearby families helped raise the walls, put on the roof, and lay the floor (if any) and then left it to the owners to apply finishing touches. At first such houses were built without nails;

wooden pegs and poles held them together. Houses had dirt floors or were floored with broad split boards. Primitive chimneys, built of grass, mud, and sticks, were placed on the outside gable side. The backs and sides of these fireplaces were lined with rocks set in mud or mud plaster. Fireplaces, which served for cooking as well as heating, were usually five feet high, three to five feet long, and two feet deep. Atop these fireplaces, big logs were set high enough so they would not catch fire.

This style of folk house, known as *single pen*, was basically a one-story house with a small loft and gable roof. Most Alabama single-pen houses had windows on either side of the chimney. Double log houses came into being as more living space was needed. Because it was difficult to enlarge a log house, the usual solution was to add another complete room at the gable side rather than in back. This had been an established custom in England, regardless of what building materials were used. If the second pen were placed against the chimney end of the original structure, this was called a *saddlebag house* (because each pen was on one side of the chimney like saddlebags on either side of a horse). If the second pen were placed next to the original pen (on the nonchimney side), this was called a *double-pen house*. If the second pen were separated from the first by a roofed open space six to ten feet wide, this was known (for obvious reasons) as a *dogtrot* or *dog run house*. Most dogtrot-type houses are found in the Piedmont (eastern hills) of Alabama, but dogtrot houses were built throughout the state, accounting for about 10 percent of its original rural houses except in extreme south Alabama.

Departing Birmingham, take Interstate 59 to Bessemer.

suggestions for background reading

Agee, James, and Walker Evans. *Let Us Now Praise Famous Men: Three Tenant Families.* Boston: Houghton Mifflin, 1960.

Blitz, John H. *Ancient Chiefdoms of the Tombigbee.* Tuscaloosa: University of Alabama Press, 1993.

Carmer, Carl. *Stars Fell on Alabama.* New York: Farrar and Rinehart, 1934. Reprint. Tuscaloosa: University of Alabama Press, 1985.

Cason, Clarence. *90° in the Shade.* Chapel Hill: University of North Carolina Press, 1935. Reprint. Tuscaloosa: University of Alabama Press, 1983.

Duffee, Mary Gordon. *Sketches of Alabama.* Edited by Virginia Pounds Brown. University: University of Alabama Press, 1970.

Dunne, Gerald. *Hugo Black and the Judicial Revolution.* New York: Simon and Schuster, 1977.

Fundaburk, Emma Lila, and Mary Douglass Foreman. *Sun Circles and Human Hands: The Southeastern Indians, Art and Industry.* Luverne, Ala.: E. L. F. Publisher, 1957.

Jackson, Harvey H., III. *Rivers of History: Life on the Coosa, Tallapoosa, Cahaba, and Alabama.* Tuscaloosa: University of Alabama Press, 1995.

Mellown, Robert Oliver. *The University of Alabama: A Guide to the Campus.* Tuscaloosa: University of Alabama Press, 1988.

Miller, Rex. *Croxton's Raid.* Fort Collins, Colo.: Old Army Press, 1980.

Searcy, Margaret. *Ikwa of the Temple Mounds.* University: University of Alabama Press, 1974. (Juvenile fiction)

Silverberg, Robert. *Mound-building of Ancient America: The Archaeology of a Myth.* Greenwich, Conn.: New York Graphic Society, 1968.

Vandiver, Frank E., ed. *The Civil War Diary of General Josiah Gorgas.* University: University of Alabama Press, 1972.

Walthall, John A. *Moundville: An Introduction to the Archaeology of a Mississippi Chiefdom.* University: Alabama Museum of Natural History, 1977.

Walthall, John A. *Prehistoric Indians of the Southeast: Archaeology of Alabama and the Middle South.* Tuscaloosa: University of Alabama Press, 1980.

Welch, Paul D. *Moundville's Economy.* Tuscaloosa: University of Alabama Press, 1991.

Wiggins, Sarah Woolfolk Wiggins, ed. *The Journals of Josiah Gorgas, 1857–1878.* Tuscaloosa: University of Alabama Press, 1995.

Wilson, Eugene M. *Alabama Folk Houses.* Montgomery: Alabama Historical Commission, 1975.

Bessemer Depot

Bessemer

Named in honor of Henry Bessemer, the English ironmaster who invented the Bessemer process of steel-making, this industrial city was founded in 1887 by Henry F. DeBardeleben, who hoped it would rival Birmingham in rapid growth. Although Bessemer never outdistanced Birmingham, it is one of Alabama's major centers of coal mining, steel-making, cast iron and clay pipe production, and manufacturing of railroad wheels.

The **Hall of History Museum**, 1905 Alabama Avenue, housed in the restored **Southern Railway Depot** built in 1916, contains displays of prehistoric fossils, pioneer lifestyles, Civil War artifacts, industrial machinery, and local history. Open Tuesday through Saturday, 10 a.m. to 5 p.m. No admission charge. The depot, on the National Register, has leaded glass windows and hand-carved woodwork.

Follow Alabama 150 to Jefferson County 20. Turn west on Eastern Valley Road at signs for Bessemer Historic Homes and Tannehill Historical State Park.

West Jefferson County Historical Society has preserved three historic farm homes, all listed on the National Register. **McAdory House** (c. 1840), one-story dogtrot style, was once the center of a 2,000-acre farm. Thomas McAdory Owen, founder of the Alabama Department of Archives and History, and Robert McAdory, first mayor of Bessemer, were born here. On the right of the main house is the boys' house where the sons slept. On the left is the travelers' house where overnight guests were accommodated.

Owen House (c. 1833), originally a two-room cottage, was enlarged in 1838. Thomas Owen brought his bride, Melissa Sadler, to a honeymoon cottage here when he was nineteen and she seventeen. During the Civil War, Owen operated a foundry near the Tannehill furnaces. The girls' bedroom upstairs can be entered only through the parents' bedroom.

Sadler House (c. 1817), originally a small log structure, was enlarged around 1838 to a two-story dogtrot style. Isaac Sadler farmed 2,800 acres of land in 1860, one of the most productive farms in Jefferson County. The house contains some original furnishings.

All three houses are open only by appointment. In December the West

Jefferson County Historical Society holds an annual open house during which these three homes are decorated with old-fashioned Christmas trimmings. For information, telephone (205) 491-5543.

Continue past Sadler House to Tannehill Historical State Park.

Tannehill Furnace

Tannehill Historical State Park

Birmingham's iron industry originated when a small forge was built here in 1829 by Daniel Hillman, an old Dutch furnaceman from Pennsylvania, beside a creek and near rich pockets of brown ore. After Hillman's death, the furnace was purchased by a cotton planter, Ninion Tannehill. The first charcoal blast furnace was added in 1855 under supervision of Moses Stroup, a noted ironmaster. Two more were added by the Confederate government in 1863.

Alabama's first blast furnaces were similar to the furnaces first built in Europe in the fourteenth century. These furnaces, made of limestone, were lined with fireproof bricks made of clay. They were shaped somewhat like cones, about thirty feet wide at the base and narrowing to a short smokestack. The blast furnace made possible a much greater output of iron and the production of cast iron objects.

Pig iron, a crude form of iron that could be cast into pots, skillets, and farm implements or refined into steel, was made in these furnaces. The ingredients of pig iron, called the *charge*, were iron ore and limestone. These materials were put in at the top of the furnace. Cords of cedar were burned in kilns to make charcoal to heat the charge. A bellows, run by water power, blasted air into the bottom of the furnace to heat the burning charcoal and melt the charge more rapidly.

As the charge melted, liquid iron separated from the slag (refuse) and collected in the hearth at the base of the furnace. This molten iron flowed into sand molds arranged around the main channel. Because such molds looked like a litter of pigs around a sow, the name *pig iron* came into use.

Tannehill's three furnaces were major Confederate suppliers, producing more than twenty tons of heavy ordnance a day, including cannonballs, gun barrels, and other munitions, which were hauled out by oxcart to the railroad at Montevallo for transport to Selma and to the Confederate army. More than 600 slaves worked in this operation. On March 31, 1865, three companies of Iowa cavalry blew up the overhead trestles, burned the foundries, cast houses, and slave houses, tore up the tramways, and knocked these furnaces out of production.

One old Tannehill furnace was re-fired as a bicentennial project in 1976. In three days the old furnace produced two and one-half tons of iron. This furnace is on the National Register.

The **Iron and Steel Museum of Alabama**, in the park, contains exhibits interpreting the iron industry in the South from frontier days through the Civil War to modern times. Open Monday through Friday, 9 a.m. to 5 p.m.; Saturday and Sunday, 10 a.m. to 5 p.m. No admission charge.

Other structures of interest at Tannehill Park are the reconstructed **John Wesley Hall Gristmill** and **Cotton Gin**, a copy of the historic Hall's Mill, which operated in this area prior to the Civil War; **Tapawingo Bridge** (1902), an iron truss structure; **Hogan House** (1835), a dogtrot; **Duncan House** (c. 1870), a single-pen cabin; a **blacksmith shop** (c. nineteenth century) and display of **early farm machinery**; and **Kimbrell Methodist Church** (c. 1905), a rural frame church. Tannehill Park is open daily from 7 a.m. to 9 p.m. Parking charge.

Accommodations: Tannehill Historical State Park contains camping facilities and picnic areas. Visitors can rent some of the old log cabins.

From Tannehill, follow signs to Interstate 59. Proceed south on Interstate 59 to Tuscaloosa. In Tuscaloosa, exit right onto McFarland Boulevard (U.S. 82 west). Just across the Black Warrior River, turn right on Rice Mine Road and follow signs to the North River development on Watermelon Road east of Lake Tuscaloosa spillway.

North River Historic Area

Developers of this handsome residential community have moved and restored several historic structures, including **Snider Log Cabin** (c. 1837), dogtrot with twin staircases leading to girls' and boys' loft bedrooms (note windows of hand-blown glass imported from Germany), twin fireplaces of native stone, and porch with handmade cedar roof shingle exposed beneath; **Old Center Church** (c. 1865–75), built of massive hand-hewn logs held together with pegs (windows of German hand-blown glass) and containing altar and two deacon chairs of solid yellow pine (this church, according to its deed, was "sometimes Baptist, sometimes Methodist"); **Gainesville Bank** (1835), oldest bank building in central Alabama (note wooden dentil work decorations on front and in interior), containing vault from the old Shelby Iron Company of Columbiana (during the mid-1800s this bank issued its own currency); **Umbria Plantation Schoolhouse** (c. 1820), one-room school for children of a cotton planter near Sawyerville (note unusual chimney built of hand-

Umbria Plantation schoolhouse

made pink grooved brick separated from building at top).

Departing North River, return to Tuscaloosa via U.S. 82 to University Boulevard exit; turn right and proceed to the University of Alabama campus.

Tuscaloosa

The site of Tuscaloosa, near the falls of the Warrior, was once a Creek trading post known as Black Warrior Town. During the Creek War of 1813–14, American troops led by General John Coffee captured and burned the town. After Creeks were forced to surrender most of their territory within the present boundaries of Alabama, white settlers started a town at this site, which they called *Tuskaloosa*, meaning "black warrior." The name honors the giant Indian chief Tuskaloosa, who led his people against De Soto and his Spaniards at the Battle of Maubila in 1540.

White pioneers from Georgia, the Carolinas, and Tennessee settled in and around Tuscaloosa because of its strategic location in a fertile farm area along a major river and Byler Road, which led to the Tennessee Valley. When Alabama became a state in 1819, Tuscaloosa, chartered December 13, 1819, drew strong support from north Alabama to become the first permanent state capital. However, south Alabamians won out. After floods virtually destroyed Alabama's first capital, Cahaba (see Cahaba), Tuscaloosa served as the capital from 1826 to 1846. But the white population of eastern Alabama grew rapidly following removal of the last Creeks in the 1830s. These new settlers eventually succeeded in moving the capital to Montgomery.

During the Civil War, a force of 1,500 Union troops under General John Croxton captured Tuscaloosa and burned four buildings on the campus of The University of Alabama where cadets trained for Confederate service.

Tuscaloosa today is an industrial center. Its major industries produce tires, chemicals, wire products, asphalt, and fabricated steel.

The University of Alabama

The University of Alabama opened its doors in 1831 with thirty-five students and four faculty members, one of whom was also president. President Alva Woods was so strict that students rioted and faculty members resigned. Eventually the president himself was asked to resign. The university began to grow under its second president, the Reverend Basil Manly, although campus life often was marked by riots and disorders as college authorities attempted to discipline students from pioneer backgrounds of much freedom.

In 1865 Union troops burned the campus, leaving only four structures untouched. After it reopened in 1871, the university expanded beyond the College of Arts and Sciences to include a law school and the Colleges of Engineering, Education, and Commerce. The first women students were admitted in 1893. That year also saw the fielding of the first football team, the "thin Red Line," which became the modern "Crimson Tide."

Between 1912 and 1937 the campus underwent extensive growth, from 400 students and sixteen buildings to 2,000 students and twenty-five buildings. Following World War II, two branch campuses in Birmingham and Huntsville began to expand into separate institutions of the University of Alabama System. During the 1970s, a new School of Communications and the Colleges of Community Health Sciences and Nursing were added in Tuscaloosa. Some 19,000 students are

enrolled in the present undergraduate and graduate programs of the University of Alabama.

Visit or write the Office of University Relations (Box 870373, Tuscaloosa, AL 35487-0373) in Rose Administration Building for an attractive *Walking Tour Guide* to the campus.

Gorgas-Manly Historic District, on the campus, includes eight buildings, among them **Clark, Manly, and Garland halls** (1886–88), brick Gothic Revival style built to complete the quadrangle with old **Woods Hall** (c. 1868), which was built after the Civil War raid and was named for the university's first president; **Gorgas House** (c. 1829), on the National Register, two-story brick Federal-style raised cottage with curved staircase to portico (one of four buildings to survive the Civil War raid); and **Jason's Shrine** (c. 1860), white stucco octagonal structure used by cadets on guard duty during the Civil War.

Gorgas House was the first permanent building on the University campus and was designed by an English architect using brick imported from

Gorgas House, Tuscaloosa

96

England as ballast in ships that returned with Southern cotton. The walls of the house are eighteen inches thick. Framing and floors are of heart pine. The structure was built with very few nails. Catches for shutters are made from horseshoes. This architectural style, known as "low country raised cottage," raises the principal rooms of the house a story above ground to remove them from damp soil. Originally designed as a hotel or college commons, the house was used as a private residence beginning in 1840. Among its notable residents was General Josiah Gorgas, who served as head of the Confederate ordnance bureau and became president of the university in 1879. His wife, Amelia Gayle Gorgas, served as university librarian for many years; the present library bears her name. Their son, Dr. William Crawford Gorgas, was instrumental in purging the Panama Canal Zone of mosquitos, thereby virtually eliminating yellow fever and malaria and allowing construction to proceed on the Panama Canal.

Gorgas House is open to the public Monday through Saturday, 10 a.m. to 12 noon and 2 to 5 p.m.; Sunday, 3 to 5 p.m. No admission charge.

Other historic sites on The University of Alabama campus include the **President's Mansion** (c. 1840), another structure that survived Croxton's raid. Its British architect chose Greek Revival but broke with the

President's Mansion, The University of Alabama

usual pattern to build a double winding staircase from the ground to the first floor and to use arches on the ground floor. This building is also a raised cottage. Note intricate iron lacework. On the National Register, the President's Mansion is open on special occasions. The **observatory** (c. 1844), also on the National Register, is another structure to survive the Civil War. It was built as a scientific observatory. The **Alabama Museum of Natural History**, located in **Smith Hall**, contains anthropological and geological displays, including a diorama of one of the old Tannehill furnaces. Open weekdays, 8 a.m. to 4:30 p.m. No admission charge.

The **Hugo Black Room**, in the law school library, is a replica of the home office of that school's most illustrious alumnus. Justice Black (see Ashland), who served on the Supreme Court from 1937 until 1971, is considered by most legal scholars to have been one of the twelve greatest justices in the history of that body. The Hugo Black Room is approximately the size of the original room in the justice's Alexandria, Virginia, home. All of its furnish-

replica of Hugo Black office

ings, decorations, and books are originals from that home office, arranged by Mrs. Hugo Black as they were at the time of her husband's death. The Hugo Black Room may be viewed Monday through Friday, 8 a.m. to 3 p.m. No admission charge.

Paul W. Bryant Museum, 300 Paul W. Bryant Drive on The University of Alabama campus, is dedicated to the memory of the university's legendary football coach Paul W. "Bear" Bryant. The museum exhibit hall traces the history of football at The University of Alabama. Highlights include memorabilia from Alabama's twelve national championship teams, Coach Bryant's famous houndstooth hat, and videos of games that allow the visitor to relive exciting plays from the past. Open Monday through Saturday, 9 a.m. to 4 p.m. Admission charged. Telephone (205) 348-4668.

Adjacent to the university campus is **Bryce Hospital** (founded 1852), also on the National Register. The central building of this institution for treatment of the mentally ill has four stories, with Doric columns support-

ing two balconies and a large round dome.

Downtown Area

Near the central business district at the west end of University Boulevard is **Capitol Park**, site of Alabama's second capitol. Only the central foundation remains of the capitol, which burned on August 23, 1923. Nearby is the **Old Tavern** (1827), on the National Register, a two-story brick stagecoach inn of French-style architecture with second-story balcony, hand-cut laths, and peg construction, frequented by legislators when Tuscaloosa was the capital. Open Tuesday through Saturday, 10 a.m. to 12 noon; Sunday, 1 to 4 p.m. Small admission charge. Also near Capitol Park is **McGuire-Strickland House** (1820), on the National Register, Tuscaloosa's oldest frame house still in use, now headquarters of the Tuscaloosa County Preservation Society. Open Monday through Friday, 8:00 to 4:30 p.m. No admission charge.

At the corner of Eighth Street and Lurleen Wallace Boulevard, **St. John**

Old Tavern, Tuscaloosa

98

the **Baptist Catholic Church** (1845), one-story brick, is the oldest Catholic church in Alabama outside of Mobile, and in fact was completed before the cathedral in Mobile. In the late nineteenth century, St. Paul's Church in Birmingham (now the cathedral church of the Birmingham diocese) was founded as a mission from St. John's.

Nearby **Druid City Historic District**, named for the giant water oaks planted here in 1826, was once an exclusive residential district. Historic structures in the district, which is on the National Register, include: **Governor's Mansion** (1834), now the University Club, two-story brick with six Ionic columns, hipped roof, and double doors upstairs and down, built by a steamboat captain and later owned by Governor Arthur Pendleton Bagby (1837–41); **Collier-Overby-Boone House** (c. 1820), 901 21st Avenue, two-story frame, once the home of former Governor Henry W. Collier (1849–53), on the National Register; **Guild-Verner House** (1822), 1901 University Boulevard, two-story brick building restored by Tuscaloosa Homebuilders Association, on the National Register; and **Mildred Warner House** (1822), 1925 Eighth Street at 20th Avenue, on the National Register, originally a two-room cabin with fireplaces at each end, later remodeled in Georgian style with basement kitchen. Restored by the David Warner Founda-

tion, the house contains furniture from Carter Hall in Virginia. Open Saturday, 10 a.m. to 6 p.m.; Sunday, 1 to 6 p.m. Free admission.

Other National Register sites in Tuscaloosa include: **Battle-Friedman House** (c. 1835), 1010 Greensboro Avenue, rose stucco over brick with six square columns and large doorway with crystal fanlight and sidelights, built by pioneer merchant Alfred Battle, later the home of the Friedman family (open Tuesday through Saturday, 10 a.m. to noon and 1 to 4 p.m.; small admission charge); **Cherokee** (c. 1860–62), 1305 Greensboro Avenue, Italianate mansion built by Robert Jemison, wealthy stagecoach operator and an early opponent of secession, now the offices of the Convention and Visitors Bureau, the Preservation Society, and the Heritage Association; **Searcy-Hobson House** (c. 1830), 2606 Eighth Street, two-story frame with square wood columns, built for Henry Minor, prominent figure in the early statehood period, later the home

Mildred Warner House, Tuscaloosa

99

of Dr. James Searcy, second superintendent of Bryce Hospital, now adapted for commercial use.

Stillman College, 3600 15th Street West, was founded after the Civil War by Presbyterians as a training school for black ministers. One of its graduates, William H. Sheppard, was made a Fellow of the Royal Geographic Society in 1893 in recognition of his efforts to introduce inhabitants of the Babuka territory of Africa to Christianity. The **library** has six noteworthy Corinthian columns, with capitals of Italian marble.

Now a four-year coeducational institution, Stillman is controlled by the United Presbyterian Church in the United States.

The **Japanese Gardens** at Gulf States Paper Corporation's national headquarters, 1400 River Road Northeast, although not of historic significance, are of interest to those wishing a glimpse of gardens designed to reflect Oriental symbolism. Their design was inspired by the gardens at Katsura Imperial Villa, Kyoto, Japan. The office building houses an outstanding collection of art. Tours of the building and the gardens are conducted Monday through Friday at 5 p.m.; Saturday, 10 a.m. to 7 p.m.; Sunday, 1 to 7 p.m. No admission charge.

From downtown Tuscaloosa, take Alabama 69 (Lurleen Wallace Boulevard northbound) across the Black Warrior River to Northport.

Northport

Northport District, on the National Register, comprises a forty-seven-block town of brick business structures and Queen Anne cottages virtually unchanged since the 1890s. **Kentuck Museum** in town features craft tools, quilts, coverlets, pottery, baskets, and furniture. Open Monday through Friday, 9 a.m. to 5 p.m.; Saturday, 10 a.m. to 4:30 p.m. Telephone (205) 333-1252. No admission charge.

Christian-Harper Home (c. 1830s), 512 Main Avenue, on the National Register, is a two-story Greek Revival raised cottage of square, handmade brick with Ionic portico. Eleven miles north of Northport off U.S. 43 is a one-half-mile portion of the original **Byler Road**, Alabama's first state toll road, which once ran from Tuscaloosa to the Tennessee River. It is marked by an Alabama Historical Association marker.

From Tuscaloosa, take Interstate 59 south to the Moundville exit. Follow Alabama 69 south to Moundville.

Watch on the left for the sign indicating **Little Sandy Baptist Church** (c. 1834), a typical country church of the pioneer era. If asked, the neighbors will direct visitors to someone who has a key.

In Moundville, note **Carthage Presbyterian Church** (c. 1859), built by slaves and characterized by harmonious simplicity.

Life at Moundville (diorama)

Moundville Archaeological Park

Human beings with a highly developed culture inhabited the middle Mississippi River Valley from around A.D. 1200 until well into the sixteenth century. They are popularly called *mound builders* although their tradition is formally known as *Mississippian*. The dominant feature of their culture was the building of huge earthen mounds that served as foundations for temples and other important buildings.

On important occasions, such as the burial of a chief, it is likely that priests stood atop these mounds to address the gathering below. The largest mound at the park is fifty-eight feet high and covers almost two acres. This and other mounds were built by people who carried baskets full of dirt up the mound, emptied them, and packed the earth with their feet.

Moundville Archaeological Park is a typical Mississippian site in that it is located near a river. It dates from A.D. 1200 to 1400. Mound builders tilled the rich soil bordering the Black Warrior River, harvesting corn, beans,

squash, and gourds. Smaller villages stretched along the Black Warrior, but Moundville was evidently the central ceremonial area for mound builders of this part of Alabama.

Among relics found at Moundville are flint axes and hatchets, arrowheads, hunting knives, bone needles, hoes, and other tools, indicating that these people were able to fell trees, hunt animals, make clothing from skins, and till the soil.

Designs on their pottery, such as feathered serpents and the hand-and-eye motif, indicate that their culture was influenced by that of Indians in Mexico. Weeping eyes, two-headed birds, and designs resembling swastikas and Greek crosses also were carved on bottles and jars by these prehistoric potters.

De Soto and his men, traveling through the Southeast in 1539–43, saw mound builders at work constructing their mounds. But sometime after the De Soto expedition, this tradition died out. Only their artifacts, their mounds, and their descendants—some of the American Indians of today—remain of the Mississippian culture.

Moundville Archaeological Park (a National Historic Landmark) contains twenty temple mounds, a reconstructed village depicting the way of life of these ancient people, and an archaeological museum featuring numerous displays on the Moundville

101

Indians. Museum open daily 9 a.m. to 5 p.m.; park open 8 a.m. to 8 p.m. Small admission charge.

Accommodations: The park offers campgrounds and a picnic area overlooking the Black Warrior River.

Continue south on Alabama 69 to Havana.

Havana

Havana Methodist Church (c. 1880), one-story frame with wide pine flooring and fine woodwork in ceiling, has had five college presidents as members. Near the church is a monument to Julia S. Tutwiler, whose father, Henry Tutwiler, operated Greene Springs Academy, one of Alabama's most progressive academies, near Havana during the antebellum era. Greene Springs, unlike most academies, had a large library, a telescope, and a chemistry laboratory. Tutwiler stressed mathematics, literary classics, and science. He also allowed his daughters and other girls from the neighborhood to attend classes with boys. Julia attended Vassar College in upstate New York and later studied in Germany. When she returned to Alabama, she endeavored to persuade the Alabama legislature to set up a school to train women teachers (see Livingston University). Miss Tutwiler campaigned for years against Alabama's practice of leasing convicts as workers for private industries. This practice did not end, however, until the late 1920s.

Located at Havana are **Cedarwood** (c. 1818), the Joseph Blodgett Stickney house, which is one of the earliest buildings in this area, and the **Whatley Home** (c. 1830s), two-story frame Georgian with Greek Revival details, where an old stagecoach line changed horses.

Leaving Havana, return to the intersection of Alabama 69 and Alabama 60. Drive south on 60 approximately 3.5 miles to Hale County 21. Follow 21 for 2.3 miles, turn left (opposite old store) and go 0.5 mile to Tanglewood.

Tanglewood

Tanglewood (c. 1859), is one of the few small plantation homes in Alabama open to the public. The home contains memorabilia of the family of J. Nicholine Bishop, an early Alabama educator whose family migrated to Alabama from North Carolina in 1819. Representative of small, simple plantation homes of Alabama in the pre–Civil War period, Tanglewood is owned by the University of Alabama. It is open by appointment through the university's Office of Land Management, telephone (205) 348-6462. No admission charge.

Tanglewood, near Havana

Leaving Tanglewood, return to U.S. 82 and continue east to Centreville.

Centreville

Centreville business district, around the 1904 Bibb County Courthouse, contains several Victorian-era stores and the **Presbyterian Church** (1859).

From Centreville, take Alabama 25 toward Montevallo. Watch for Brierfield Ironworks Park signs about twenty miles east of Centreville.

Brierfield
Ironworks Park

Bibb Naval Furnaces, or Brierfield Furnaces (c. 1861–88), were among the principal producers of iron for the Confederate foundry at Selma. Nearby Brierfield, founded in the 1840s, was a boom town of its day. Union troops led by General James H. Wilson destroyed these furnaces on their way to Selma in the spring of 1865. Rebuilt in 1868, the furnaces operated until 1888 when steel nails were introduced. General Josiah Gorgas, former chief of Confederate ordnance, was in charge of these furnaces for a few years after the war.

Old Brierfield Furnace

Ruins in the park are listed on the National Register. Open daily 7 a.m. to 5 p.m. No admission charge.

Brierfield

Brierfield is three miles south of Alabama 25 on Alabama 139.

Now virtually a ghost town, this onetime boom town contains a few of its original homes, mostly in poor condition except **Montebrier** (c. 1850s), one-and-one-half-story restored Gothic Revival, on the National Register.

Departing Brierfield, return to Alabama 25 and follow signs to Montevallo.

Montevallo

Settled in 1815 by one of the veterans of General Andrew Jackson's Indian fighters, this community originally was called Wilson's Hill. In 1825, Wilson's Hill was one of the towns considered for Alabama's capital, but Tuscaloosa was chosen instead. The **University of Montevallo**, founded in 1895 as a women's college, is now a coeducational university.

King House, interior

103

King House, Montevallo, exterior

King House (c. 1823), on campus, was the Federal-style "mansion house" of Edmund King, first owner of the land on which the university stands. It is said to be the first brick house and the first house with glass windows in this part of the state. Union general James H. Wilson used this house as headquarters when he led his forces through Montevallo during the Civil War. On the National Register, King House is open on special occasions.

Reynolds Hall (c. 1851) once housed Montevallo Male Institute. In front of this building, men from this vicinity were mustered into Confederate service, receiving a flag made by the women of Montevallo.

Leaving Montevallo, continue on Alabama 25 to Interstate 65, then proceed north to Birmingham.

TOUR 9
East Central Alabama

From Birmingham

Childersburg

Sylacauga

Horseshoe Bend

Talladega

Ashland

Cheaha State Park

Piedmont

Anniston

Jacksonville

Return to Birmingham

gristmills

covered bridges

"gold rush" towns

antebellum mansions

Indian battleground

nature trail

museums

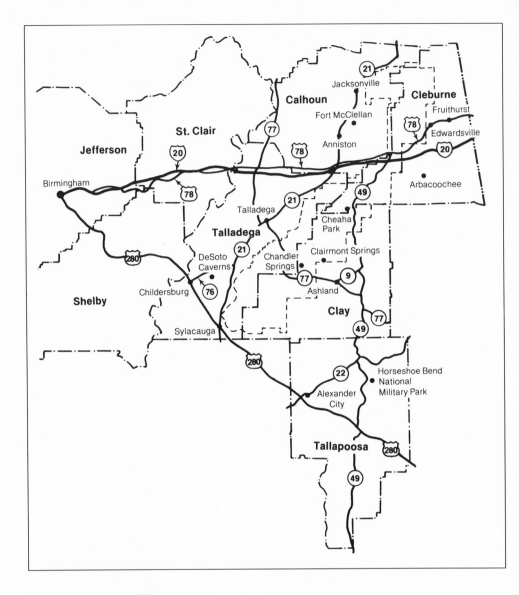

Ridge, Valley, and Piedmont

Home of the Upper Creeks

Creeks once occupied the largest part of what is now Alabama. The word *Creek* was a nickname given to these Indians by British traders because their villages were located along creeks. Actually the proper name for these In-

dians is *Muskogees*. The Creeks were not a nation but a confederation. Many smaller groups of Indians, such as the Alabamas, the Maubilians, the Euchees, and the Hitchiti, became part of this confederation. European traders spoke of these groups as Upper and Lower Creeks. Upper Creeks, mainly Muskogees and Alabamas, lived along the Alabama, Coosa, and Tallapoosa rivers. Lower Creeks lived nearer the Gulf Coast.

As white settlers began to move into this region at the start of the nineteenth century, the Creeks became increasingly hostile. Many did not wish to adopt the ways of whites as government agents urged them to do under a new Indian policy instituted by President George Washington. Indian agents were supposed to instruct Indians how to plow, raise cotton, weave, spin, care for domestic animals, and become skilled in carpentry or blacksmithing. Indians also wanted to keep their lands. Unfortunately for them, they had granted the American government the right to maintain horse paths through their territory over which white pioneers were allowed to travel to the region around Mobile. These horse paths became highways of settlement.

The great Shawnee Indian leader, Tecumseh, leader of the Creeks, came to Alabama in 1811 to try to unite all Indians against the white Americans. Scornfully he compared their lives as farmers and traders with the traditional ways of their ancestors. After Tecumseh's visit, the Creeks divided. Most Upper Creeks, called Red Sticks because of their bright red war clubs, wanted to resist white encroachment. Most Lower Creeks, more accustomed to whites, were inclined toward peace. This division led to the Creek War of 1813–14, which ended after the Battle of Horseshoe Bend (see Horseshoe Bend). In the treaty that followed this war, Creeks ceded about three fifths of present Alabama to the federal government, thereby opening the way of white settlement.

However, Creeks still owned more than five million acres in eastern Alabama. In 1832 a few of their leaders, under pressure, signed the Treaty of Cusseta, agreeing to cede this land if any Creeks who wished to stay would be allowed to choose homesteads. But troubles constantly broke out between Creeks and white settlers. Eventually most of these 23,000 Creeks were forcibly moved from Alabama to new homes in the West.

Leaving Birmingham, take U.S. 280 southeast toward Childersburg.

suggestions for background reading

Brantley, William H., Jr. *Battle of Horseshoe Bend in Tallapoosa Co., Ala., March 27, 1814*. Birmingham: Southern University Press, 1955.

Corkran, David H. *The Creek Frontier, 1540–1783*. Norman: University of Oklahoma Press, 1956.

Piedmont Scenery

Foscue, Virginia O. *Place Names in Alabama*. Tuscaloosa: University of Alabama Press, 1989.

Garrett, Mitchell B. *Horse and Buggy Days on Hatchet Creek*. University: University of Alabama Press, 1957. Reprint 1982. (Locale: Clay County)

Gates, Grace. *The Model City of the New South: Anniston, Alabama, 1872–1900*. Huntsville: Strode, 1978. Reprint (paper). Tuscaloosa: University of Alabama Press, 1996.

Halbert, H. S., and T. H. Ball. *The Creek War of 1813 and 1814*. Chicago: Donohue and Haneberry, 1895; reprint ed., edited by Frank L. Owsley, Jr. University: University of Alabama Press, 1969. Reprint (paper) 1995.

Hamilton, Virginia Van der Veer. *Hugo Black: The Alabama Years*. Baton Rouge: Louisiana State University Press, 1972. Reprint (paper). Montgomery: Black Belt Press, 1996. (Locale: Ashland)

James, Marquis. *Andrew Jackson: The Border Captain*. New York: Grosset and Dunlap, 1933.

Mason, David P. *Five Dollars a Scalp: The Last Mighty War Whoop of the Creek Indians*. Huntsville: Strode, 1975. (Fiction)

Milham, Charles G. *Gallant Pelham, American Extraordinary*. Washington, D.C.: Public Affairs Press, 1959. (Locale: Piedmont)

Nixon, H. C. *Lower Piedmont County: The Uplands of the Deep South*. New York: Duell, Sloan, and Pearce, 1946. Reprint. Tuscaloosa: University of Alabama Press, 1984. (Locale: Piedmont)

Owsley, Frank Lawrence, Jr. *Struggle for the Gulf Borderlands: The Creek War and the Battle of New Orleans, 1812–1815*. Gainesville: University Presses of Florida, 1981.

Pope, Virginia Voss. *Fruithurst: Alabama's Vineyard Village*. Albertville: Thompson Printing Co., 1971.

Remini, Robert V. *Andrew Jackson and the Course of American Empire, 1767–1821*. New York: Harper and Row, 1978.

Rosengarten, Theodore. *All God's Dangers: The Autobiography of Nate Shaw*. New York: Alfred A. Knopf, 1975.

Sanguinetti, Elise. *The Last of the Whitfields*. New York: McGraw Hill, 1962. Reprint. Tuscaloosa: University of Alabama Press, 1984. (Fiction)

Sulzby, James F., Jr. *Historic Alabama Hotels and Resorts*. University: University of Alabama Press, 1960. Reprint (paper) 1989.

Childersburg

Thought to be one and one half miles northeast of Childersburg was Coosa, also called *Coca* and *Cosa*, an ancient capital of the Creeks. In 1540 De Soto and his weary followers rested for twenty-five days in Coosa. At this point, two of his men, a white man named Feryada and a black man named Robles, decided to desert. Another Spanish expedition, passing through this area twenty years later, found the two men living peaceably in what is now Talladega County.

During World War II Childersburg became a boom town because a large powder-making plant was built in the vicinity.

Immediately to the right after leaving U.S. 280 on Alabama 76 will be **Butler-Rainwater House** (c. 1890), 1000 First Street Southwest, two-story frame, whose geometric porch and gable trim are excellent examples of Eastlake styling.

Departing Childersburg, continue on Alabama 76 east to Talladega County 36, then

Butler-Rainwater House, Childersburg

left three miles (bear to the right when road splits) to Talladega County 46. Kymulga Gristmill is at this intersection.

Kymulga Gristmill

Once nearly every Alabama community had a gristmill. Farmers came in wagons to bring their corn to these mills to be ground into meal. The miller charged one eighth of a bushel of meal, called the toll, as his price for doing the grinding.

In most mills the grindstone was turned by power from a large wheel moved by the weight of water. Mills fell into disuse after the Civil War when farmers began to grow more cotton and less corn. Also, larger mills using gasoline-powered engines helped put water mills out of business.

However, a few of the old mills still remain. Like Kymulga, they are operated occasionally so visitors can see the old way of grinding and may purchase fresh, water-ground meal.

Kymulga Mill (c. 1867), on the National Register, is open Saturdays for grinding and Sundays for tours. The three-and-one-half-story frame structure once housed five sets of stones powered by four turbines, an unusually large operation.

Nearby **Kymulga Covered Bridge** (c. 1860), also on the National Register, once carried Georgia Road over Talladega Creek. The wooden, 105-foot span, double-beam structure is in poor condition.

Nearby on Talladega County 46 is **Robinson-Baker House** (c. 1885), presumably built by James Baker, owner and operator of the mill during the nineteenth century. This one-and-one-half-story structure has tower, gingerbread, and rambling floor plan.

Return to Alabama 76. Turn east to De Soto Caverns.

De Soto Caverns

This prehistoric complex of onyx caves was sacred to the Creek Indians, who believed that their forefathers had come out of this cavern to form the Creek nation. While resting in this vicinity in 1540, Spaniards visited these caves and recorded them in the journals of the De Soto expedition. In 1797 Benjamin Hawkins, an Indian agent, reported this natural wonder to President George Washington.

Inside the cave is an ancient burial ground containing evidence that prehistoric people lived here more than 2,000 years ago. One rock bears the name of I. W. Wright, an Indian trader from South Carolina, and the date,

Kymulga Covered Bridge

1723. According to local lore, the Creeks, angry at the desecration of their sacred place, killed and scalped Wright.

During the Civil War, De Soto Caverns were mined by Confederates to make gunpowder from saltpeter. Cave soil, often rich in calcium nitrate, can be processed to produce potassium nitrate (commonly called *saltpeter* or *niter*), which makes up 75 percent of gunpowder. Workers placed soil in a wooden vat and thoroughly saturated it with water. The nitrate-enriched water filtered into a leaching trough where it was allowed to stand until soil impurities settled to the bottom. Then it was taken from the cave and boiled in large kettles with a mixture of potash or wood ashes (potassium carbonate). This process converted the calcium nitrate into potassium nitrate (niter). Finally the water was boiled and the niter crystals allowed to dry before being made into gunpowder. De Soto Caverns also provided bat guano, rich in nitrate, which was used in making saltpeter when other sources became scarce.

The caverns are open daily, April through September, Monday through Saturday, 9 a.m. to 5 p.m.; Sunday, 12:30 p.m. to 5 p.m.; April through September, open until 5:30 p.m. Admission fee.

Leaving De Soto Caverns, follow Alabama 76 east toward Talladega.

At milepost 16 on the right, note **Morris-Holmes House** (c. 1857), two-story frame with dentil molding and two-story portico supported by four octagonal columns.

At the intersection of Alabama 76 and Alternate U.S. 231 near Winterboro, note historic marker signifying that this stretch of road was once part of the **Central Plank State Road** (c. 1850), one of several wooden toll roads that once crossed Alabama. These privately or semiprivately owned roads fell into disuse because they were too expensive and difficult to maintain.

Several miles farther north on Alternate U.S. 231 are other markers denoting the site of **Mardisville**, a United States land office for the sale of lands ceded by the Creeks in 1832, and the site of part of the **Jackson Trace**, an old Indian trail widened by Andrew Jackson and his troops during the Creek War.

Talladega option: Continue north on Alternate U.S. 231 toward Talladega (see Talladega below).

Sylacauga option: If you prefer, proceed to Sylacauga rather than Talladega. Return to Childersburg and follow U.S. 280 south to Sylacauga, or proceed south from Winterboro to Sylacauga on Alternate U.S. 231.

Sylacauga

Sylacauga is located on a solid deposit of some of the hardest, whitest marble in the world. The bed is ap-

Marble Pits, Sylacauga

Court building and the Lister Hill Center for Biomedical Communications in Washington, D.C.

To view the marble pits, turn west off U.S. 280 onto Tallapoosa County 6 (Quarry Road). Proceed one mile to the quarry area. Small marble chunks and chips can be picked up along the road; polished slabs may be purchased at plant offices.

proximately 32 miles long by 1.5 miles wide and 400 feet deep. It is the only known commercial bed of mandre cream marble in the world.

Marble is basically limestone that has been changed by the force of tremendous pressures and heat within the earth. Indians who once lived in this area used marble for their arrowheads. The earliest marble quarries in Alabama were opened in the 1830s by skilled stonemasons from Scotland. They took orders for tombstones, mantels, doors, and window sills, shipping their wares to other towns over the old Central Plank State Road, which led to Wetumpka.

In 1900 Guiseppe Moretti, an Italian sculptor, came to Sylacauga to purchase and develop a marble quarry. His *Head of Christ*, displayed in the Alabama Department of Archives and History in Montgomery, was the first work of sculpture to be carved from Sylacauga marble. Moretti later fashioned the huge iron statue of Vulcan, now the symbol of Birmingham.

Sylacauga marble, a beautiful white or translucent rock with faint green lines, has been used in many fine structures, including the U.S. Supreme

Marble is drilled out of the ground by channeling machines that utilize chisel-edged steel bars to make cuts two inches wide and several feet deep. The blocks are lifted from the pit by cranes to the surface of the quarry. Then they are transported to the plant where saws with sets of parallel blades cut them into slabs. The slabs are then polished with carborundum and finer abrasives.

The town is on the south edge of Talladega National Forest, and the timber industry is important in the area.

Sylacauga Cemetery, East Fort Williams Street, contains tombstones made from local marble and carved by early Scottish stonemasons.

Sylacauga is also a major center of textile manufacturing. Group tours of Avondale Mills operations may be arranged through that company's public relations office in Sylacauga. Telephone (205) 249-1363.

Departing Sylacauga, continue south on U.S. 280 to Alexander City. Turn east off U.S. 280 onto Alabama 22 and travel eighteen miles to New Site. Horseshoe Bend National Military Park is five miles south on Alabama 49.

Horseshoe Bend National Military Park

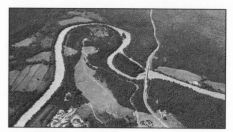

Horseshoe Bend

By mid-1813 the four-month-old civil war that included Upper and Lower Creek Indians had grown into a major war involving the U.S. militia. Mobilizing his Tennessee militia, Andrew Jackson set out in late 1813 to drive southward into the Upper Creek or "Red Stick" country between the Coosa and Tallapoosa rivers, where there were many white settlements. Supply delays, short-term enlistments, and even mutinies hampered the army's operations from Fort Strother in the vicinity of present-day Ragland. In March 1814, Jackson's army, resupplied and reinforced, set forth again.

Meanwhile, many Red Stick warriors had built a refugee village called Tohopeka inside the "horseshoe bend" of the Tallapoosa River where they hoped to be protected by the encircling river, the magic of their prophets, and a log barricade across the open end of this peninsula. On March 27 Jackson sent General John Coffee, with 700 men and 600 Cherokee and Lower Creek allies, to cross the Tallapoosa and surround the bend. With the rest of his army (about 2,000 men) on the peninsula Jackson then ordered an artillery bombardment of the barricade. After some of Coffee's Cherokees crossed the river and assaulted the

Red Sticks from the rear, he immediately ordered a frontal charge on the barricade.

Besieged from both sides, the 1,000 Red Stick warriors, led by Menawa, fought until almost all were dead. Menawa, although severely wounded, managed to escape. Jackson's losses were 49 killed and 154 wounded.

Remnants of the hostile Creeks, including the famous Red Eagle, surrendered to Jackson in April 1814 at Fort Jackson (earlier known as Fort Toulouse) near present-day Wetumpka. In August, the Treaty of Fort Jackson was signed, ending the Creek War officially and forcing the Creek nation to cede some 20 million acres of land, including much of present-day Alabama, to the United States.

For Andrew Jackson the victory at Horseshoe Bend was the first step to national fame and the White House. For the Creeks the war's end set in motion events that eventually would force them to give up their ancestral hunting grounds and move to a strange new territory west of the Mississippi River in the 1830s. To white pioneers the victory at Horseshoe

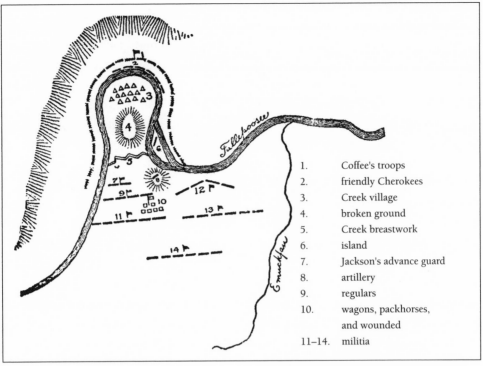

1.	Coffee's troops
2.	friendly Cherokees
3.	Creek village
4.	broken ground
5.	Creek breastwork
6.	island
7.	Jackson's advance guard
8.	artillery
9.	regulars
10.	wagons, packhorses, and wounded
11–14.	militia

Jackson's sketch of the Battle of Horseshoe Bend

Bend meant that a vast new wilderness now was open to settlement. Within the next five years the one-time homeland of the Creeks would become part of the new state of Alabama.

Horseshoe Bend National Military Park, operated by the National Park Service, includes the entire battlefield of this historic encounter. Its **museum** contains a diorama of the battle and Creek life. A three-mile tour road, hiking trails, and outdoor exhibits and markers interpret battlefield sites. A flintlock rifle demonstration in Tennessee militia costume and historical talks are given on Sundays and upon request throughout the week. Open daily 8 a.m. to 5:00 p.m. No admission charge. For special group tours and other information, telephone (205) 234-7111.

Accommodations: The nearest camping facilities are at Wind Creek State Park, six miles south of Alexander City, on the shores of Lake Martin. The park is open daily. Small admission fee. Comfortable motels may be found in Dadeville and Alexander City. Cheaha State Park and Talladega National Forest, both fifty miles north of Horseshoe Bend Park on Alabama 49, offer camping and Cheaha Lodge (dining, lodging). End Alternate Route.

Departing Horseshoe Bend, follow Alabama 49 north and rejoin Tour 9 at Lineville (see Gold Rush Towns below).

Talladega

Indian trails leading to the Creek capital at Coosa once passed through this vicinity, perhaps because of the big spring from which thousands of gallons of water flow daily. On November 9, 1813, Andrew Jackson and 2,000 of his Tennessee volunteers defeated 1,000 Creeks at the Battle of Talladega, a victory celebrated by American artists and poets for two decades thereafter. Creek lands in the Talladega area were ceded in 1831. Promoters of a town near the big spring began laying off streets and offering lots for sale. Prospectors lived in log hotels and drove out to look over the former Indian lands. Attracted by opportunities in law, medicine, and politics, educated and ambitious young men from Tennessee, Kentucky, Georgia, and as far away as Maine flocked to the area around Talladega.

Talladega today is a busy center of industry and education.

Talladega College was founded immediately after the Civil War by two former slaves, William Savery and Thomas Tarrant, who organized a school in one room of a residence near the present campus. In 1866, the Alabama superintendent of education reported a "flourishing school" at Talladega. The Freedmen's Bureau helped support this school in its earliest days but the American Missionary Association later took responsibility for its operation. Unlike Tuskegee Institute, founded by Booker T. Washington to encourage blacks to learn vocational skills, Talladega College was dedicated to the philosophy of providing a liberal arts education for its students. It is still operated by the American Missionary Association.

Swayne Hall (c. 1857), one of Alabama's National Historic Landmarks, was originally a Baptist high school for boys. Slave labor was used in its construction. In 1862, the hall, empty because of the war, was used as a temporary prison for sixty-five Union officers captured at the Battle of Shiloh. When the building was offered for sale in 1867, it was purchased by the American Missionary Association as the new home of Talladega College. For years, the hall served as library, classroom facility, offices, and housing for students. Freedmen from surrounding areas held mass meetings here, proud that such a large structure was available to blacks.

DeForest Chapel (c. 1903), one-story brick Gothic Revival, is named for the Reverend Henry Swift DeForest, president of Talladega College from 1880 to 1896. His son, Lee, perfected the radio tube, thereby helping to make possible radio, sound motion pictures, and television.

Swayne Hall and DeForest Chapel are open daily 8 a.m. to 4 p.m. No admission charge.

114

The Alabama Institute for the Deaf and Blind is the outgrowth of the Alabama Institute for the Deaf established by the legislature in 1860. In 1867 a Department of the Blind was opened. The institute, largest of its kind in the United States, now also includes departments for the adult blind and deaf and the Helen Keller School of Alabama for the treatment of deaf-blind children. More than 1,200 children and adults, most of them from Alabama, are treated here. **Manning Hall** (c. 1850), originally the Masonic Female Institute, a three-story brick structure, is now the administration building.

Talladega Court Square Historic District, on the National Register, comprises some thirty structures surrounding the courthouse. Most are fine examples of Victorian "boom town" architecture. **Talladega Passenger Depot** (c. 1906), one-story brick with unusual bellcast hipped roof of tile, serves as chamber of commerce offices today.

Talladega is noted for handsome homes and tree-shaded streets, especially, along South Street East and East Street South. Part of this section, on the National Register, is known as the "Silk Stocking District" because of the wealth of its residents.

Fort Lashley site, corner of Fort Lashley Avenue and South Street, marks the location of a trading post in which 14 whites and around 100 friendly Indians were besieged by hostile Creeks in 1813. According to lore, a friendly Indian clad in a hog skin sneaked out of this stockade and made his way through the besiegers to tell Andrew Jackson of their plight. In the battle that followed, Jackson's men defeated the Creeks and lifted the siege.

From Talladega, follow Alabama 21 toward Anniston.

Watch for **Curry House** three miles from Talladega on the left. Jabez Lamar Monroe Curry was a congressman (1857–61) from the Talladega area prior to the Civil War and an advocate of secession. He became speaker pro tempore of the house in the Confederate Congress but was defeated in 1863 by Marcus Cruikshank of Talladega, who sympathized with the "peace party" that sought to bring an end to the war. Curry attributed his defeat to the fact that many people in this district had opposed secession and were disheartened by the progress of the war. After the war's end, Curry became director of the Peabody Fund, established by George Peabody to improve southern education. He served as American ambassador to Spain from 1885 to 1888, having previously been minister to Spain in 1855. Curry's statue is in Statuary Hall in the Capitol at Washington, D.C.

His home (c. 1838), one-story frame with front and side veranda, is made of hand-hewn boards and shingles and slave-made brick. It is a

Faith Manor, Talladega

National Historic Landmark in addition to being on the National Register.

Just west of the Curry House, follow Talladega County 93 northeast.

Idlewild (c. 1829), on the left, two-story brick structure with colonnade, was the birthplace of Betsy Hamilton, a local author.

Jemison-Turner House (c. 1836–37), about four miles beyond Idlewild on the left, was built by Robert Jemison, operator of an early stagecoach line in antebellum Alabama and an early opponent of secession. The one-story Greek Revival cottage with steamboat design wing became the home of an overseer who operated the nearby mill and the 700-acre Jemison plantation.

Follow Talladega County 93 until it crosses a creek. Turn right and continue on paved road 1.4 miles. Turn left on chert road one-half mile to Faith Manor.

Faith Manor (c. 1833), the **Elston-Barta House**, on the National Register, was originally the center of a 700-acre plantation. The two-story brick dwelling is a well-proportioned example of the earliest form of Georgian

architecture in Alabama and resembles the architecture of the Carolina seaboard in the eighteenth century. Open by appointment. Telephone (205) 362-1406. Admission charge.

Follow Talladega County 93 to nearby Interstate 20 and return to Birmingham, or return to Talladega via Talladega County 93 and Alabama 21 and resume Tour 9.

From Talladega, take Alabama 77 toward Ashland. Just past Waldo, after the road crosses a creek, is Waldo Historic District.

Waldo Historic District
Sorghum Making

Waldo Town Park, on Highway 77 five miles south of Talladega, is the site of an annual sorghum-making festival known as "sopping days." Held in late September or early October, the festival features the old process of making sorghum syrup. Sorghum, biscuits, and sausage are sold by the Waldo fire department. For information, call (205) 362-8493.

Alabama pioneers sweetened their meals with molasses made from sorghum cane, a plant resembling corn, because sugar was scarce and expensive. Planted in late spring, sorghum cane is ready for harvest in the fall when its seeds turn red and hard. Molasses making starts soon after the cane is cut so that the juice will not become sour.

Pioneers took their cane to a mill whose owner collected every fourth

116

gallon as his fee. A cane mill consisted of two or three large metal crusher rollers mounted on a wooden frame. Gears connected these rollers to a long wooden arm, or "sweep," to which a mule or horse was hitched. As the animal walked around the mill, these gears turned the rollers. Stalks of cane were pushed between the rollers, mashing the cane to a pulp. The juice dripped into a barrel covered by a cloth filter. Juice was boiled three or four hours in a large metal pan until it thickened and changed color from green to caramel. Then the syrup was filtered again, poured into containers, cooled, and sealed to await the long winter ahead.

Waldo Covered Bridge (c. 1858) nearby, one-span, 115-foot-long Town truss type, is in poor condition.

Old-Time Resorts

Leaving Waldo, continue on Alabama 77 toward Ashland. Turn east on old Alabama 77 at sign for Chandler Springs. Turn right at sign for Chandler Springs Baptist Church.

Chandler Springs was a modest antebellum resort near three mineral springs containing potassium, sodium, magnesium, calcium, iron, and other minerals believed to have healthful properties. Families came to this hotel before and after the Civil War to take the waters, dance, bowl on the lawn, and listen to the bullfrogs. Those who did not own summer cottages stayed at a frame hotel that burned in 1918. Nothing remains today of the old summer colony except the springs.

Those interested in old-time resorts may continue on old Alabama 77 past twin lakes on either side of the highway. Watch for a sign on the left for Odum Scout Trail. Turn left three miles to Clairmont Springs.

Clairmont Springs Historic District was one of the favorite watering places in early twentieth-century Alabama. Here visitors came by train to rest, eat fried chicken and fried ham, and drink water from mineral springs containing iron, sulphur, alum, arsenic, and other minerals believed to have medicinal value. Creek Indians had drunk from these same springs. Maria Forge, one of the first iron ore furnaces in Alabama, was operated near here by the Riddle brothers from Pennsylvania, who stamped their ore with a boar's head crest and claimed that it equaled the finest ores of Sweden. A 500-pound hammer, lifted by water-powered bellows, was used to forge the iron.

Clairmont Springs Hotel (c. 1908), two-story frame fifty-room building that closed in 1973, was the last mineral spa resort hotel to operate in Alabama. The hotel is in dilapidated condition, as are a number of the summer cottages and the old bathing pool nearby, yet Clairmont is the best preserved of Alabama's old time watering places.

Return to old Alabama 77 and continue east to Ashland.

Ashland

Ashland is the county seat of Clay County. This remote section of Alabama has produced several widely known political figures, among them U.S. Supreme Court justice Hugo L. Black; U.S. senator Claude Pepper of Florida; Joseph C. Manning, one of Alabama's leading Populists during the 1890s; Hiram Evans, Jr., imperial wizard of the Ku Klux Klan during the 1920s; and Henry J. Carwile, a candidate for governor during World War II who drove a red, white, and blue Model-T Ford.

Justice Black, who served on the high court from 1937 until shortly before his death in 1971, briefly became a member of the Klan when he sought to succeed in politics during the 1920s. In 1926 the Alabama Klan, then at the zenith of its political strength, helped elect Black to the U.S. Senate, where he served until President Franklin D. Roosevelt appointed him to the Supreme Court. Black took part in a number of major Court decisions, including its ruling to outlaw segregation in public schools. In **Clay County Courthouse** (c. 1906), also on the National Register, Black tried his first cases as a fledgling lawyer. The Hugo L. Black Memorial Courtroom has been restored to resemble its appearance in the 1920s.

Clay County has one of the largest graphite deposits in the United States.

Clay County Courthouse

Five miles west of Ashland, nearly fifty graphite mines once operated, employing 2,500 workers. The mines closed in the late 1920s after Congress (despite the protests of Senator Hugo Black) refused to enact a protective tariff, thereby enabling graphite from Madagascar and other foreign countries, mined by low-cost labor, to enter the United States.

Leaving Ashland, follow Alabama 9 to Lineville.

Gold Rush Towns

Miners searching for gold (but often finding only pyrite or mica) started a brief gold rush in Alabama during the 1840s. Numerous private mines operated in the Lineville area. Several companies mined pyrite, often called *fool's gold*, in the little community of Pyriton. Other nearby "gold rush" towns include Goldville in Tallapoosa County and Arbacoochee and Edwardsville in Cleburne County. When richer deposits of gold were discovered in California, Alabama's brief gold rush ended. Recently, however, a number of Alabamians have shown new interest in prospecting for gold in the Talladega National Forest area, once the gold mining center of the state.

Leaving Lineville, follow Alabama 49 to Cheaha State Park.

Cheaha State Park and Talladega National Forest

Cheaha Mountain, 2,407 feet above sea level, is the highest point in Alabama. This peak is probably the cone of a much higher ancient peak of sandstone that resisted erosion. Geologists call such peaks monadnocks, meaning mountains of rock that resist erosion. Stone Mountain, near Atlanta, is another well-known monadnock.

Accommodations: Cheaha State Park includes cottages, a motel, and campground facilities. Outstanding views.

Departing Cheaha State Park, follow Talladega Scenic Drive, Alabama 49, through Talladega National Forest, which contains the southernmost thrusts of the Appalachian mountain chain into northeastern Alabama. This drive offers a number of scenic overlooks from which to view the rolling Alabama countryside. It resembles Virginia's Blue Ridge Parkway and Skyline Drive in that it is little traveled, sparsely settled, and follows the crests of hills and mountains. Talladega Scenic Drive, however, is only about twenty miles long. When it ends at U.S. 78, turn west toward Anniston.

Shoal Creek Church

Side Trip: Gold Mining Towns, Old Log Church, Pinhoti Trail, Victorian Homes.

Follow Interstate 20 east to Heflin exit. Turn south on Alabama 9 and ask locally for directions to Arbacoochee.

Arbacoochee was a thriving boom town during Alabama's gold rush of the 1840s. All that remains of Arbacoochee is a dilapidated two-story brick building, which probably served as a general store, and some of the mining pits. Local residents are not eager to point out the sites of the old gold mines.

Return north to U.S. 78 and proceed through Heflin to Edwardsville, another former gold rush boom town. Beyond Edwardsville on U.S. 78, turn left at the sign for the Coleman Lake area of Talladega National Forest. Continue six miles, turn right at the sign for Shoal Creek Church. Follow this dirt road a few hundred yards.

Shoal Creek Church, a well-preserved, early-nineteenth-century hand-hewn log church with original benches, still is used for community gatherings and "dinner on the grounds." Unlike Clay Bank Log Church (see

119

Ozark), Shoal Creek Church is still in a forest setting far from modern intrusions. Its outdoor tables and benches provide a good picnic site.

Pinhoti Trail, a foot trail through the mountains, valleys, and ridges of the Talladega National Forest, passes near this church. When it is completed from Piedmont to Sylacauga, the Pinhoti Trail will link with the Appalachian Trail, which extends from Georgia to Maine. In Alabama the trail follows a route used by hunters and by war parties when Creeks and Cherokees fought to establish a boundary between their nations in the early nineteenth century.

The word *Pinhoti* is derived from the Creek words *pinwa* (turkey) and *huti* (home). As in all compound Creek words, the second syllable is dropped. The trail is blazed by marks on trees resembling turkey tracks. Maps are available at Talladega National Forest ranger stations, at Cheaha State Park, or by writing the U.S.D.A. Forest Service, 2946 Chestnut Street, Montgomery, AL 36107; telephone (205) 832-4470.

Return to U.S. 78 and turn east toward Fruithurst.

Fruithurst

In the mid-1890s a group of northern investors acquired large land holdings in this area in hope of establishing a colony of vineyardists and winemakers. The town of Fruithurst, whose name connotes the harvesting of fruit in a wooded grove, was incorporated in 1896. Its financiers built an elaborate eighty-room clubhouse in an effort to attract more investors. Groups of Swedes moved here from Minnesota to labor in vineyards and wineries.

However, Alabama's weather, soil, and prohibitionists doomed this experiment to failure. Soon the Alabama Fruit Growers and Winery Association went bankrupt. Its clubhouse, later moved to nearby Borden Springs and operated as a summer resort, burned in 1935. All that remains of this turn-of-the-century vineyard colony are about a dozen Victorian homes scattered throughout a small village.

Leaving Fruithurst, return to Interstate 20 and turn west toward Anniston.

Anniston

Anniston was created after the Civil War by the Tyler and Noble families to be an industrial area of the New South. Merging northern capital and southern talent, the little town that grew up around the Woodstock Iron Company's charcoal iron furnaces and cotton mill became an experiment in utopian community building.

The town was first called by the company name, *Woodstock*, which had been selected because of the proximity of a village named Woodstock to Oxford, England. (The company property was close to Oxford, Alabama.) When the postal authorities reminded the town's proprietors that there was another Woodstock near Tuscaloosa, a new name had to be chosen. The resulting "Anniston" honored Annie, the wife of Alfred Tyler.

The founders divided the town into business, industrial, and residential sections. The community was further segregated occupationally as operatives lived in cottages adjacent to the mills and furnaces. The Tylers and Nobles used company profits for community improvements, such as paved and tree-lined streets, parks, schools, churches, and an opera house for entertainment. The town soon gained a reputation as "the model city."

For a decade it was a closed, private company. By 1883, outside pressures, including the coming of the Georgia Pacific Railroad, forced the town to open to the broader public. New business opportunities attracted industries, commercial activities, and people. Anniston became the most rapidly growing community in Alabama in the 1880s and in the process the parent company gradually lost control of the town.

Iron and textiles provided the industrial base for the town, with numerous and diverse products. In the 1880s Anniston was the site of one of the world's largest rolling stock plants, which turned out railroad cars from engine to caboose. The cast iron pipe

St. Michael and All Angels, Anniston

industry began in that same decade. Anniston pipe could soon be found in the water and sewerage systems of Jerusalem, Tokyo, Mexico City, Havana, and Honolulu. By the 1920s Anniston was the world's largest producer of cast iron pipe.

Anniston also is known as a military center. Army officials first recognized the advantages of climate and location during the Spanish-American War. A temporary encampment named Camp Shipp housed troops until after the final peace settlement. Fort McClellan was built during World War I, and the Anniston Army Depot was added during World War II.

Anniston could never compete in size with the larger Birmingham, partly because of the lack of coke in the iron-making process. The town remains, however, a good example of the New South's industrializing hopes.

121

Moreover, the founders' model city image was accepted by their contemporaries and still persists as the town's motto.

The **Episcopal Church of St. Michael's and All Angels** (1888), 18th Street and Cobb Avenue, was built by John Ward Noble, one of Anniston's founders, as a place of worship for foundry workers and stonemasons who had come from England. Designed by the architect who drew the original plans for St. John the Divine in New York City, the Norman-Gothic masonry church features a ceiling hand-carved by Bavarian wood carvers. Angels' heads, carved at the end of the grain rather than on the flat of the wood, all turn so that every angel looks directly toward the altar of Carrara (Italian) white marble. The ceiling is a replica of ship ribs.

Except for the marble and alabaster on the altar and reredos, all materials used in this church, including pine and sandstone, are native to Alabama. Every stone in the building was cut by hand. In the parish hall is a series of English lithographs depicting the history of Christianity from Stonehenge to the preaching that preceded the first prayer book in English. This set of the lithographs is believed to be the only one now in existence.

Open daily 9 a.m. to 4 p.m. No admission charge.

Other sites of interest in Anniston include **Anniston Inn Kitchen** (1883),

African display, Anniston Museum of Natural History

120 West 15th Street, all that remains of the massive Anniston Inn built during Anniston's boom period, now a women's clubhouse and on the National Register; **Crowan Cottage** (1887), 1427 Woodstock Avenue, two-story, shingled structure in the Richardsonian style; **Noble-Roberts-Parker Cottage** (1887), 900 Leighton Avenue, on the National Register, brick cottage restored as an office; **Grace Episcopal Church** (c. 1885), 1000 Leighton Avenue, Gothic Revival designed by George Upjohn; and **Tyler Hill District**, containing a dozen homes of the 1890s era.

Departing Anniston, take Alabama 21 north toward Jacksonville.

Anniston Museum of Natural History, a large, handsome building located at 800 Museum Drive near the intersection of Alabama 21 and U.S. 431, contains a variety of displays, including the Lagarde African Hall, with lions, cheetahs, and a rogue elephant; Ornithology Hall, exhibiting hundreds of species of birds in their natural habitats; Egyptian mummies, a prehistoric Pteranadon, and free nature films. Open Tuesday through Friday, 9 a.m. to 5 p.m.; Saturday, 10 a.m. to 5 p.m.; Sunday, 1 to 5 p.m. Closed Monday. Admission charge. Telephone (205) 237-6766.

Fort McClellan

During the Spanish-American War, army technicians discovered that the Choccolocco Mountains formed an excellent background for artillery firing. After study by the War Department, Camp McClellan was established in 1917. Its name honored Major General George B. McClellan, commander of the Union army from 1861 to 1862. After World War I, Camp McClellan became a permanent post and was redesignated Fort McClellan. Approximately 500,000 men were trained at Fort McClellan during World War II, including a company of Japanese-Americans who helped familiarize other troops with the fighting style and methods of Japanese soldiers.

The Women's Army Corps School was founded at Fort McClellan in 1952. Two years later this became the first permanent home of the Women's Army Corps Center. In 1977 the U.S. Army Military Police School was moved from Georgia to Fort McClellan. In 1978 Congress disestablished the Women's Army Corps. The Department of the Army relocated its Chemical School at Fort McClellan in 1979. Fort McClellan's average military population was about 10,000.

Edith Nourse Rogers Museum, Building 1077 near the intersection of Fifth Avenue and Third Street close to Gallaway Gate, depicts the history of women's role in the military through exhibits of photographs, uniforms, flags, guidons, and personal memorabilia. Open Monday through Friday, 8 a.m. to 4 p.m.; weekends by appointment. No admission charge.

Military Police Corps Museum, Building 3182 on 23rd Street, documents the history of the Military Police Corps, using dioramas and photographs, from its beginning to the present. Open Monday through Friday, 8 a.m. to 4 p.m.; weekends and holidays by request. No admission charge.

Continue on Alabama 21 north to Jacksonville.

Jacksonville

Home of Jacksonville State University, Jacksonville, settled in 1822, was originally known as June Bug. Its present name honors General Andrew Jackson, who led his Tennessee volunteers through this territory during the Creek War of 1813–14. Union forces invaded and damaged Jacksonville in 1862.

Among homes and structures of interest in Jacksonville are **Crook Rowan House** or **Ten Oaks** (1850), 805 South Pelham Road, planter's townhouse; **Walker-Daugette House** or **The Magnolias** (c. 1850), 603 North Pelham Road, two-story brick

Dr. J. C. Francis Museum

and one-time home of Clarence W. Daugette, president of Jacksonville State University from 1899 to 1942; **Boxwood** or **Clark-Ide House** (c. 1840), 300 North Pelham Road, once the home of a frontier doctor and used as headquarters by Federal troops during the Reconstruction era (now a fraternity house); **First Presbyterian Church** (1861), near the square, used as a hospital during the Civil War; **Old Tavern** (1838), Crow Corner, oldest business building in Jacksonville and once a "house of entertainment"; and **St. Luke's Episcopal Church** (1856), 103 Chinabee Street, one-story board and batten after an Upjohn design.

Dr. J. C. Francis Medical Museum, 100 Gayle Street, has been restored by the Alabama Historical Commission and is on the National Register. Dr. Francis, a native of Tennessee, moved to Jacksonville in 1837 when this was only a small village. The front room of his two-room office served as a waiting room and apothecary, while the back room was used for examinations. His medical practice was typical of that of the rural southern family doctor of that time. He went by horseback or buggy whenever he was called.

The museum contains an interesting period collection of surgical instruments, medical kits, medicines, pharmaceutical bottles, and supplies, as well as the journal of Dr. Francis with its recommended treatments for such ailments as ulcers, chilblain, and mortification. Open by prior appointment only. Please call R.S.V.P. telephone: (205) 435-7611, extension 8. No admission charge.

In the **cemetery**, South Church and Mays streets, a handsome statue marks the grave of Major John Pelham, a gifted artillery leader (called "Gallant Pelham" by General Robert E. Lee), who gave his life for the Confederacy at the age of twenty-four.

Departing Jacksonville, return via Alabama 21 toward Fort McClellan and Anniston. About two miles south of Jacksonville, watch for a sign indicating the route to White Plains and Rabbittown. Turn right onto a small road between two buildings on Alabama 21 across from the White Plains-Rabbittown Road. Follow this road one mile to Aderholt's Mill on the left at the bridge.

Aderholt's Mill (c. 1836), a three-story structure of slave-made bricks, once had a giant water wheel that furnished the power to grind corn and wheat, crush feeds, thrash peas and beans, make syrup, gin cotton, saw lumber, and even make furniture and caskets for the local community. After the Civil War, the wife of one of the millers was dashed to death when her sweeping skirts were caught in the mill machinery. In 1934 the old water wheel was removed and an enclosed turbine wheel installed. This unusual brick mill, operated until the early 1970s, is in sound condition.

Return via Alabama 21 to Interstate 20.

Directly across from the entry point on the highway is an old cotton mill with workers' houses in parallel rows nearby. (For a brief history of the cotton mill movement, see *Textile Towns and Mills*, Tour 12.)

Four miles farther on Interstate 20, turn right at the Coldwater exit.

Proceed toward Coldwater one fourth of a mile, turn right at the first intersection, and proceed less than one mile to **Coldwater Covered Bridge** (c. 1900). This sixty-foot, one-span modified Kingsport-truss bridge (see *Blount County*), roughly constructed with the use of nails, is deteriorating.

Return to Interstate 20. To see a larger example of a late-nineteenth-century mill village, exit Interstate 20 at Pell City.

About two miles west of this exit is an old mill still in operation. Houses of the original village surround the mill. In the mid-twentieth century, owners of mills like this sold these houses to individual owners. As can be seen, pride of ownership has resulted in additions and personal touches to houses that once were almost identical.

Leaving Pell City, follow Interstate 20 west to Birmingham.

Capitol dome, interior (p. 132)

TOUR 10

Montgomery

first capital of the Confederacy

first White House
of the Confederacy

antebellum mansions

civil rights movement sites

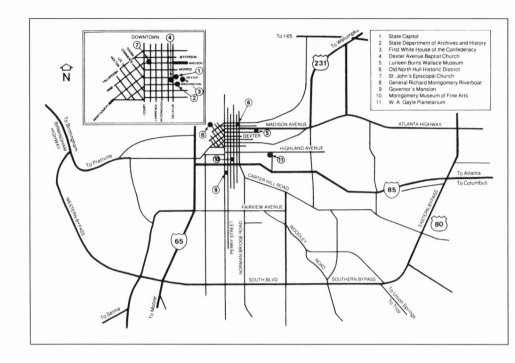

Located on the Alabama River near the Federal Road, Montgomery was incorporated in 1819, a village of less than a hundred houses and stores. The city's name honors General Richard Montgomery, who lost his life in the Benedict Arnold expedition against Quebec during the American Revolution. (Montgomery County was named for Major Lemuel P. Montgomery, who was killed at the Battle of Horseshoe Bend during the Creek War.)

The town resulted from the merger of two towns built by rival groups of land speculators after this rich river bottom area was offered for sale in 1817. One group of Georgians built a town called East Alabama. Another group of New Englanders founded a town called New Philadelphia. Their

bitter rivalry ended when the two towns were merged and named Montgomery.

Montgomery became Alabama's most important inland shipping point for cotton. During harvest, Court Square was jammed with wagons, mules, horses, farmers, and brokers. Many early planters doubled as lawyers, physicians, bankers, hotel owners, and merchants. As they prospered, they replaced their log houses with Greek Revival cottages and some mansions. By 1846 Montgomery had become important enough to supersede Tuscaloosa as Alabama's capital. During the 1850s, William Lowndes Yancey, who practiced law in Montgomery, convinced most of the town's citizens that their economic and political interests would be best served by

128

secession from the Union. For four months in 1861, Montgomery served as capital of the Confederacy, thereby earning its nickname "the cradle of the Confederacy." However, the capital soon moved to Richmond to be closer to Confederate armies in the field. Its remote location saved Montgomery from Federal invasion until the closing days of the Civil War. General James H. Wilson's raiders briefly occupied the city in April 1865.

During the New South era, Montgomery installed an electric trolley system and built an impressive terminal to handle railroad passengers and freight. Factories, mills, and military bases added to the city's growth and prosperity. In 1910 Wilbur Wright established and briefly conducted a flying school on the present site of Maxwell Air Force Base.

In 1955 and 1956 black citizens of Montgomery attracted national attention by their boycott of segregated buses. The young leader of this boycott, Dr. Martin Luther King, Jr., was to become internationally known as the head of many nonviolent protests against segregation and denial of civil rights. Montgomery was the goal of a famous civil rights march from Selma in 1965. Some 25,000 marchers, whites as well as blacks, converged on Dexter Avenue to protest Alabama's restrictions against black voting rights. This march strongly influenced Congress to pass the Voting Rights Act of 1965, which declared barriers to voting to be unconstitutional.

Montgomery was also the political base from which George C. Wallace launched his campaigns for the presidential nomination in 1964, 1968, and 1972.

suggestions for background reading

Fitzgerald, Zelda Sayre. *Save Me the Waltz.* New York: Scribner's Sons, 1932. Reprint. Carbondale: Southern Illinois Press, 1967. (Fiction)

Flynt, J. Wayne. *Montgomery: An Illustrated History.* Woodland Hills, Calif.: Windsor Publishing Co., 1980.

Jackson, Harvey H., III. *Rivers of History: Life on the Coosa, Tallapoosa, Cahaba, and Alabama.* Tuscaloosa: University of Alabama Press, 1995.

Mayfield, Sara. *The Constant Circle.* New York: Delacourt, 1968.

Milford, Nancy. *Zelda.* New York: Harper and Row, 1970.

Southerland, Henry deLeon, Jr., and Jerry Elijah Brown. *The Federal Road through Georgia, the Creek Nation, and Alabama, 1806–1836.* Tuscaloosa: University of Alabama Press, 1989. Reprint (paper) 1990.

Downtown Montgomery

Maps and a pamphlet describing the historic sites along a driving or walking tour of Montgomery are available at the **Thompson Mansion** (c. 1850), 401 Madison Avenue at the corner of North Hull Street. This antebellum mansion, featuring Greek Revival, Italianate and other early Victorian architectural influences, was moved from its original site in Tuskegee in the

Lucas Tavern, Montgomery

1980s. Now a visitor information center, it includes a video presentation. Telephone (334) 262-0013.

Nestled close by is **Old Alabama Town**, 310 North Hull Street, including more than three blocks of nineteenth-century structures representative of life in central Alabama. Among these structures are **Lucas Tavern**, which once stood on the old Federal Road at Waugh and in which General Lafayette spent the night en route to Montgomery in 1825; a **log cabin** (c. 1820s); a **two-room dogtrot** house that was the home of William Lowndes Yancey at the time of his death in 1863; **Presbyterian Church** (c. 1880s), simple clapboard church built by members of a black congregation; **shotgun house** (c. 1897), representing black urban life in the late nineteenth century; **Pintlala Grange Hall** (c. 1875), representing the Grange movement among farmers in the late nineteenth century and site of the last statewide Grange meeting in 1892; and a **doctor's office**, in which Dr. Thomas Duncan, who graduated in 1892 from Alabama Medical College

in Mobile, practiced until his death in 1938. Here, too, are a **cotton gin**, a **drugstore museum**, **blacksmith shop**, **print shop**, and **grist mill**. The **Ordeman-Shaw House Museum** (c. 1848), on the National Register, is an Italianate-style townhouse that has been restored to depict the lifestyle of a Montgomery middle class family in 1850. Included in the complex are the original slave quarters and kitchens, an 1840s barn, gardens planted in period shrubs and trees, a wash house, chicken yard, and vegetable garden. Old Alabama Town is open Monday through Saturday, 9:00 a.m. to 3:30 p.m.; Sunday, 1:00 to 3:30 p.m. Admission charge.

The nearby streetscape has several restored period houses, used as offices and not open to the public, including **Mayor Reese House** (c. mid-1850s), Greek Revival cottage with boxed Doric columns; **DeWolf-Cooper Cottage** (c. 1856), a Gothic Revival clapboard cottage; **Davis-Cook House** (c. 1857), large one-story dwelling with Greek Revival and Italianate details.

Nearby on the corner of Perry and

Ordeman-Shaw House

130

St. John's Episcopal

Madison streets is **St. John's Episcopal Church** (c. 1855), of Gothic design but without the usual slave gallery because an older church structure was given to black Episcopalians. Among rectors of St. John's were the Right Reverend Nicholas Hamner Cobbs, first bishop of the Diocese of Alabama and an opponent of secession, and the Reverend Edgar Gardner Murphy, who led a movement against child labor during the 1890s and early 1900s. While Montgomery was the capital of the Confederacy for four months in 1861, many prominent Confederate government leaders worshiped here. President Jefferson Davis, although not an Episcopalian at that time, rented a pew for members of his family who belonged to that denomination. The church is on the National Register.

Nearby on the corner of Bibb and Coosa streets is the **Murphy House** (c. 1851), on the National Register, Greek Revival with Corinthian columns and marble portico, used as headquarters for the Union army in 1865. Period rooms are open to visitors Monday through Friday during office hours of the City Waterworks Board, which is housed here. No admission charge.

In the area around Court Square on Dexter Avenue are the **McMonnies Fountain** (c. 1885), built over one of Montgomery's oldest wells; **Klein & Son** (c. 1856), designed after a Venetian palazzo, originally the office of the Central Bank of Alabama, strongest bank in the state prior to the Civil War; and **Winter Building** (c. 1841), Italianate design, once the office of the Southern Telegraph Company from which the order to fire on Fort Sumter was transmitted, thereby initiating hostilities between the North and South. The Winter Building is on the National Register.

On the lower two blocks of **Commerce Street**, a warehouse and commercial area, buildings constructed during the New South era following the Civil War are being restored. Nearby **Union Station** (c. late nineteenth century), Romanesque Revival

Murphy House

131

Union Station

Capitol, interior of dome

with handsome oak woodwork and mosaic tile floors, has also been restored and is a National Historic Landmark.

Cottage Hill Historic District (c. 1870–90), bounded by Holt, Goldthwaite, Clay, and Clayton streets, includes approximately ninety-five one- and two-story Victorian dwellings. This in-town residential district is undergoing restoration by private owners and small commercial enterprises. The district is on the National Register.

Capitol and Vicinity

The location of Alabama's capital was a hot political issue during the early years of statehood. St. Stephens, first territorial capital, and Cahaba, first permanent state capital, were located in south Alabama. Huntsville in north Alabama served as tempo-

The Capitol, exterior

rary state capital while Cahaba was being built. After Cahaba was abandoned as the state capital, north Alabama residents managed to win a fight to move the capital to Tuscaloosa in 1826.

In 1846 the capital moved again. Powerful south Alabama politicians persuaded the legislature to designate Montgomery as the capital. In 1849 fire destroyed a large portion of the first capitol built on what was known as Goat Hill in Montgomery. In 1851 a new capitol was constructed on this site. Alabama's historic decision to secede from the Union was made in the House of Representatives chamber in this building. A star on the west portico marks the spot where Jefferson Davis was inaugurated president of the Confederacy. The Confederate government was organized here while Montgomery served as capital of the Con-

Restored interior chamber in Capitol

First White House of the Confederacy

federacy for four months in 1861. The historic Selma-to-Montgomery civil rights demonstration of 1965 ended at the capitol steps. The capitol is a National Historic Landmark. In 1992 the Alabama Historical Commission completed a restoration of the interior of the capitol. Guided tours daily from 9 a.m. to 4 p.m. except major holidays. No admission charge.

Rice-Semple-Haardt House

Other historic sites near the capitol include **Rice-Semple-Haardt House** (c. 1855), moved from 725 Monroe Street to the corner of High and Court streets, Greek Revival with Victorian Gothic arches on second-story gallery, listed on the National Register. On the south side of the capitol is the **First White House of the Confederacy** (c. 1835), Italianate-style, two-story dwelling (moved from its original site) in which Confederate president Jefferson Davis and his family lived in 1861. It is on the National Register. Open Monday through Friday, 8 a.m. to 4:30 p.m.; open Saturday and Sunday for groups of ten or more by appointment only. Telephone (334) 242-1861. Donations accepted. The **Alabama Department of Archives and History** building next door houses a museum containing exhibits of a variety of items related to Alabama history and the Alabama Hall of Fame. Open Monday through Friday, 8 a.m. to 5 p.m.; Saturday 9 a.m. to 5 p.m.; reference room closed Mondays. No admission charge.

Dexter Avenue Baptist Church

Civil Rights Memorial

Just down Dexter Avenue from the capitol at the corner of Decatur Street is a National Historic Landmark, **Dexter Avenue Baptist Church** (c. 1885), 454 Dexter Avenue, the second Baptist church built for a black congregation in Montgomery. Dr. Martin Luther King, Jr., while serving as pastor of this church in 1955, led the Montgomery boycott against segregated bus transportation and thus began a career that culminated in his national leadership of the civil rights movement. Downstairs is featured a mural depicting events and people associated with Dr. King's career. Open Monday through Friday, 9:30 a.m. to noon and 1 to 4 p.m.; Saturday 10 a.m. to 2 p.m. Closed on Sundays and when facilities are in use.

Telephone (334) 263-3970. No admission charge.

The **Civil Rights Memorial**, one block south of Dexter Avenue Baptist Church on the corner of Washington and Hull streets, is a tribute to the 40 Americans who died during the Civil Rights Movement from 1954 to 1968. Designed by Maya Lin, the architect of the Vietnam Memorial in Washington, the circular black granite table records the names of these Americans and chronicles the history of the movement in lines that radiate like the hands of a clock. Water emerges from the table's center and flows evenly across the top. On a curved black granite wall behind the table are engraved the words from the Bible that Dr. Martin Luther King, Jr., often quoted: "We will not be satisfied until justice rolls down like waters and righteousness like a mighty stream." Open 24 hours a day; no admission charge.

Perry Street

William Lowndes Yancey law office, now the Lanier Building, corner of Perry and Washington Streets, where the famous secessionist orator practiced law from 1846 until his death in 1863, is on the National Register.

Teague House (c. 1848), 468 South Perry Street, Greek Revival with Ionic columns and marble portico, was a private residence until 1955. One of antebellum Montgomery's most pretentious homes, this was one of the houses used as headquarters by General James H. Wilson's raiders when Union troops occupied Montgomery in 1865. From its portico General Wilson read a proclamation declaring Montgomery to be under martial law. Now the home of the Alabama Histori-

Governor's Mansion

cal Commission, the Teague House is on the National Register. Reception rooms with period furnishings are open to the public during office hours on weekdays.

House of the Mayors (c. 1830s), 532 South Perry Street, was the home of two Montgomery mayors and a mayor of nearby Fort Deposit. Restored in 1978–79, it is now the office of Montgomery's United Way.

Governor's Mansion (c. 1907), 1142 South Perry Street, twentieth-century Neoclassical Revival, on the National Register, has been the official residence of Alabama governors since 1950. Open Tuesday through Thursday, 9:30 to 11 a.m. and 2 to 2:30 p.m. by appointment. No admission. Telephone (334) 834-3022.

Other Montgomery Historic Sites

Scott and Zelda Fitzgerald Museum, 919 Felder Avenue, is the one-time home of author F. Scott Fitzgerald and his wife, Montgomery native Zelda Sayre Fitzgerald. Museum hold-

Teague House, Montgomery

Scott and Zelda Fitzgerald Museum

ings focus on the personal artifacts which were a part of the couple's public and private lives. Visitors may also view a twenty-five minute video on Scott and Zelda and their Montgomery connection. Open Monday through Friday, 10 a.m. to 2 p.m.; Saturday and Sunday, 1 to 5 p.m. No admission charge. Tours available by appointment. Call (334) 264-4222 or (334) 263-4916.

W. A. Gayle Planetarium, 1010 Forest Avenue in Oak Park, offers a variety of programs on the stars, sun, moon, and planets. Open certain weekends at 2 p.m.; school shows, September through May. Call for information: (334) 241-4799.

Montgomery has five institutions of higher learning. **Huntingdon College**, 1500 East Fairview Avenue, operated by the Alabama/West Florida Conference of the Methodist church, was founded in Tuskegee in 1845 and moved to Montgomery in 1909. Originally a women's college, Huntingdon admitted its first male students in 1932. **Alabama State University**, 915

South Jackson Street, a predominantly black institution, was founded in 1874. **Auburn University at Montgomery**, established in 1967, is seven miles east of downtown Montgomery on Interstate 85. **Troy State University** operates a branch campus at 215 Montgomery Street. **Alabama Christian College** is located at 5345 Atlanta Highway.

The **Alabama Shakespeare Festival** is located in the Wynton M. Blount Cultural Park off Woodmere Boulevard. This internationally acclaimed theater is the southeast's fastest growing attraction, and one of the largest and most productive regional theaters in North America, annually attracting over a quarter of a million visitors from all 50 states and over 50 foreign countries. ASF operates virtually year-round with world-class theater productions, concerts, and educational programs, and is the only American theater invited to fly the flag seen over England's Royal Shakespeare Company. English-style grounds surround the theatre, offering visitors a spectacular view and scenic picnic sites. Handicapped accessible. For indi-

Alabama Shakespeare Festival

136

Montgomery Museum of Fine Arts

vidual tickets and backstage tours, call (334) 271-5353. For group rates call (334) 271-5330.

Montgomery Museum of Fine Arts also lies within the Wynton M. Blount Cultural Park. Noted for its outstanding collection of 19th and 20th century paintings in the Blount Collection, the Museum also houses a collection of southern regional art and American and Old Master prints, as well as hosting a diverse selection of traveling exhibitions each year. Free admission. Handicapped accessible. Open Tuesday through Saturday, 10 a.m. to 5 p.m.; Thursday, 10 a.m. to 9 p.m.; Sunday, noon to 5 p.m. Group tours available with minimum three weeks notice. Call (334) 244-5700.

Chantilly (c. 1836), in the Mt. Meigs area about seven miles east of Montgomery on Vaughn Road, is a remarkable example of the early settlement of Montgomery County. On the old Federal Road in the rich Tallapoosa River region, Mt. Meigs was a prosperous community of planters, many of whom had migrated from South Carolina and Virginia. Originally a square structure with two-story front portico, the house has a pedimented front gable and delicate colored glass sidelights. In the early 1850s, two large rooms were added, one on each side, and the front portico was replaced with a long verandah. Other changes have been made over the years, but Chantilly remains a fine example of the composite Georgian/Federal architecture that was replaced in the South by Greek Revival and Italianate.

Sturdivant Hall, Selma (p. 154)

TOUR 11
Western Black Belt

From Montgomery

Lowndesboro

Hayneville

Camden

Cahaba

Selma

Demopolis

Livingston

Eutaw

Greensboro

Marion

Return to Montgomery

planter homes

antebellum churches

sites of civil rights
demonstrations

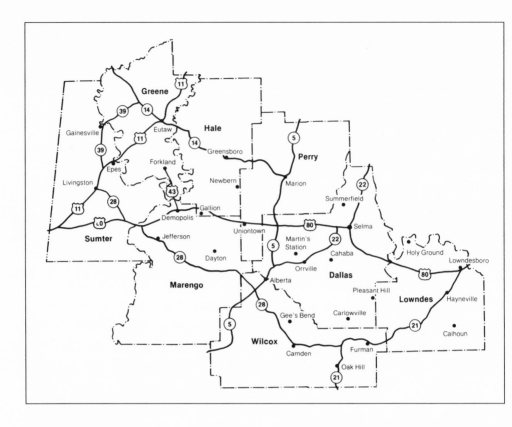

Alabama's Black Belt

Andrew Jackson's defeat of the Creek Indians at Horseshoe Bend in 1814 opened the heartland of Alabama to white settlement. In the land rush that followed, the richest prize was bottomland near the Alabama River. At the Alabama land sales of 1815 and 1817 held in Milledgeville, Georgia, and St. Stephens in Washington County, would-be settlers and big-time speculators purchased government land worth almost one million dollars.

Soon the river valleys of Alabama filled with settlers. Latecomers and those unable to purchase bottomland were forced to settle for the dark, gummy prairie nearby. Part of this area was covered with a heavy growth of cane, hence the nickname *canebrake* for the portion around Demopolis and Marion. After slaves cleared away the cane, these clay soils, underlain with limestone, proved as fertile as the river bottoms. Named for the color of its dark soils, the Black Belt became the major cotton-producing center of Alabama. This fertile crescent stretches across south central Alabama in a northwesterly direction.

Because lands yielded bountifully, most Black Belt planters prospered. James Tait, who came to Wilcox

County from Georgia in 1818 with his father, Charles Tait, owned six plantations on both sides of the Alabama River and 311 slaves by 1851, making him one of Alabama's major slave-owners and landholders. Several former Tait plantation mansions survive in Wilcox County.

Successful planters enlarged their original log houses or built new homes in the popular Greek Revival style. Some chose to live in neighborly clusters around towns such as Lowndesboro, Gainesville, Dayton, Eutaw, Greensboro, Marion, and Carlowville. Other planters erected spacious homes on their isolated plantations to accommodate big families and a constant stream of guests.

Many of these old mansions remain today. Some, such as Sturdivant Hall in Selma and Gaineswood and Bluff Hall in Demopolis, have become museums of value to their communities and to visitors. But to sense the isolation of plantation life, one must drive through the countryside and search for the old homes.

During the 1960s, because its black majorities were largely voteless, the

slave cabin in the Black Belt

Black Belt became a center for civil rights demonstrations. Names like Hayneville, Camden, Marion, and Selma appeared in national headlines. In 1965, U.S. 80 between Selma and Montgomery was the scene of a famous five-day march by civil rights demonstrators that influenced Congress to pass the Voting Rights Act of 1965.

Cattle, lumber, soybeans, and pond-raised catfish are major products of the Black Belt today, although cotton still covers many fields in the early fall. Because machines have replaced "stoop" labor and federal quotas have cut back production, most tenants and sharecroppers have left the area in search of city jobs. Many of those who remain live in poverty despite the efforts of cooperatives, the appearance of major new industries such as chemical plants, and the occasional opportunity to obtain new jobs on the huge Tennessee-Tombigbee Waterway.

One can get some notion of the Black Belt from antebellum times to the civil rights revolution by taking U.S. 80 from Montgomery through Selma to Demopolis. But for a real sense of the history of this region, one must leave this heavily traveled road and plunge deep into Lowndes, Dallas, Wilcox, Perry, Hale, Marengo, Greene, and Sumter counties.

Departing Montgomery, take U.S. 80 west as far as Lowndesboro.

Taken in leisurely fashion, this is a one-week tour. If confined to Selma, Demopolis, Eutaw, Greensboro, and Marion, it could be completed in two or three days. Preferable time of year: spring or fall.

Greek Revival Architecture

Temple building, using columns, began with the ancient Greeks at the time of the Doric order (600 B.C.) and lasted until the Corinthian order (100 B.C.). During these 500 years, the Greeks erected magnificent temples, such as the Parthenon, in and around Athens, using Doric, Ionic, and Corinthian columns. The Romans later built variations of such temples, like the Pantheon in Rome. Tuscan columns were a Roman innovation.

Thomas Jefferson, more than any other American, is credited with having revived Greek architecture in this country. His efforts to do so were based upon the natural kinship between Greek democracy and that of the early United States. The Greek Revival influence may be seen at Jefferson's Virginia home, Monticello, as well as at the University of Virginia, an institution he founded. It is reflected as well in the architecture of the United States Capitol and the Supreme Court building in Washington, D.C.

Wealthy planters, with numerous slaves to make bricks and plaster and to fell timber, as well as the means to import marble from Italy and fine furniture from Europe and the East, brought the Greek Revival style to Alabama. Many designed their own houses; others employed professional architects. Still others relied upon master carpenters who built identical houses in village after village, using architectural handbooks to determine the Greek details of columns. In hope of achieving coolness despite Alabama's subtropical climate, these houses were built with wide halls, high ceilings, and generous verandahs. Another Alabama innovation was the use of wrought iron on balcony railings, exterior staircases, fences, and gates. As one student of Alabama's mansions put it, these builders "fashioned Greek Revival mansions from red clay and pine trees and they did it well."

(See Glossary of Architectural Terms.)

suggestions for background reading

Adelman, Bob. *Down Home: Wilcox County.* New York: McGraw-Hill, 1972.

Baldwin, Joseph G. *Flush Times in Alabama and Mississippi.* New York: Appleton, 1853. (Locale: Gainesville)

Brantley, William H. *Three Capitals: A Book About the First Three Capitals of Alabama, St. Stephens, Huntsville, and Cahawba.* Boston: Merrymount Press, 1947.

Brown, Virginia Pounds, and Laurella Owens. *Toting the Lead Row: Ruby Pickens Tartt, Alabama Folklorist.* University: University of Alabama Press, 1981. (Locale: Livingston)

Carmer, Carl. *Stars Fell on Alabama.* New York: Farrar and Rinehart, 1934. Reprint. Tuscaloosa: University of Alabama Press, 1985.

Fry, Anna M. Gayle. *Memories of Old Cahaba.* Nashville, 1908. Reprint. Huntsville: Strode, 1972. (Locale: Cahaba)

Gamble, Robert S. *The Alabama Catalog, Historic American Buildings Survey: A Guide to the Early Architecture of the State.* Tuscaloosa: University of Alabama Press, 1986.

Gamble, Robert S. *Historic Architecture in Alabama: A Primer of Styles and Types, 1810–1930.* Tuscaloosa: University of Alabama Press, 1990.

Gosse, Philip Henry. *Letters from Alabama.* London: Morgan and Chase, 1859. Reprint. Tuscaloosa: University of Alabama Press, 1993. (Locale: Pleasant Hill)

Hammond, Ralph. *Antebellum Mansions of Alabama.* New York: Bonanza Books, 1951. (Includes many Black Belt mansions)

Jackson, Harvey H., III. *Rivers of History: Life on the Coosa, Tallapoosa, Cahaba, and Alabama.* Tuscaloosa: University of Alabama Press, 1995.

Jackson, Walter M. *Alabama's First U.S. Vice President, William R. King.* Decatur: Decatur Printing Co., 1952. (Locale: Selma)

Jones, James Pickett. *Yankee Blitzkrieg: Wilson's Raid Through Alabama and Georgia.* Athens: University of Georgia Press, 1976. (Locale: Selma)

Jordan, Weymouth O. *Hugh Davis and His Alabama Plantation.* University: University of Alabama Press, 1948.

King, Coretta Scott. *My Life with Martin Luther King, Jr.* New York: Holt, Rinehart, and Winston, 1969. (Locale: Marion)

Kolchin, Peter. *First Freedom: The Responses of Alabama's Blacks to Emancipation and Reconstruction.* Westport, Conn.: Greenwood Press, 1972.

Lancaster, Clay. *Eutaw: The Builders and Architecture of an Antebellum Southern Town.* Eutaw: Greene County Historical Society, 1979.

Liddell, Viola Goode. *A Place of Springs.* University: University of Alabama Press, 1979. Reprint (paper) 1982. (Locale: Camden)

National League of Pen Women. *Historic Homes of Alabama and Their Traditions.* Birmingham: Birmingham Publishing Co., 1935. Reprint. Birmingham: Southern University Press, 1969. (Includes many Black Belt mansions)

Rawick, George P., ed. *Alabama and Indiana Narratives.* Vol. 6 of *The American Slave: A Composite Autobiography.* Westport, Conn.: Greenwood Press, 1972. (Includes many Black Belt narratives.)

Rogers, William Warren, and Ruth Pruitt. *Stephen S. Renfroe: Alabama's Outlaw Sheriff.* Tallahassee, Fla.: Sentry Press, 1972. (Locale: Sumter County)

Smith, Winston. *Days of Exile.* Tuscaloosa: W. B. Drake and Son, 1979. (Locale: Demopolis)

Sterne, Emma Gelders. *Some Plant Olive Trees.* New York: Dodd, Mead, and Co., 1937. (Fiction. Locale: Demopolis)

Trelease, Allen W. *White Terror: The Ku Klux Klan Conspiracy and Southern Reconstruction.* New York: Harper and Row, 1971.

Webb, Sheyann, and Rachel Nelson, as told to Frank Sikora. *Selma, Lord, Selma.* University: University of Alabama Press, 1980. (Locale: Selma)

Lowndesboro

Lowndesboro is the jewel of Alabama's planter villages. First settled in 1815, this small community attracted wealthy planters who desired neighbors and sociability. Within a mile or two, thirty-five to forty homes sprang up, ranging in style from raised cottages to classic Greek Revival mansions. By the late 1850s, Lowndesboro, with its business district (destroyed by fire in 1927), two military academies, and female academy, was a flourishing town that attracted visitors from Montgomery and nearby villages. After the Civil War, most Lowndesboro homes gradually fell into disuse and disrepair. In recent years, however, many have been restored by preservation-minded owners. In late March or early April of each year, Lowndesboro citizens sponsor an annual pilgrimage during which several homes are opened to visitors.

Lowndesboro Historic District, on the National Register, includes some twenty structures. Among them are **Meadowlawn** (c. 1853), two-story elegant frame mansion with portico supported by thirteen columns and extending around two sides of the house; **Old Homestead** (c. 1823), large two-story frame mansion with front and side porticos; **The Pillars** (c. 1850), two-story L-shaped Greek Revival with two major porticos; **Reese-Meadows House** (c. 1850), two-story L-shaped structure with two porticos; **Presbyterian Church** (c. 1850), end-gable frame structure with Greek Revival portico topped by a long spire; **African Methodist Episcopal Church** (c. 1830), frame church with the copper dome from Alabama's first state capitol at Cahaba as its steeple and containing a slave gallery.

From Lowndesboro, take Alabama 21 south to Hayneville.

Hayneville

Lowndes County Courthouse (c. 1856), a Greek Revival two-story stucco and wood building on the National Register, is one of four antebellum courthouses still in use in Alabama. It was enlarged and modified in 1905.

One of the tragic deaths of the civil rights movement of the 1960s oc-curred in Hayneville. On August 20, 1965, Jonathan Daniels of Keene, New Hampshire, a twenty-six-year-old Episcopal seminarian and volunteer worker in the civil rights movement, was shot to death by a white deputy sheriff in front of a Hayneville store. Daniels is listed on an honor roll of "martyrs of today" in England's famed Canterbury Cathedral.

Brewer House (c. 1832), a one-story frame dwelling, was once the home of Willis Brewer, a newspaper editor, state auditor and legislator, and author of *History and Resources of Alabama*.

Leaving Hayneville, continue on Alabama 21 southwest toward Camden.

South of Hayneville, take Lowndes County 33 to Calhoun.

The **Principal's Residence** (c. 1900), on the National Register, is one of three remaining buildings from Calhoun School, founded on the advice of Booker T. Washington in 1892 as a vocational school for blacks. The school operated for half a century.

Return to Alabama 21 and continue southwest. At Beechwood, take Lowndes County 12 to Pleasant Hill.

Pleasant Hill

The Englishman and tutor Philip Gosse taught in this lonesome countryside during the 1830s. The **Underwood-Mayo House** (c. 1845) in this small community has a two-story

144

portico supported by both square and round Doric columns and topped by a pediment with sunray louvre. The rear ell of this house includes a raised dining room above a basement brick kitchen (now abandoned) from which hot food was brought up a stairway.

Belvoir (c. 1825) on Dallas County 12 near Pleasant Hill, a two-story frame house with hipped roof, was originally the center of a large plantation owned by Reuben Saffold, member of the 1819 Alabama Supreme Court and political leader during the early era of statehood.

Note **Pleasant Hill Baptist Church** (c. 1850), with its open belfry, and **Pleasant Hill Presbyterian Church** (1851), with its unusual domed belfry. Both contain slave galleries.

From Pleasant Hill follow Lowndes County 7 east to Lowndes County 85 and turn south. Proceed to Lowndes County 4, then east to Carlowville.

Carlowville

This nineteenth-century rural village, on the National Register, spreads along Lowndes County routes 85 and 4. Carlowville, once the social and commercial center of south Dallas County, has no business center today. Visitors must search for its antebellum homes behind thickets and along country lanes. Among them are **The Homestead** or **Alison-Wade House** (c. 1849), built from handmade brick

in late Georgian style; **Camellia Hall** or **Youngblood House** (c. 1833), two-story frame remodeled in the 1920s to Neoclassical; **Lone Live Oak** (c. 1838), boyhood home of the late Tennessee senator Kenneth D. McKellar; **Rumph-Alison House** (c. 1840), home of Dr. Samuel Alison, who served Carlowville for seventy years.

Easier to find are two antebellum churches. **Carlowville Baptist Church** (c. 1834), originally Federal with added Greek Revival portico, contains a slave balcony and raised pulpit. Note the knife marks on its old doors. **St. Paul's Episcopal Church** (c. 1839), originally Greek Revival but enlarged and Gothicized, contains its first musical instrument, an old melodeon, in the choir balcony. Its exterior columns were handmade on local plantations for a total of five dollars.

From Carlowville take Alabama 89 south to Alabama 21; turn east to Furman.

Furman

Two antebellum churches on Wilcox County 59 south of Furman are of interest. The Greek Revival **Methodist Church** (c. 1858) includes original hand-hewn and -dressed doors and benches, and original chandeliers and wall lamps. Note the six box columns and the unusual octagonal bell tower. (Request a key at the store just down the road.) The **Baptist Church** (c. 1858–60), handpegged, contains a slave balcony. The baptistery was added as a separate building in 1887.

Four miles south of Furman near Wilcox County 59 are three prehistoric Indian mounds known as **Drake Field Mounds**.

Hawthorne House (c. 1852), with pedimented double central portico and crowfoot banister, was the boyhood home of the Confederacy's youngest general, John Herbert Kelley.

Continue south on Wilcox County 59 and turn north on Alabama 10 to Oak Hill.

Oak Hill

In this small community are several antebellum homes, including the **Dale Home** (c. 1848), once a Presbyterian manse and birthplace of Governor Benjamin Meek Miller (1931–35); **Ramsey-Bonner Home** (c. 1838), two-story frame with shed-roof porch built by Dr. A. C. Ramsey, a Methodist circuit rider; **Fox Home** (c. 1840s), one-story Greek Revival altered by Victorian-style additions; **Mc-Williams-James Home** (c. 1840s–1850s), near intersection of Alabama 10 and 21; **Jones-Williamson Home** (c. 1840s–1850s), about one mile south of Alabama 21. **Bethel Associate Reformed Presbyterian Church** (c. late 1800s) is one of four churches of this denomination remaining in Alabama.

Continue northwest to Camden on Alabama 10.

Camden

Camden, incorporated in 1832, was built to serve as county seat of Wilcox County and named by an early settler to honor his hometown of Camden, South Carolina. The original settlement grew up on land donated by Thomas Dunn that was located near an abundant spring about four miles from the Alabama River. By the 1850s, Camden had developed into an enterprising political, social, and intellectual center of south Alabama. Wilcox Female Institute attracted students from throughout the South.

The focal point of Camden is Courthouse Square. The two-story brick **courthouse** (c. 1859) with bracketed cornice and Italianate influence is one of Alabama's four antebellum courthouses still in use. (The others are in Lowndes, St. Clair, and Perry counties.) A bronze plaque at the entrance honors Private Enoch H. Cook who, with ten sons and two grandsons, served in the Confederate army—possibly the largest number of soldiers furnished by one family. Of the thirteen, five were killed in action. Note small frame **law offices** (c. 1850) nearby.

During the civil rights era, this courthouse was the scene of a number of demonstrations, some of which were led by Dr. Martin Luther King, Jr., and his close associate, Dr. Ralph Abernathy, a native of Camden. At the time, not a single black in Wilcox or

Lowndes counties, both almost 80 percent black, had the right to vote.

Wilcox Female Institute (1849), on Church Street, one of the oldest women's school buildings in Alabama, has been restored and serves as headquarters of the Wilcox Historical Society. It is on the National Register. **Dale Masonic Lodge** (c. 1847), on Broad Street, was chartered in 1827.

Among Camden's antebellum homes are **Jones-McIntosh House** (c. 1860), Broad Street, Greek Revival cottage; **Sterrett-McWilliams House** (1851), Clifton Street, superb example of eclecticism; **Dunn-Bonner House** (c. 1832), Broad Street, built by Thomas Dunn, who donated the land for Camden; **Beck-Creswell House** (c. 1840), Broad Street and Bridgeport Road, two-story frame with Federal influences and double central portico; and **Bagby-Lidell House** (1853), 403 Broad Street, two-story frame with central portico, home of Arthur Pendleton Bagby, governor of Alabama (1837–41); U.S. Senator (1841–48); and minister to Russia (1848).

Accommodations: Roland Cooper State Park on Alabama 41 north of Camden contains modern cottages, camping facilities, and golf course.

To get a sense of plantation life in the lower Black Belt, take Alabama 10 west from Camden four miles to the Possum Bend vicinity. Turn left at Possum Bend store on Clifton Ferry Road for 1.9 miles to **White Columns** (1859–60), the Felix Tait plantation, striking, two-story Italianate-influenced structure with two porticoed entrances and bracketed cornices. At the end of Clifton Ferry Road, turn left on Alabama 221 one mile to **Liberty Hall** (c. 1843), two-story frame with portico supported by two Ionic and two Doric columns. A large dining room is separated from the main house by a gallery. Return to intersection with Alabama 10. Turn left on Wilcox County 33 for 1.3 miles to **Countryside** (c. 1855–56), the Robert Tait-Ervin House, a T-shaped, two-story structure with continuous one-story verandah across the front and partially along each side. Return to intersection of Alabama 10. Turn west about two miles on Alabama 10 to **Cook Hill** (1833–35), two-story frame (high on a hill to the left) with shed-roof verandah and end exterior chimney. Its builder, Daniel Cook, moved from North Carolina to Wilcox County by covered wagon in the 1820s. Returning to Camden, turn left on Wilcox County 19 about four miles to **Mathews-Tait Home, Yopon** (c. 1845), with four fluted Doric columns lining its large verandah.

Return to Camden and take Alabama 28 north toward Catherine.

Watch for abandoned antebellum homes at (1) the River Bluff intersection, (2) near the junction of Alabama 28 and Wilcox County 19, and (3) at Miller's Ferry. Note plantation bell, used to summon slaves to the fields, beside the Miller's Ferry post office.

Below the bridge over the Alabama River is a pleasant picnic spot. Note **Miller's Ferry Lock and Dam** downstream.

Turn north on Alabama 5 at Catherine. Several old homes are scattered around the hamlet of Gastonburg. At Alberta, turn right on Gee's Bend Road. Note cotton gin near railroad tracks. If cotton is being ginned, pause to watch this process. Continue to Gee's Bend.

Gee's Bend

The road to Gee's Bend winds through tableland for about ten miles to an isolated peninsula surrounded on three sides by the Alabama River. Also known as Boykin, Gee's Bend is an almost wholly black community composed of rural homes, cotton fields, a school, post office, two day-care centers, and two stores. Many of its residents have been told, by means of oral tradition, that they are descended from slaves smuggled illegally from Africa to Mobile long after the international slave trade was prohibited in this country in 1808.

During the Great Depression, the Roosevelt administration authorized government purchase of a large portion of the land in this bend. Tracts were parceled out for a token price to enable black residents to become landowners. Nonetheless, the great majority of the natives of Gee's Bend contin-

ued to exist in poverty. Under a later social program, VISTA, volunteers came to Gee's Bend to teach its farmers new methods of cultivation and how to raise hogs. Presently a group of Mennonites lives just outside the bend.

By far the most successful endeavor to improve the lives of these people has been the **Freedom Quilting Bee**. In a small concrete block building, women of Gee's Bend and other communities gather to piece colorful quilts for sale in fashionable Eastern stores. The cooperative divides its profits among its workers. Visitors are welcome to drop in on the quilting bee. If a quilt is too expensive, visitors can always buy a potholder as a memento of the trip to this remote area of the Black Belt.

Return to Alberta. Turn north toward Orrville via Alabama 5 and 22. (Watch carefully for the intersection where Alabama 5 turns north toward Marion. Follow Alabama 22 east at this point.)

At Martin, take Dallas County 3 one mile north to Martin's Station to view **St. Luke's Episcopal Church** (c. 1853), a one-

Freedom Quilting Bee

story, board and batten Gothic Revival structure said to have been designed by Richard Upjohn of New York, first president of the American Institute of Architects, but probably based on one of Upjohn's published designs. This small church was moved from Cahaba in the late 1800s to escape possible destruction by floods.

Orrville

On the main street of Orrville, note the **Mills-Albritton House** (c. 1854), two-story frame with four exterior chimneys and full-width portico with eight octagonal columns and balcony, and the **Smith-Sutton House** (c. mid-1800s), two-story frame with pedimented portico and two Doric columns. Nearby **Bland-Chestnutt-Turner House**, antebellum two-story frame with Greek Revival embellishment, has a one-story verandah with six heavy square columns and entablature.

At the second yellow flashing light in Orrville, turn right toward Molette's Bend. Continue about five miles to the intersection of this paved road with a major gravel road. Take the gravel road to **McMillan-Oxford House** (c. 1858), recently restored three-story frame that commands a stunning view of the Alabama River from its porches and rooms. This was once a well-known stop for steamers plying the Alabama River. Ask directions to

Molette Cemetery and **Molette House** (c. 1817), the latter a pioneer structure. William P. Molette, who bought this rich tract of land in 1817, became Dallas County's largest slave-holder. He owned 307 slaves, many of whom spoke only African dialects.

Return to Orrville. Take Alabama 22 toward Selma. Watch for Cahaba marker. Turn right to the site of Alabama's first permanent capital (1820–26).

Cahaba

Alabama's first governor, William Wyatt Bibb, who owned a large river plantation in Autauga County, believed that Alabama's future greatness lay along the Alabama River. Other early leaders of the state, including powerful Huntsville men, wanted to locate the capital at Tuscaloosa on the Warrior-Tombigbee system. Ignoring his opponents, Bibb obtained a large land grant from the U.S. government and persuaded the 1818 Alabama legislature to approve a location at the confluence of the Cahaba and Alabama rivers as Alabama's capital. (The original spelling was Cahawba, but the modern spelling Cahaba is used in this book.)

While Cahaba was being built, Huntsville served as temporary capital. When the statehouse was completed in 1820, Cahaba became Alabama's seat of government. In 1821 steamboats began to make the journey

Cahaba historic marker

from Mobile to Montgomery, often stopping at the new capital. General Lafayette, touring America in 1825, arrived at Cahaba by steamboat. Later, elaborate homes sprang up along Cahaba's streets, including the Perine house, with twenty-six rooms, ballroom, and conservatory, and the Crocheron mansion, with its huge reception area and a dining room that could seat 75 to 100 guests. At Bell Tavern, planters gambled at billiards, poker, and real estate.

Floods and yellow fever doomed Cahaba. The waters of the Alabama and Cahaba rivers surged into the capitol in 1822. Tall tales circulated of water so high that legislators floated by boats to their meeting rooms on the second floor. Shortly thereafter they voted to move the seat of government to Tuscaloosa. In the flood of 1833, the old capitol collapsed. Its copper dome was later salvaged and moved to a Lowndesboro church.

During the Civil War, Cahaba was proposed as the site of a large Confederate prison, but Andersonville, Georgia, judged more secure, won this dubious distinction. However, more than 2,000 Northern prisoners of war were packed in low tiers like chicken roosts within "Castle Morgan," an old cotton warehouse in Cahaba where Capital Street meets the river.

At the end of the war, the seat of Dallas County was moved to the safe bluffs of rival Selma. Residents of Selma moved columns, balustrades, and bricks from the abandoned homes of Cahaba to adorn their new houses. By the 1870s Cahaba was deserted except for a few dozen blacks who took up residence amid the moldering cornices, plasters, and paneling in its remaining mansions.

Preservation of this historic site, listed on the National Register, is in process. The **Old Cahawba Archaeological Interpretive Park** includes a picnic area, hiking trails, interpretive signs, and welcome center. The park is open daily 9 a.m. to 5 p.m. Free admission. Telephone 1-800-628-4291 or (334) 872-8058. The only original structures remaining are **Judge Fambro**

150

House (c. mid-1800s), a one-story frame in poor repair, and Barker slave quarters. See the site of **Castle Morgan**; **columns of Crocheron House**; historical markers and street signs; the **Perine Well**, the only remnant of massive Perine House, from which water was piped through the walls to provide an early air-conditioning system. Gravestones from the early 1800s show the devastating effect that yellow fever had on the town. The origin of the **Cahawba Mounds**, two extensive mounds (c. 1750) at entrance to the site of Cahaba, has not been definitively ascertained.

Return to Alabama 22. Turn northeast toward Selma.

Selma

Hernando de Soto, leading his famed march through Alabama in 1540, allegedly spent several days in the vicinity of present Selma. French explorers led by Bienville (the founder of Mobile) fought Indians at this site in 1702. Another French explorer named this place *Écor Bienville*, meaning "Bienville Bluff." The first American settlers, arriving around 1809, called the place High Soapstone Bluff because of the chalky appearance of these bluffs.

William Rufus King, a future vice-president of the United States who owned a large plantation at King's Bend a few miles from Selma, helped organize the land company that plotted lots in Selma. Incorporated in 1820, Selma was named by King, who had a taste for literary epics. He discovered the Greek word *selma*, meaning "seat" or "throne," in one of his favorite epics, *The Poems of Ossian*.

In the 1820s, Selma became a major river port. During the "flush times" of the cotton kingdom in the 1830s, eight steamers at once might be observed taking on cotton and passengers at Selma's wharfs. Selma also became the great slave market of the Black Belt. Each week from September to April, dozens of slaves, accompanied by overseers and guards, were marched to a large three-story building on Water Street for the sales. Planters came from miles around to purchase field hands, skilled blacksmiths, or housemaids. By 1840 slaves outnumbered whites in Dallas County by two to one. When the Civil War came, Dallas County was 76 percent black.

Deep within the South, the river town of Selma, having also the best railroad connections in Alabama, be-

Steamboat landing at Selma

151

came a major supply base for the Confederacy. Some 10,000 men, women, and children were employed in its ordnance industries. The Selma arsenal, largest in the South except for that of Richmond, produced cartridges, horseshoe nails, shovels, canteens, and uniforms. Coal and pig iron, brought to Selma by railroad, were made into cannon and arms for the battlefields of Virginia. Brooke cannon, powerful muzzle-loading guns used aboard ships and for harbor defense, were cast at the Selma Naval Works under the command of a Virginian who bore the Welsh name of Catesby ap Roger Jones. The Selma Naval Works also produced ironclad rams, such as the famed *Tennessee*, sent downriver for the defense of Mobile.

Selma's isolation saved it from invasion early in the war. But in April 1865, Union general James H. Wilson, with 9,000 troops and cavalry, headed for Selma, which was defended by only 3,000 troops (many of them vagrants, boys, or old men) under the command of Confederate general Nathan B. Forrest. In the Battle of Selma, 400 Federal soldiers were wounded and 20 Confederates died, including the local Presbyterian pastor. On Sunday, April 2, 1865, Wilson's victorious raiders moved into town. Disobeying orders, they set fire to storehouses, most of the business district, and many private homes. Selma was more heavily damaged than almost all other Alabama towns combined—indeed, was almost as devastated as Atlanta or Richmond. The Civil War still seems a recent event to Selma's white residents, who hand down from generation to generation tales of how the house or the family silver was saved and how the Lady Banksia rose at the First Presbyterian Church shed its petals when the body of the minister was brought back from the battlefield.

Exactly 100 years after this battle, Selma experienced the second major upheaval in its history. In 1965, to dramatize the fact that only 0.9 percent of Dallas County black adults were permitted to vote, Dr. Martin Luther King, Jr., chose Selma as the focus of voting rights demonstrations. For weeks, blacks marched daily from Brown Chapel African Methodist Episcopal Church to the Dallas County courthouse. Mass arrests of these demonstrators made national headlines. The Selma demonstrations climaxed on Sunday, March 7, 1965, when marchers crossed the Edmund Pettus Bridge and were met by state troopers and sheriff's posses armed with tear gas and billy clubs and were driven back into Selma. The spectacle at Pettus Bridge, seen on television, aroused a national storm of indignation. Thousands of sympathizers, whites as well as blacks, poured into Selma from all over the nation. Determined to make their dramatic protest, these demonstrators received permission for another march from federal district judge Frank M. Johnson, Jr., in Montgomery. President Lyndon Johnson called the Alabama National Guard into federal service to protect the marchers during their five-day trek along U.S. 80 to Montgomery. This march led Congress to pass the Voting Rights Act of 1965, which banned various educational tests that had been used to bar black voters, and which empowered federal examiners to supervise elections. Today the right to vote is freely exercised in Selma.

Accommodations: Several comfortable motels are on U.S. 80 west. Paul M. Grist State Park, seventeen miles north on Alabama 22, offers primitive camping facilities.

Water Avenue Historic District, a six-block area between Franklin and Lauderdale streets, is one of the South's few remaining antebellum riverfront streets. It is on the National Register. Among its structures is the **St. James Hotel** (c. 1837), Alabama's only surviving example of an early river hotel, now under restoration. Other structures reflect Italianate influence. Note iron balconies and railings. The building at 1012 Water Av-

Edmund Pettus Bridge

enue, formerly a cotton warehouse, houses the National Voting Rights Museum and offers a view of historic **Edmund Pettus Bridge**, where the civil rights confrontation of 1965 took place. At the foot of Water Avenue is the **L. & N. Depot**, judged one of twelve depots of architectural significance in Alabama, now a museum.

Old Town Historic District, also on the National Register, contains numerous old homes as well as the site of the Confederate arsenal and naval foundry. The **Old Dallas County Courthouse** or **Smitherman Building** (c. 1840s), 109 Union Street, served as a Confederate hospital and later a community hospital and is now a museum containing a collection of Civil War relics and displays of Selma-

Water Avenue, Selma

L. & N. Depot, Selma

153

manufactured munitions salvaged from the Alabama River, as well as coin collections and old glass. It is open Monday through Friday, 9 a.m. to 5 p.m. Small admission charge.

The old courthouse and the **U.S. Courthouse** and **Federal Building** on Alabama Avenue are on the National Register. The arch in front of the Federal Building honors Selma's U.S. senators John Tyler Morgan and Edmund Winston Pettus. Nearby is another National Register site, **Saint Paul's Episcopal Church**, 210 Lauderdale Avenue. Built to replace a church destroyed by Wilson's raiders, the present structure (c. 1871–84) is one of four Alabama churches designed by Richard and R. M. Upjohn in Gothic Revival style to resemble English cathedrals. Open by appointment.

Other locations open to the public include **Live Oak Cemetery** (c. 1829), also on the National Register, on West Dallas Avenue, the burial place of prominent Alabamians, including Vice-President William Rufus King (1852), U.S. senators John Tyler Morgan (1877–1907) and Edmund Pettus (1897–1907), Confederate navy captain Catesby ap Roger Jones, and Confederate general William Hardee. Note the large Confederate monument.

Sturdivant Hall (c. 1853), 713 Mabry Street, is one of the Black Belt's most handsome mansions. Listed on the National Register, this Greek Revival structure, with modified Corin-

Sturdivant Hall

thian columns in front and Doric columns in the rear, occupies with its outbuildings nearly a city block. Completed at a cost of $69,000, the ten-room mansion epitomizes the setting enjoyed by wealthy Black Belt families in the 1850s. Now a house museum, it is open Tuesday through Saturday, 9 a.m. to 4 p.m.; Sunday, 2 to 4 p.m. Small admission charge.

Next door is **White-Force Cottage**, once the home of Martha Todd White, a half-sister of Mary Todd Lincoln. The Sturdivant Museum Association, which owns Sturdivant Hall, restored the cottage. **Morgan House**, 719 Tremont Avenue, once the home of Confederate general and U.S. senator John Tyler Morgan, is on the National Register. It contains offices of the Cahawba Project and is owned by the Alabama Historical Commission. Open by appointment.

Information for self-guided tours of both these historic districts may be obtained at the **Selma-Dallas County Chamber of Commerce**, 513 Lauderdale Street. Selma offers an annual pilgrimage of historic homes each March or early April. A reenactment of the 1865 Battle of Selma is staged in April. Each October the city sponsors an arts and crafts and Tale Tellin' festival in the riverfront historic district.

Sites of significance in the civil rights movement of the 1960s are **Brown Chapel African Methodist Episcopal Church** (c. 1906), 410 Martin Luther King, Jr., Street. This byzantine-influenced structure was the site of mass meetings led by Dr. Martin Luther King, Jr., whose monument stands in front and marks the beginning of the Martin Luther King, Jr., Street Walking Tour. Open Monday, Wednesday, Friday, 9 a.m.–1 p.m. The **First Baptist Church**, 709 MLK, Jr., Street, was financial headquarters of the movement. The Edmund Pettus Bridge is also a landmark of this phase of the voting rights movement. The present **Dallas County Courthouse** on Alabama Avenue was the objective of many marches in 1964 and 1965. **Selma University**, on Lapsley Street between Minter and Philpot avenues, is one of the oldest black junior colleges in Alabama. It was founded in 1878 by the Alabama Colored Baptist Convention to train ministers and teachers.

Departing Selma, proceed north on Broad Street, turn right on Alabama 14 and U.S. 80 to Range Street.

One-half mile south is the scene of

Brown Chapel A.M.E. Church

the Battle of Selma (on the left at Trinity Lutheran Church). A portion of the breastworks has been preserved and a stone marker erected.

Return to U.S. 80. Turn west toward Uniontown and Demopolis.

Uniontown

For a glimpse of one of the Black Belt's most ambitious mansions, turn left off U.S. 80 at the first traffic light in Uniontown, bear left, and cross the railroad tracks. In a grove of trees on the right is **Pitts' Folly** (c. 1852–53), a two-story, L-shaped structure with fourteen massive Doric columns of plaster-covered brick across the front and east side and two solid walnut Doric columns at the entrance. The house got its name because many neighbors considered that it was indeed a folly to build such a huge mansion. Its superstitious builder, Philip Henry Pitts, deliberately left his house unfinished.

Returning to U.S. 80, note the small frame **post office** (c. 1850), restored at the intersection with Alabama 61. Turn right on 61 three blocks to **Uniontown United Methodist Church** (c. 1858), with three-bay facade. Continue one-half mile to **Westwood** (c. 1836–40), on the right beyond a cemetery, an unusual frame mansion of Italianate style distinguished by a projecting central bay. Known as "the Mecca of Canebrake society," Westwood was built by a railroad developer, James L. Price, and was the long-time residence of Alexander Davidson, an Alabama legislator (1885–89). It is on the National Register.

Dayton

Those who have developed a taste for planter villages should leave U.S. 80 at Faunsdale and drive south for eight miles on Alabama 25 to Dayton. **Dayton Cemetery** (c. 1830s), on the left one-half mile past a church, is noteworthy for its many elaborately carved Victorian Gothic monuments. The **Catlin Tomb** (c. 1857) marks the gravesite of John D. Catlin, one of Marengo County's wealthiest early settlers. **Dayton United Methodist Church** (c. 1851) has a pedimented portico supported by four round Doric

columns on square piers. Among notable houses in this tiny community are **Magnolia Grove** (c. 1836); **Pegram House** (c. 1848); **Stewart-Gaines House** (c. 1857); and **Bittersweet** (c. 1847). For directions, inquire locally.

Return to U.S. 80 and continue west toward Demopolis.

Gallion
(formerly Prairieville)

Nine miles east of Demopolis, near the intersection of U.S. 80 and Alabama 69, watch on the right for **St. Andrew's Episcopal Church** (1853–54), a National Historic Landmark as well as a National Register listing. This one-story red structure, built as a parish church, reflects the Gothic Revival style of architecture popular in the 1850s. Variously called *Carpenter*, *Steamboat*, or *Downing* Gothic, the style is typified by board and batten siding and decorative bargeboards. Its interior symbols are works of art. Interior walls were finished with tobacco

St. Andrew's Episcopal Church, Gallion (drawing)

juice stain. The church was built by two black master carpenters.

St. Andrew's, like St. Luke's Episcopal Church at Martin's Station (see *Gee's Bend*), is said to have been designed by Richard Upjohn of New York, first president of the American Institute of Architects. (It is more likely that both St. Andrews and St. Luke's were based on some of Upjohn's many published plans for rural Gothic churches.) The charming small church is open by appointment and on special occasions. Contact Trinity Episcopal Church in Demopolis at (334) 289-3363. An annual church service and dinner on the grounds take place here in late September or early October.

Return to U.S. 80 and proceed west to Demopolis.

Demopolis

In 1817 a group of unlikely pioneers stepped from barges onto the shores of what is now Marengo County. They put up rough cabins along the white bluffs of the Tombigbee River and named their settlement Demopolis ("city of the people").

These 400 men and women had been supporters of Napoleon Bonaparte. When their leader was exiled to St. Helena, they fled from France to America where they hoped to grow olive trees and make wine. Congress granted them 92,000 acres (at two dollars an acre) in the Alabama wilderness, but the settlers had trouble locating the boundaries of this grant.

Among these colonists were men who had led the great armies of France during the Napoleonic wars. Lieutenant General Lefebvre Desnouettes had been at Napoleon's side during the famous retreat from Russia. Colonel Nicholas Raoul had accompanied the former emperor on his escape from Elba. Women in this party, with their silk dresses, satin slippers, and parasols, were more suited to the drawing rooms of Paris than to the log cabins of Alabama.

With the help of friendly Choctaws, the immigrants learned to plant corn, beans, and squash. Colonel Raoul became the owner of a Tombigbee River ferry. General Desnouettes built a log museum to house his swords, battle flags, pistols, and bronze statue of Napoleon. To clean the thick cane from their land, the French hired indentured servants from Germany.

But the Germans proved unwilling or unable to clear the fields. The settlers found that frost killed their olive trees and that their grapes withered or ripened too soon. Twice these colonists were forced to move—once because they had settled outside the boundaries of their grant.

Gradually the French pioneers became discouraged. Some returned to France; others moved to New Orleans or Mobile. Little remains of their experiment as members of a "vine and

157

olive colony" except a few jujube trees (perhaps planted after the olive trees failed), a handful of descendants, and some place names commemorating Napoleon's great battles: *Marengo, Aigleville, Arcola,* and *Hohenlinden* (shortened to *Linden*).

Each December Demopolis celebrates **Christmas-on-the-River**. Bluff Hall, glowing with candlelight, is adorned with native greenery, fruit, and traditional decorations. Guides in period dress describe the old home's history. The festival includes an evening parade of floats on the Tombigbee River and a children's parade through downtown Demopolis. The river parade takes place on the first Saturday in December. The Bluff Hall party, called "Christmas in the Canebrake," is held the preceding evening.

Accommodations: Demopolis has several comfortable motels. Primitive campsites are available at Chickasaw State Park, nine miles south of Demopolis on U.S. 43, and at Foscue Creek Park in Demopolis.

Demopolis Town Square (1819) has existed since Demopolis was organized. One of the oldest town squares in Alabama, it is on the National Register. Included are three structures: **City Hall** (c. 1820), a two-story brick structure with portico that has been a tavern, post office, boys' school, and library; the **Presbyterian Church** (c. 1843) two-story brick structure with Doric pilasters, later a courthouse, opera house, and now the fire department; and the **Pavillion** (c. 1880), frame octagonal gazebo with lattice trim.

Demopolis has a number of interesting homes and sights. Its outstanding home is **Gaineswood**, 805 Whitfield Street East, which is on the National Register as well as being a National Historic Landmark. Gaineswood often has been compared to Monticello, Thomas Jefferson's home in Virginia. Like Jefferson, the builder of Gaineswood took a great interest in the construction of his home. Serving as his own architect, General Nathan Bryan Whitfield built Gaineswood between 1843 and 1861, around an existing two-room log house. Gaineswood developed into Alabama's most unusual Greek Revival mansion. Once the center of a 1,400-acre plantation, Gaineswood is now part of the city of Demopolis. It is one of the few house museums in the South to contain its original furniture. The interior includes an elaborate drawing room

Gaineswood

Bluff Hall

with Corinthian columns, vis-à-vis mirrors, and coffered ceiling. Operated by the Alabama Historical Commission, Gaineswood is open to the public Monday through Saturday, 9 a.m. to 5 p.m.; Sunday, 1 to 5 p.m. Closed on the major holidays. Admission charge. Telephone: (334) 289-3220.

The other house museum in Demopolis is **Bluff Hall** (c. 1832), North Commissioners Avenue, which was built as a townhouse by Francis Strother Lyon, a lawyer, cotton planter, and politician. Originally this was a plain Federal townhouse. By 1850 the columned front portico and rear wing had been added and the structure painted white to conform to the popular taste for Greek Revival. Bluff Hall was named for the high chalk bluff of the Tombigbee River upon which it stands. Operated by the Marengo County Historical Society, it is listed on the National Register. Bluff Hall is open Tuesday through Saturday, 10 a.m. to 5 p.m.; Sunday, 2 to 5 p.m. Small admission charge. Telephone: (334) 289-1666. Next door is a craft

shop featuring, among other handmade articles, split-oak baskets, an early Alabama craft.

Also on the National Register are the **Curtis House** (c. 1830s), 510 North Main Street, a two-story brick residence considered an early example of an antebellum planter's townhouse; **Foscue House** (1840), on U.S. 80, an unusual brick country residence built by a wealthy planter; **Lyon Hall** (1853), Main and Franklin streets, built by George Gaines Lyon, Yale graduate, lawyer, and planter, in Greek Revival style with two-story portico and six Doric columns joined by cast iron porch railings; **Ashe Cottage** (c. 1850s), North Commissioners Avenue, Gothic Revival with later gingerbread touches; **White Bluffs**, site of the 1817 landing of the French founders of Demopolis; and **Glover Mausoleum** (c. 1840) in Riverside Cemetery, one of the largest mausoleums in Alabama.

Jefferson

Another small planter community, Jefferson, on Marengo County 21 about ten miles south of Demopolis, typifies many such antebellum centers. The **Jefferson Historic District**, containing about twenty structures dating from the late 1840s and early 1850s, is on the National Register. Its structures include an antebellum store; Baptist church; Methodist church; and Hildreth, Bryan, and Grant homes.

Forkland

Well worth a special effort is a side trip to the Forkland vicinity off U.S. 43 north of Demopolis. **St. John's-in-the-Prairies Episcopal Church** (c. 1859), a charming, one-story board and batten structure now on the National Register, was moved from the prairie area of present Hale County in 1878 and rebuilt. Nearby are the **Glover House** (c. 1840), one-story board and batten cottage, and an early-nineteenth-century tavern. Ask directions to **Thornhill** (c. 1833), a two-story frame mansion with six massive Ionic columns built by carpenters brought from Virginia by the owner, James Innes Thornton (family schoolhouse is on the grounds), and to **Rosemount** (c. 1832–39), considered by many to be Alabama's most beautiful antebellum mansion. Although not open to the public, Rosemount may be glimpsed from the road. Its outstanding exterior feature is a thirty-by-fifteen-foot cupola from which Rosemount's masters kept watch on their slaves in the fields. Rosemount's great interior hall, extending sixty feet across the house, was the scene of many musicales, dances, and receptions. The twenty-room mansion was planned and built by Williamson Allen Glover, who came to this rich Black

Belt area with his parents when he was thirteen years old. His sister, Mary Ann, became the first wife of James Thornton, master of neighboring Thornhill. Rosemount is on the National Register.

From Demopolis, head west on U.S. 80. Fifteen miles from Demopolis, take Alabama 28 to Livingston.

Three miles east of Livingston is **Oak Manor** (c. mid-1800s), two-story frame with Italianate eave brackets and full-width double verandah supported by six Doric columns.

Livingston

Courthouse Square, recently restored, is one of the most attractive small town squares in Alabama. **Sumter County Courthouse** (c. 1900), on the National Register, is Beaux-Arts style with an eight-sided domed cupola. At one corner of the square was once a well bored by a mule turning an auger. Its water was reputed to have medicinal value. The site of the well (which is now covered by a pavilion) long has been a gathering place for Sumter County politicians. On New Year's Eve, men and boys of Livingston, costumed in outlandish garb, take part in the annual Dud Parade down Main Street to the well, where prizes are awarded. **Sumter County Commissioners Office** (c. 1836), one-story brick with Italianate influence and unusual brickwork, was

Alamuchee covered bridge, Livingston

originally the office of the probate judge and later a library. Ruby Pickens Tartt, well-known Alabama folklorist, served as librarian here during the 1930s.

Livingston University (c. 1840) was originally a college for girls known as Alabama Normal College. Miss Julia Tutwiler, one of Alabama's leading nineteenth-century educators, persuaded the Alabama legislature to establish this school to train women teachers. She was head of the school from 1890 to 1910. None of the original buildings remains. One of the oldest covered bridges in the south, **Alamuchee Covered Bridge** (c. 1861), has been relocated on the Livingston University campus. It is an eighty-foot-long, one-span, Town-truss bridge (see *Blount County*).

Among Livingston's interesting sights are **Little House** (c. 1852), on West Main Street, one-and-one-half-story frame with six fluted Doric columns on its front verandah; **Pleasant Ridge** (c. 1842), West Main Street, two-story frame with double portico supported by fluted Doric columns; and **St. James Episcopal Church** (c.

1843), Spring and Monroe streets, frame Greek Revival with Victorian embellishments.

Departing Livingston, take U.S. 11 north to Epes.

Epes

A road to the left of U.S. 11 leads to the site of **Fort Tombecbé**, on the bluffs of the Tombigbee River. (Ask locally for directions.) This fort was established by the French in 1736, surrendered in 1763 to the English and renamed Fort York, then ceded to Spain in 1783. A new fort was built, named Fort Confederation (1794–97). Later a site nearby was used by Americans as a trading post with the Choctaw Indians. This site, which is on the National Register, offers an excellent view of the chalk (limestone) bluffs.

Leaving Epes, take U.S. 11 south to Alabama 39. Turn north onto 39 and follow it 11 miles to Gainesville.

Gainesville

This small community was the third largest town in Alabama in 1840,

Chalk Cliffs of the Tombigbee River

boasting a population of nearly 4,000. As one of the northernmost Alabama landings on the Tombigbee River, Gainesville was a thriving port for steamboat traffic, shipping 6,000 bales of cotton a year to Mobile. It was incorporated in 1835 on land that belonged to Choctaw Indians before the Treaty of Dancing Rabbit Creek. The town was named for Colonel George Strother Gaines, who as an American agent to the Choctaws helped negotiate this treaty. During Gainesville's boom, the twenty-room American Hotel, now vanished, was the social and business center of western Alabama. One of Gainesville's early settlers was Joseph G. Baldwin, a young Virginia lawyer who wrote his recollections of this bustling era in his book *Flush Times of Alabama and Mississippi*. The economic stagnation that set in after the Civil War helped preserve Gainesville's mid-nineteenth-century flavor, as did its isolation from main highways.

With the completion of the Tennessee-Tombigbee Waterway, Gainesville appeared to be on its way to a second boom. One of the first dams of this project is located near the present village. "Tenn-Tom," as the waterway is called, provides an alternative to the Mississippi River for barge traffic from the Ohio Valley to the Gulf of Mexico. Environmentalists have criticized the project as being destructive of a scenic river and its natural surroundings. Other opponents declared that Tenn-

Tom, which cost more than one billion dollars, is an expensive boondoggle for American taxpayers. But its proponents claim that the waterway means jobs and prosperity along the Tombigbee and will triple the tonnage passing through the port of Mobile. Those interested in the waterway may wish to make the short side trip via Alabama 14 to Pickensville. The **Tom Bevill Visitor Center**, located in an antebellum-style mansion, contains displays that relate to the history and development of the Tombigbee River and the Waterway. Moored beside the center is the snagboat U.S.S. *Montgomery*, one of the last steam-powered stern-wheelers to ply the rivers of the South. The Center and the snagboat are adjacent to the Tom Bevill Lock and Dam, where visitors are invited to watch the lockage of vessels traveling between the Gulf of Mexico and the riverports of mid-America.

While in the vicinity, those interested in World War II memorabilia will want to visit the recently opened Aliceville Museum and Cultural Arts Center. Housed in what was once the

Tom Bevill Visitor Center

Coca-Cola bottling works, the museum displays artifacts from some of the German POWs who were held at Camp Aliceville during World War II. Admission charged.

Gainesville Historic District, nominated for the National Register, includes the **Confederate discharge site** where Confederate general Nathan B. Forrest and his forces were paroled in May 1865 after four years of military service; **Gainesville Presbyterian Church** (c. 1837), frame Greek Revival with slave balcony; **Lewis-Long Home** (c. 1835), Main Street east of Lafayette, two-story frame Federal style with Greek Revival embellishments and adjoining plantation offices; **The Magnolia** (c. 1845), corner of Webster and Pearl streets, two-story frame with four extremely large Ionic columns and garden enclosed by a brick wall; **Gainesville Methodist Church** (1872), late Greek Revival; **Saint Alban's Episcopal Church** (1879), Carpenter Gothic; **Colgin Hill** (1832), originally log, now covered with weatherboarding, reputed to be the oldest house in Gainesville; **American Hotel ice cellar** (1850), twenty-foot-deep cellar used to store ice and other provisions for patrons of that hostelry; and **Confederate Cemetery** (c. 1862), containing graves of 177 unknown Confederate soldiers, a monument, and Civil War cannon.

Leaving Gainesville, follow Alabama 39 north and 14 east to Eutaw.

Eutaw

Eutaw was founded in 1838 by the people of Greene County after a close and vigorously contested vote over the location of the seat of county government. The new town was laid out by Asa White, who donated to the county a twenty-acre lot that would accommodate the new public buildings on a central square. The new seat of justice was to be surrounded by commercial lots that would be auctioned to raise money to construct buildings for the judicial functions necessary in a growing and prosperous community. The people named the new town *Eutaw* in commemoration of the final defeat of the British in the southern campaign at Eutaw Springs, South Carolina, at the end of the American Revolution. Its handsome Greek Revival architecture is a reminder that Eutaw was once a center of comfortable living among planters who prospered on rich land that had belonged to the Choctaw Indians. The prosperity ended with the collapse of the Confederacy in 1865.

The predominantly black population of Greene County, as a consequence of the Voting Rights Act of 1965, has elected a black sheriff and other black county officials. Although proceeds from dog racing have added to tax revenues, Greene County continues to rank as one of the nation's poorest counties.

Eutaw's most striking mansion is

Kirkwood, Eutaw

Kirkwood (1857–60), Kirkwood Drive, now restored to its original dignity. One of the last great mansions to be built in the Black Belt during the antebellum era, Kirkwood was left incomplete due to the Civil War blockade. This four-story mansion with cupola and columns along two sides is on the National Register. Kirkwood contains the Victorian furnishings bought by its original owner, Foster M. Kirksey, at the time of his second marriage in 1860. The house has eight carved Italian marble mantels. Bohemian glass, depicting the four seasons, flanks the front entry. Kirkwood is now a "bed and breakfast." Reservations may be made with its present owner, Mary Swayze. Telephone (205) 372-9009.

Other National Register sites in Eutaw are **Greene County Courthouse** (c. 1869–70), rebuilt after it was deliberately burned in 1868 to destroy indictments against members of the Ku Klux Klan (and said to be the last Greek Revival public building

constructed in Alabama); **Coleman-Banks House** (c. 1847), 430 Springfield Avenue, two-story frame structure with original brick kitchen and smokehouse to the rear; and the **First Presbyterian Church** (c. 1851), considered an excellent example of a carpenter's version of Greek Revival. The sanctuary has a slave gallery at the rear.

Forty-four antebellum structures in Eutaw are on the National Register as a thematic district. Interesting homes nominated include **Dunlap-Ward House** (c. 1844), with a slave house (a rarity in the Black Belt) still standing in the rear; **Mesopotamia Female Seminary College** (c. 1845), Main Street and Wilson Avenue, boarding school for girls until 1911 and now a branch of the predominantly black Miles College in Birmingham; **Perkins-Spencer House** (c. 1850), two-story frame built at the peak of the Greek Revival period and almost identical to the Coleman-Banks House; **Webb-Reese House** (c. 1854), 244 Wilson Avenue, with four two-story Ionic columns and original colored glass sidelights at the entry.

Just north of Eutaw on Highway 14 are the adjacent plantation homes of the Pippen and Carpenter families, both built in the mid-1850s, each with impressive colossal octagonal columned porticos.

Departing Eutaw, take Alabama 14 east to Greensboro.

Greensboro

Three years before Alabama achieved statehood, a few log houses occupied the site of what was to become Southern University, forming a community known as Troy. Incorporated in 1823, the village, its name changed to Greensboro, boasted twenty kerosene street lamps and a newspaper. Located on the northern edge of the western Black Belt, Greensboro became the focal point of its area as did Camden on the extreme southern fringe of this region of rich soil. Because this cotton trading center contained no industry, Wilson's raiders of 1865 passed Greensboro by, leaving its fine old homes intact. Three Alabama governors, Israel Pickens (1821–25), John Gayle (1831–35), and Thomas Seay (1886–90), came from Greensboro. Their homes still stand.

The pride of antebellum Greensboro was Southern University, founded by the Methodist Church and chartered by the Alabama legislature in 1856. The college opened in 1859, but soon all but fourteen of its students and a few faculty members were drained away to Confederate service. Southern University never recovered from the war. In 1918 it was consolidated with Birmingham College in Birmingham to form Birmingham-Southern College. The **President's Home** still stands in Greensboro but the main building was destroyed by a storm in 1973.

In recent years, a number of Greensboro's nineteenth-century mansions and cottages have been restored by new owners, many of whom have chosen to spend their retirement years in this pleasant old town.

Greensboro Historic District, which includes the commercial and residential sections adjacent to and including Main Street, contains numerous nineteenth- and early twentieth-century structures. Its most historically interesting home is **Magnolia Grove** (c. 1840), 1002 Hobson Street, on the National Register, a two-story brick Greek Revival mansion that was the birthplace and home of Richmond Pearson Hobson, a hero of the Spanish-American War. Occupying the head of Greensboro's Main Street, Magnolia Grove was built by Colonel Isaac Croom, who with his wife, Sarah, came to Alabama from North Carolina. Now owned by the Alabama Historical Commission, this house has been restored as a public museum. Magnolia Grove contains a museum room in which hangs a portrait of Ad-

Magnolia Grove, Greensboro

miral Hobson who, as a navy lieutenant in his twenties, led a daring effort to bottle up the Spanish fleet. Hobson and his men managed to blow up their ship, the *Merrimac*, and escape the explosion in a raft. But because the *Merrimac* sank widthwise instead of lengthwise across the harbor entrance, the Spanish fleet was able to emerge and fight American naval forces at the Battle of Santiago. Captured by the Spanish, Hobson and his men were held as prisoners of war for thirty-three days. Hobson later served in the U.S. House of Representatives and became a leader of the national prohibition movement. In 1933 he was awarded the Congressional Medal of Honor for his exploits during the Spanish-American War. The museum room also contains the nameplate and captain's chair from the *Merrimac*. Open Wednesday through Saturday, 10 a.m. to 4 p.m.; Sunday, 1 to 4 p.m. Small admission fee. Telephone: (334) 624-8618.

Among Greenboro's handsome homes are the **Gayle-Tunstall-Sledge House** (c. 1829), 1801 Main Street, two-story brick with brick servants' house and kitchen; **Johnston-Torbert House** (c. 1828), 1101 South Street, two-story brick with one-story central pedimented portico; **Glencairn** (c. 1837), 705 Erwin Drive, two-story frame built by Colonel John Erwin, early Alabama lawyer and leader in the secession movement; and **Magnolia Hall** (c. early 1850s), 805 Otts Street, two-story frame considered one of the finest examples of the temple form of Greek Revival architecture in this region.

Accommodations: There are comfortable motels in Greensboro.

From Greensboro, take Alabama 61 south eight miles to Newbern.

Newbern

Admirers of the simple dignity of rural antebellum churches will find this short trip well worthwhile. The tiny hamlet of Newbern possesses two handsome churches. **Newbern Presbyterian** (c. 1848), a one-story frame church with mortise and peg construction and hand-hewn timber, is an example of an early attempt at Greek Revival style. **Newbern Baptist** (c. 1849), two-story frame building, has solid poplar Doric columns. Note also **Walthalia** (c. 1854–56), one-story frame home with verandah built by slaves, and **Newbern town bell**.

Slave gallery in church

Return north on Alabama 61 to Greensboro and turn east on Alabama 14 toward Marion.

Watch for **Carlisle Hall** (c. 1858) on the left one mile west of the Francis Marion High School. Reportedly the brick and pinkish sandstone used in this house was imported from Europe, as were twelve marble mantels. In the antebellum period many ships brought over loads of brick as ballast; some streets in Mobile are paved with European brick. Wooden houses predominate in and around Marion because the soil in the area does not lend itself to brickmaking. Walls in Carlisle Hall are twenty-eight inches thick. A highly individual house, Carlisle Hall, with its three-story brick tower, stands apart from the predominantly Greek Revival neighboring mansions. Its architects, Richard Upjohn and Son, used a variety of styles. The balcony rail suggests Moorish influence while its overhanging copper roof follows Japanese temple lines. Romanesque arches were used over doors and windows.

Marion

Like Greensboro, Marion was a center of planter society and education. Originally known as **Muckle's Ridge** for an early settler who built a cabin nearby in 1817, this is one of the oldest towns in Alabama. Within the city limits are ninety-six antebellum structures. The town's name was changed in 1822 to honor Francis Marion, "Swamp Fox" of the American Revolution. Marion Female Seminary (1836), Judson Female Institute (1838; later Judson College), and Howard College (1842; for male students), were organized in antebellum Marion. After the Civil War, **Lincoln Memorial School**, corner of Lee and Lincoln streets, was founded by Congregationalists to educate newly freed blacks. During the twentieth century, Coretta Scott, later the wife of Dr. Martin Luther King, Jr., and Daisy Fuller, later the wife of Andrew Young, former mayor of Atlanta and former United States ambassador to the United Nations, attended this school.

During the 1960s, Marion was the scene of several voting rights demonstrations by Perry County blacks. One skirmish between Alabama State Troopers and black demonstrators led to the shooting death of Jimmy Lee Jackson, a black youth, in a cafe near the courthouse.

Perry County Courthouse (c. 1854), constructed of white painted brick, has six Ionic columns, portico with a clock in the pediment, black iron railing around the balcony, and front gable outlined with dentils. **Judson College**, one of the oldest colleges for women in America, was founded by Baptists in 1838. It is the only women's college in Alabama today. Its first president, Milo P. Jewett, was one of the first proponents of elec-

Jewett Hall, Judson College

tive courses in colleges, a radical idea in that era. He left Alabama to become the first president of Vassar College in Poughkeepsie, New York. The **Alabama Women's Hall of Fame**, which houses bronze plaques honoring outstanding women leaders of this state, is located in the Judson College Library. It is open weekdays, 8 a.m. to 10 p.m., from September to June and at other times by appointment. No admission fee.

Nearby **Marion Military Institute** occupies the site of old Howard College, forerunner of present-day Samford University in Birmingham. This all-male junior college prepares young people for the army, navy, and air force academies and is the site of the **Alabama Military Hall of Honor**. Bronze plaques honoring Alabamians who have distinguished themselves in the armed forces of the United States are displayed in the **Marion Military Institute Chapel**. Open daily; no admission fee. During the Civil War, the chapel and Old South Hall were used as Confederate hospitals.

Homes of interest in Marion include **King-Barron-Arbuthnot House** (c. 1856), 1001 Washington Street, home of Porter King, the Confederate captain to whom General Barnard E. Bee, upon watching General Thomas J. Jackson and his forces withstand heavy Union attack at Manassas, remarked "Look at Jackson, standing like a stone wall," thereby giving Jackson his famous nickname. The house is noted for the simplicity of its slender, fluted Doric columns as well as for upper and lower double doors, both with transoms, sidelights, and corner pilasters. **Hanna-Weissinger-Warren House** (c. mid-nineteenth century), Lafayette Street, T-shaped two-story frame, has side entrance and beaded cornice trim above the columns. **King-Sledge House** (c. 1830), 321 Clay Street, is a raised cottage with later Victorian trim on its porches. **Moore-Avery House** (c. 1835), 508 Green Street, was the home of Alabama's first Civil War governor, Andrew B. Moore,

Marion Military Institute Chapel

who ordered the seizure of Fort Morgan and Fort Gaines before Alabama seceded from the Union. In the **Lea-Thatcher Home**, Green Street, General Sam Houston, president of the Republic of Texas, married Margaret Moffette Lea in 1840.

Churches of interest include **Siloam Baptist Church** (c. 1849), Washington Street. In an earlier structure, the Baptist State Convention of 1844 adopted the "Alabama Resolutions" that resulted in the separation of southern and northern Baptists in 1845. **Marion Presbyterian Church** (c. 1877), Washington Street, was organized in 1832. **St. Wilfred's Episcopal Church** (1908), Washington Street, has a cemetery in the rear containing graves of Confederate soldiers and of William Brooks, president of the Alabama Secession Convention of 1861. **Marion Methodist Church**, Washington Street, organized in 1819, occupied its present sanctuary in 1886.

Marion Female Seminary, across from Marion Elementary School, was founded in 1836 and is now owned by the Perry County Historical Society. It is on the National Register. In this building Nicola Marschall, musician and artist, designed the first Confederate flag.

State Fish Hatchery

Take Alabama 175 north about seven miles from Marion to **Marion State Fish Hatchery**,

Marion Presbyterian Church

a facility of interest to all who enjoy fishing and to those interested in the history of Alabama's natural resources. The hatchery dates to 1932. As a Works Progress Administration project in the late 1930s, it underwent added construction. The land is owned by the federal government and is leased to the state. Here the Fisheries Section of the Alabama Conservation Department propagates about five million warm-water fish annually, including bass, catfish, bluegill, and sunfish. These fish are used to stock public lakes and reservoirs owned by the state. Research in fish nutrition, pond fertilization, aquatic plant control, and hybridization is conducted at the adjacent Southeastern Fish Cultural Laboratory of the U.S. Fish and Wildlife Service. Special group tours of the hatchery may be arranged on advance notice. Perry Lake Recreation Area, on the east side of the hatchery property, offers picnic facilities and fishing. It is open free of charge during daylight hours from March 1 through October 31.

On the Cahaba River east of the hatchery is one of the alleged sites of Chief Tuskaloosa's capital, the city mentioned by De Soto's chroniclers as where De Soto took Tuskaloosa prisoner, thereby infuriating the chief and his followers and leading to the Battle of Maubila.

Leaving the hatchery, follow Alabama 14 east to Sprott and then south to Suttle. Turn east on Dallas County 6 and proceed to Summerfield.

Summerfield

Several historic homes and a church remain of what was once a residential, educational, and commercial town. Summerfield has much the same quiet, unspoiled quality as the north Alabama community of Mooresville. Centenary Female College, chartered here in 1841 by Methodists, was a widely known institution that closed after the Civil War because many planters lacked the means to educate their daughters. Centenary was a forerunner of a present-day Methodist institution, Huntingdon College in Montgomery. Nothing remains of a large central building that once dominated the Centenary campus at Summerfield.

Note several antebellum houses on Centenary and Main streets, including **Swift-Moore-Cottingham House** (c. 1850), two-story frame with hipped roof and pedimented full-height portico with four square Doric columns; **Childers-Crow House** (c. 1827), two-story frame dogtrot with partially enclosed verandah and tapered square columns; **Sturdivant-Moore-Cain House** (c. 1838), two-story frame with Federal details, including fanlights and sidelights, and **Andrews-Brady House** (c. early 1800s), one-and-one-half-story frame enclosed with picket fence. **Summerfield Methodist Church** (c. 1845), one-story frame with gabled roof and belfry, exemplifies the simplicity of many antebellum village churches.

Departing Summerfield, turn south on Dallas County 37 toward Selma. Watch for the Valley Creek sign three miles south of Summerfield.

Turn left on Dallas County 65 to **Valley Creek Presbyterian Church** (c. 1858), two miles from the intersection on the right. This simple but handsome two-story brick structure, on the National Register, has ground-level entry and curved stairs to a second-floor sanctuary.

Return to Dallas County 37 and continue two miles south toward Selma.

Watch on the right for **Kenan Home** (c. 1826), two-story frame with strong Federal influence. Note wing additions on either side of the central section. The house survived an attempt by Union soldiers to burn it in

Valley Creek Presbyterian Church

April 1865. The parlor floor contains a jagged black ring mark where members of Wilson's raiders set fire to a pile of furniture. Legend has it that a slave put out the fire.

One-half mile south of Kenan Home, turn left at Y on an unpaved road and proceed one hundred yards to **Kenan's Mill** (c. 1825), a turbine mill powered by water from Valley Creek. In operation until 1968, the mill still is used occasionally to demonstrate the old process of grinding cornmeal. Across the swinging bridge is a former charcoal kiln. For the experience of fording a shallow stream, follow this road a few hundred yards to **Kenan's Ford**, one of the few fords on a public road in Dallas County.

Returning to Dallas County 37, continue south to U.S. 80. Follow U.S. 80 through Selma toward Montgomery.

Near Tyler Crossroads is a marker commemorating the alleged passage of De Soto and his Spanish followers along the south side of the Alabama River in 1540. At the intersection of Lowndes County 23 and U.S. 80 is a marker commemorating the Battle of the Holy Ground, which took place in 1813 near White Hall. In 1965 this stretch of U.S. 80 was the scene of the famous Selma-to-Montgomery march by civil rights demonstrators.

Holy Ground

Those interested in the Creek War may wish to search for this site by following Lowndes County 23 toward the Alabama River. This fifty-acre neck of land was the home of the principal prophets of the Creek Nation who assured their followers that no white man could ever invade their stronghold. However, General F. L. Claiborne's army, moving north from Fort Deposit, successfully stormed the Holy Ground, driving its defenders into the river or swamps. William Weatherford, the Red Stick leader, is said to have escaped by jumping his horse, Arrow, from a twelve-foot bluff into the Alabama River and swimming Arrow to safety on the opposite shore.

Return to U.S. 80 and continue to Montgomery.

Brownfield House, Opelika (p. 181)

TOUR 12
South Central Alabama

From Montgomery

Tuskegee

Auburn

Opelika

Tallassee

Wetumpka

Return to Montgomery

Tuskegee University

planter homes

Auburn University

covered bridge

textile towns and mills

Fort Toulouse-Jackson

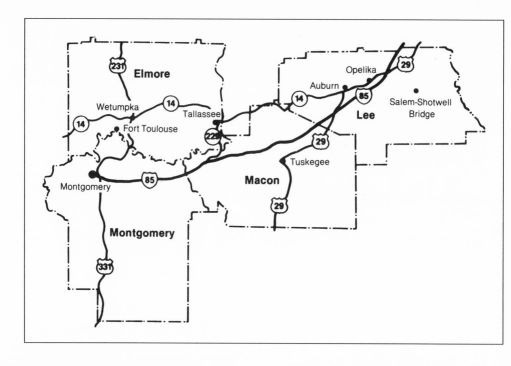

Tuskegee University

The eastern end of Alabama's Black Belt—so named for the color of its fertile soil—is less well known for Greek Revival mansions than the western Black Belt. Although the eastern end of this fertile crescent still contains a number of elaborate planter homes, the major site of historic interest on its northern edge is a world-famous school. Tuskegee Institute (now called Tuskegee University), founded by Booker T. Washington on July 4, 1881, celebrated its centennial in 1981. Begun in a dilapidated church and shanty, the school grew into an internationally famous institution by the time of Washington's death in 1915. Its energetic principal won widespread financial support among people of wealth and influence in both the North and South. Andrew Carnegie, Collis P. Huntingdon, and John D. Rockefeller were among the benefactors whose names now appear on major campus buildings.

Washington's goal was to model his school after Hampton Institute in Virginia where he had been educated. He set three objectives for Tuskegee: to produce black teachers, to teach craft and occupational skills, and to stress high moral character and absolute cleanliness for both students and faculty. This philosophy not only attracted support from philanthropists but caught the attention of two U.S. presidents; both William McKinley and Theodore Roosevelt visited Tuskegee during their administrations.

Booker T. Washington's accomplishment, however, was not always greeted with acclaim. Some blacks, notably W. E. B. Du Bois, felt that Tuskegee Institute's emphasis on vocational training in skills such as farming, cooking, brickmaking, and dressmaking would tend to keep blacks in subordinate roles. Du Bois, who became Washington's most severe critic, faulted Tuskegee's leader for not advocating more liberal arts education for blacks and for not speaking out more strongly for civil rights. (Although Washington combated racial injustice behind the scenes, his critics knew little or nothing of this activity.)

During World War II, black pilots were trained at Tuskegee and formed the 99th Pursuit Squadron. Today Tuskegee University attracts numerous visitors from emerging and underdeveloped nations interested in adapting Tuskegee's vocational emphasis to the needs of schools in their countries. However, Tuskegee's own curriculum has changed with the times. Washington's successor, Robert Russa Moton, led Tuskegee to establish a college department in 1927, adding liberal arts courses as well as programs in such areas as social work, veterinary medicine, and nursing. Other programs added to meet contemporary needs include the schools of arts and sciences, agriculture and home economics, engineering and architecture, and business. Additionally, Tuskegee has a job core program on campus de-

signed specifically to offer a "second chance" for young people who have experienced problems at home or in society at large. The main campus has grown to 161 buildings on 168 acres and an academic community of nearly 5,000 students, faculty, and staff.

suggestions for background reading

Elliott, Lawrence. *George Washington Carver: The Man Who Overcame.* Englewood Cliffs, N.J.: Prentice Hall, 1966.

Goodson, Martia Graham, ed., with foreword by Harry V. Richardson. *Chronicles of Faith: The Autobiography of Frederick D. Patterson.* Tuscaloosa: University of Alabama Press, 1991.

Harlan, Louis R. *Booker T. Washington: The Making of a Black Leader.* New York: Oxford University Press, 1972.

Jackson, Harvey H., III. *Rivers of History: Life on the Coosa, Tallapoosa, Cahaba, and Alabama.* Tuscaloosa: University of Alabama Press, 1995.

Jakeman, Robert J. *The Divided Skies: Establishing Segregated Flight Training at Tuskegee, Alabama, 1934–1942.* Tuscaloosa: University of Alabama Press, 1992.

McMurray, Linda. *George Washington Carver: Scientist and Symbol.* New York: Oxford University Press, 1981.

Millman, R. G. *The Auburn University Walking Tour Guide.* Tuscaloosa: University of Alabama Press, 1991.

Pound, Merritt B. *Benjamin Hawkins—Indian Agent.* Athens: University of Georgia Press, 1951.

Washington, Booker T. *Up From Slavery: An Autobiography.* New York: Doubleday, Page and Co., 1901. Reprint. Garden City, N.Y.: Doubleday and Co., 1963.

Woodward, Thomas S. *Woodward's Reminiscences of the Creek or Muscogee Indians Contained in Letters to Friends in Georgia and Alabama.* Montgomery: Barrett and Wisibey, 1859. Reprint. Mobile: Southern University Press, 1966 and 1970.

Tuskegee Institute National Historic Site

Leaving Montgomery, take Interstate 85 east. Tuskegee Institute National Historic Site is located on Alabama 126 adjacent to the town of Tuskegee. When approaching via Interstate 85, exit onto Alabama 81 south. Turn right at the intersection of Alabama 81 and 126. In two blocks you will come to the visitor orientation center, Grey Columns.

Grey Columns, Tuskegee

Grey Columns (c. 1857), the Varner-Alexander Home, is a two-story masonry Greek Revival structure with an octagonal cupola, six protruding interior chimneys, and a columned portico around three sides. It has been described as the finest mansion in this area. President Theodore Roosevelt was entertained here during his visit to Tuskegee Institute in 1905. Adapted to southern living patterns, the house has floor-to-ceiling windows and a T-shaped floor plan that allows air to circulate freely through the rooms. Its owners, the Varners, realizing the value of black workers imbued with the virtues of hard work, cleanliness, honesty, and sobriety, cooperated in the building of nearby Tuskegee. The Varner family gave the school the old brick molds used to build Grey Columns so students could construct their own classrooms and administrative buildings. Open daily 9 a.m. to 5 p.m., the center is administered by the National Park Service. No admission charge. There is an environmental trail system behind the mansion.

Tuskegee University campus may be toured by car or by following a walking tour laid out by the National Park Service in a brochure available at Grey Columns. Among the interesting sights on campus is the statue *Lifting the Veil* (c. 1922), depicting Washington's accomplishments in freeing members of his race from ignorance. Tuskegee University is a National Historic Landmark.

Also of interest is **Carver Museum**. George Washington Carver, born in slavery like Booker T. Washington,

Carver Museum, Tuskegee

was Tuskegee's most famous faculty member. In 1896 Carver, who had worked his way through school and earned a master's degree in agriculture from Iowa Agricultural College, accepted Washington's invitation to head the new Department of Agriculture at Tuskegee. For forty-seven years, Carver taught, wrote, and worked in his laboratory at Tuskegee. Determined to find new crops (other than cotton) that would flourish in the South, Carver developed 300 different peanut products, 118 new ways to use sweet potatoes, and many other uses for plants. Henry Ford came to pay tribute to Carver when this museum was dedicated in 1941. After Carver's death in 1943, Congress designated January 5 of each year as George Washington Carver Day. Carver Museum contains many examples of the

The Oaks, Tuskegee

work of this great black scientist whose experiments in rotating cotton with other crops helped to revolutionize southern agriculture. Open daily 9 a.m. to 5 p.m. No admission charge.

Booker T. Washington and George Washington Carver are buried in **Tuskegee Institute Cemetery**.

On the edge of the Tuskegee campus, the home of Booker T. Washington, **The Oaks** (c. 1899), fifteen-room two-story brick, is also a museum. Tours scheduled at 9, 10, and 11 a.m. and 1 to 4 p.m. daily. No admission charge.

The town of **Tuskegee** contains numerous antebellum homes once occupied by planters of the district. Also of interest is **Moton Field**, known as the "Cradle of Black Aviation." The 99th Pursuit Squadron, the 332nd Fighter Group, and the 442nd Bomber Group of black pilots were trained at this field during World War II when it was operated by Tuskegee Institute as a flying school. It is now a city air field.

Macon County 10 south of Tuskegee follows approximately the same route as the old **Federal Road**, along

Lifting the Veil statue

which many wagonloads of white settlers traveled in the early 1800s through Creek territory to settle in Washington County north of Mobile. Portions of the old trace are still visible near Creek Stand and Hurtsboro. **Creekwood** (c. 1838) at Creek Stand, a two-story frame structure with verandah, was once a stopping place on the Federal Road.

Leaving Tuskegee, follow U.S. 29 to Tuskegee National Forest.

The smallest of Alabama's national forests, Tuskegee contains a walking trail that follows the route taken by the famed naturalist William Bartram in his travels through Alabama in 1776 and 1777 to study wildlife, plants, and Indians. Traveling by horseback or canoe, Bartram noted the natural flora and fauna of this wilderness region and sent drawings and reports back to England, where they are housed today in the British Museum of Natural History. Other portions of the **Bartram Trail** have been marked in Butler and Lowndes counties. When the Bartram Trail is completed from Charleston, South Carolina, to Baton Rouge, Louisiana, it will touch fourteen Alabama counties. Tuskegee National Forest has no accommodations for camping or picnicking.

Departing Tuskegee National Forest, follow U.S. 29 northeast to Auburn.

Accommodations: Chewacla State Park, just south of Interstate 85 in the Auburn vicinity, contains cottages and picnic shelters. There are comfortable motels in Auburn.

Auburn and Opelika

Settled in 1836 by Georgians, Auburn took its name from the village described by Oliver Goldsmith in his poem *The Deserted Village* as "sweet Auburn, loveliest village of the plain." East Alabama Male College, founded by the Alabama Methodist Conference in 1856, became a land-grant institution known as the Agricultural and Mechanical College of Alabama under the Morrill Act passed by Congress in 1862. The name was changed to Alabama Polytechnic Institute in 1899 and to Auburn University in 1960.

Over 21,000 students attend Auburn, giving it the largest on-campus enrollment in Alabama. The university offers course work leading to the bachelor's degree in 138 fields, the master's degree in 52 fields, and the doctorate in 19 areas. Instruction is organized within eleven schools: Agriculture, Architecture and Fine Arts, Arts and Sciences, Business, Education, Engineering, Home Economics, Nursing, Pharmacy, Veterinary Medicine, and the Graduate School.

Auburn University Historic District includes **Auburn University Chapel** (c. 1850), on the National Register, brick one-story Greek Revival, built by slave labor and later

Langdon Hall, Auburn

Crenshaw House, Auburn

"gothicized"; **Langdon Hall** (c. 1846), two-story frame remodeled to one-story brick with Doric portico; **Samford Hall** (c. 1888), South College Street, on the National Register, four-story brick structure of Italianate design with extensive terra-cotta and limestone ornamentation; and **the Lathe** (c. early 1860s), just north of Samford Hall, once used to make cannon in the Confederate munitions plant in Selma. The **Alabama News-paper Hall of Fame** is located in the Ralph Draughon Library.

Other sites of historic interest in Auburn include the **Crenshaw House**, 371 North College Street, a Victorian home built circa 1890 by Auburn University mathematician and professor Bolling Hall Crenshaw on former Creek Indian land, features bay windows and delicate gingerbread trim. The Crenshaw House is located in Auburn's **Old Main and Church Street Historic District** listed on the National Register. Tours are available year-round to small groups. Call for an appointment, (334) 821-1131; **Halliday-Cary-Pick House** (c. 1848), 360 North College Street, brick and clapboard raised cottage with entrance from second-story porch; **Auburn Depot** (c. 1904), Mitchum Avenue, partially destroyed by Union raiders under General Lovell Rousseau in 1864, now restored and renovated as offices; **Ebenezer Baptist Church** (c. 1870), corner of Thach Avenue and Auburn

Samford Hall, Auburn

Ebenezer Baptist Church, Auburn

Drive South, on the National Register, one of the first black churches organized in Alabama after the Civil War; **"Pebble Hill" Scott-Yarbrough House** (c. 1847), 101 DeBardeleben Street, on the National Register, one-story frame raised cottage with hipped roof, built by Nathaniel J. Scott, who founded the town of Auburn; and **Toomer's Drugstore** (c. 1894), corner of Magnolia and College streets, with a marble and silver-plated soda fountain that traditionally has been a gathering place for Auburn students.

Leaving Auburn, take Alabama Highway 14 west seven miles to Loachapoka.

The first store built when the Western Alabama Railroad from Montgomery was extended to reach Loachapoka in 1845, houses the **Lee County Historical Society Museum**, 6500 Stage Road. This former trade center building, on the National Register, was the main structure in the Loachapoka commercial district. The 17-inch thick walls are built of fieldstone, cement, and a mixture of lime, salt, and field clay. During the Civil War, it served as a Confederate armory, and Confederate President Jefferson Davis ate at the Havis Hotel across the street from the trading center. Loachapoka was twice raided by Federal troops during the war and the trade center was emptied of the ammunition and supplies it held by Rousseau's Raiders in July of 1864. Now a museum, it houses a collection of artifacts depicting the chronological history of Loachapoka from the time of the Creek Indians through the twentieth century, with particular emphasis on Creek Indian culture. Open by appointment only; telephone (334) 887-5560 or 1-800-321-8880.

Return to Auburn and take U.S. 29 east toward Opelika.

Turn left on east University Drive, about one and one-half miles, turn right on Shelton to **Noble Hall** (c.

Noble Hall, near Auburn

Brownfield House, Opelika

Heritage House, Opelika

1854) on the National Register. This Greek Revival plantation home with Doric columns, features two-story verandahs front and rear, and handhewn woodwork.

Return to U.S. 29 and continue to Opelika.

In Opelika is the **Cullars-Burkhead-Webb House** (c. 1906), 114 North Ninth Street, a Victorian mansion; the **Brownfield House**, 611 North Eighth Street, (c. 1850), built by Dr. Robert Styles Brownfield, one of the area's first physicians, the wooden-framed dog trot structure was relocated and renovated by the Opelika Historical Preservation Society. It is available by reservation for special events and tours; **Lee County Courthouse** (c. 1897), 215 South Ninth Street, a two-story, neoclassical revival structure of red brick with central section and two wings, is on the National Register; the **Heritage House** (c. 1913), 714 Second Avenue, has an eight-foot wraparound terrace supporting six Corinthian columns on the front. These columns extend to the height of the top story and form a semicircle in the center of the terrace. Now a bed and breakfast, it can be toured by appointment. Telephone (334) 705-0485.

Leaving Opelika, take Alabama 169 for four miles to Spring Villa Road, then left one mile.

Spring Villa (c. 1850), two-story frame Gothic Revival, on the National

Lee County Courthouse, Opelika

Spring Villa, Opelika

181

Register, was once the center of Spring Villa plantation, which also included a private racetrack and a lake. The house is now the centerpiece of a park owned by the city of Opelika. The original home burned in the late 1920s but was rebuilt in 1934 by the Civil Works Administration of the New Deal. Legend has it that William Penn Yonge, who built the original Spring Villa, was stabbed to death by one of his slaves on the thirteenth step of the spiral staircase of his house because he was a harsh taskmaster.

Accommodations: Family campgrounds at Spring Villa park. Comfortable motels in the Opelika area.

Return to Interstate 85 heading east. At U.S. 280, turn south and proceed seven and one-half miles. Turn left on Lee County 83 and proceed one and one-half miles. Turn right at the sign for Mt. Spring Baptist Church on unpaved road; drive one-fourth mile to Salem-Shotwell Covered Bridge.

Salem-Shotwell Covered Bridge (c. early 1900s), one of Alabama's fifteen remaining covered bridges (see *Blount County*), a one-span, seventy-five-foot Town-truss bridge, is remarkably well preserved (except for initials carved on its sides), probably because of its remote location. Still in everyday use, it experiences little traffic on this back country road. The bridge is unusual in that the round wooden pegs used in its construction are intact.

Return to Interstate 85 and continue east toward Lanett.

Textile Towns and Mills

After the Civil War, promoters of a New South, who aimed to balance agriculture with industry, were determined to make local cotton into cloth in the south rather than continuing to ship raw material to mills in New England. New cotton mills were built and older ones expanded in Alabama during the 1890s. Northern mill operators, attracted by low-cost labor and nearby raw cotton, began to move to Alabama and other southern states. By 1900, 9,000 men, women, and children were employed in Alabama cotton mills.

This work force was composed almost entirely of whites who had mortgaged and lost their farms after the Civil War. Mill workers lived in villages where houses, church, school, and other community buildings were owned by the mill. Rent was free or only a dollar or so a week.

Wages were low because workers were not unionized and because Alabama had ample workers to replace any who might strike. Also, working hours were long: the average mill employee worked sixty-six hours a week; children often worked twelve hours a day. An Episcopal minister in Montgomery, the Reverend Edgar Gardner Murphy, persuaded the Alabama legislature in 1907 to limit the workweek of children to sixty hours and set the minimum age of child workers at twelve. Eventually child labor was outlawed by the Fair Labor Standards Act passed by Congress in 1938.

Many mill workers today own their own houses. Their work conditions and pay scales have been upgraded considerably since the 1930s, although efforts by unions to organize Alabama mill workers have met with stiff resistance by management.

Alabama textile mills were concentrated in the valley of the Chattahoochee River to make use of its abundant water resources. Major mill communities in this area are Lanett, Fairfax, Opelika, Pepperell, Shawmut, and Langdale. U.S. 29 between Auburn and Opelika passes the well-spaced, neat homes of a large mill community, Pepperell. Once owned by the mill, these homes now show individual touches of personal ownership. Although mills are not open to visitors except by special arrangement, numerous textile outlets in this vicinity sell products at bargain prices.

From Lanett, follow U.S. 29 north toward West Point, Georgia.

West Point Lake, shared by Alabama and Georgia, was constructed under the Flood Control Act of 1962 to provide power, recreation, fish and wildlife protection, and navigation, as well as to control flooding of the Chattahoochee River. This project, begun in 1965, was handled by the U.S. Army Corps of Engineers. The dam and powerhouse area of this 25,900-acre lake includes a mall with benches and fountains, fishing pier, pathway, and scenic footbridge leading to recreation areas.

West Point Dam Visitor Center and Powerhouse Exhibits Lobby houses exhibits illustrating the history of the Chattahoochee Valley and the Army Corps of Engineers. The powerhouse has an audio-slide tour of the dam and exhibits on electricity and water power.

Accommodations: Burnt Village Park campground contains camping facilities and a marina. Open year-round. Follow Stateline Road six miles north of Lanett.

Returning from Lanett, follow Interstate 85 toward Montgomery. Take the Alabama 229 exit north eleven miles to Tallassee.

Tallassee

Two ancient Indian settlements once stood on either side of the Tallapoosa River near present Tallassee. On the east bank stood Tukabatchee where the Creeks kept their copper and brass ceremonial disks under priestly guard and where important meetings were held. A large boulder in a city park commemorates this settlement. Members of the De Soto expedition of 1540 noted the existence of the towns of Tukabatchee and Tallassee on the opposite bank. In 1775 William Bartram described Tukabatchee as consisting of 386 houses strung along the river for four miles. From 1686 to 1836 this was the most important town and the political center of the Upper Creeks. Here in 1811 Tecumseh, the great Shawnee leader and ally of the British, appealed to the Creeks to join other Indian nations in war against the United States. After the defeat of the Creeks at Horseshoe Bend (see *Horseshoe Bend National Military Park*), Tallassee developed rapidly as white settlers poured into this area.

On the banks of the Tallapoosa River are **Tallassee Mills** (c. 1844), the second oldest textile factory in Alabama and the only one still in continuous operation. In 1864, General Josiah Gorgas, chief of ordnance for the Confederacy, ordered that a carbine shop be set up here to replace a similar operation in Richmond, Virginia, threatened by northern armies. Its goal to produce 6,000 carbines a year was never achieved. In 1864 General James H. Wilson's Union raiders passed within ten miles of here, missing the armory because their map was faulty. Thus this was the only Confederate armory not destroyed during the Civil War.

Leaving Tallassee, follow Alabama 14 west to Wetumpka.

Near the small crossroads of **Wallsboro** (north of Wetumpka on U.S. 231) before the American Revolution lived Lachlan McGillivray, a Scottish Indian trader who married an Indian maiden, Princess Sehoy, who was of French, Spanish, and Creek descent. Their son, Alexander McGillivray, inherited membership in the important Wind Clan of the Creek Nation through his mother. When the revolution broke out, Lachlan McGillivray returned to Scotland after his property was confiscated by the Americans. Alexander, however, remained to become the most important Indian leader since Chief Tuskaloosa at the time of De Soto's passage through Alabama 200 years earlier. Alexander McGillivray influenced the Creeks to remain loyal to the British. Later he negotiated treaties with both the Spanish and the Americans, always seeking a better deal for himself and his people. To find the site of McGillivray's plantation, turn right at Wallsboro on an ungraded road and proceed one mile to Thelma Baptist Church. Beside the church a rose quartz marker denotes the probable site of the McGillivray plantation of 1740.

Wetumpka

Wetumpka is located at the fall line where the Coosa River drops in shoals and rapids from higher ground to the plains. During the early settlement of the United States, towns and villages sprang up at the fall line of rivers where cargoes and passengers had to be unloaded from boats. Early industries also were located on the fall line to make use of the water power of falls and rapids. In 1846 Wetumpka was seriously considered as a possible site of Alabama's capital, but her neighboring city, Montgomery, eventually won out.

Wetumpka's most famous citizen was William Lowndes Yancey, a powerful orator and leader of the secessionist movement in Alabama. At the Democratic National Convention of 1860, Yancey led most southern delegates, including those from Alabama, in a walkout from the hall, thereby breaking the Democratic party into factions and contributing to the election of the Republican candidate, Abraham Lincoln.

Places of historic interest in Wetumpka include **First Presbyterian Church** (c. 1856–57), northwest corner of North Bridge and West Bridge streets, on the National Register, a one-story board and batten Gothic Revival church where Yancey attended services; the **First United Methodist Church** (c. 1854), 306 West Tuskeena Street, also on the National Register, recently restored to its original Greek Revival style; the **L. & N. Depot**, Broad Street between Tuskeena and Coosa streets, on the National Register; and the **old Alabama State Penitentiary** (c. 1840), one mile north of Wetumpka on the west side of U.S. 231, on the National Register, which was the first penal institution in Alabama.

Departing Wetumpka, follow U.S. 231 south toward Montgomery to the Fort Toulouse–Jackson Park turn-off three miles south of Wetumpka.

Fort Toulouse (c. 1717), also the site of Fort Jackson, was built by the French as an outpost for Indian trade. The fort was located on a bluff near the juncture where the Coosa and Tallapoosa rivers come together to form the Alabama River. It is on the National Register and is also a National Historic Landmark. At this site, later known as Fort Jackson, William Weatherford (Red Eagle), leader of the Red Sticks, surrendered to General Andrew Jackson following the Battle of Horseshoe Bend in 1814. The Alabama Historical Commission manages this park, which offers partial reconstructions of two historic forts. Artifacts from various historic eras of the forts are displayed at the Visitors' Center museum.

Nearby, the **William Bartram Arboretum** has walkways that meander through wildflower fields and a forest. It is named in honor of the eighteenth-century naturalist who visited this site more than 200 years ago and described Alabama flora and fauna in his *Travels of William Bartram*. Open April through October, 6 a.m. to 9 p.m.; November through March, 8 a.m. to 5 p.m. Admission charged. Guided tours are available by appointment. Write park official at 2521 West Fort Toulouse Rd., Wetumpka, AL 36092, or telephone (334) 567-3002. Campground and picnic areas also are available. The campground is open year round. Call for availability.

Leaving Fort Toulouse-Jackson, continue south on U.S. 231. Turn east on Willow-spring Road and left on Jasmine Hill Road.

Jasmine Hill (c. 1930), although not of historical significance, is a unique garden featuring reproductions of famous Greek works of art. The private collection of its owners, Benjamin and Mary Fitzpatrick, evolved as this Alabama couple made more than twenty trips to Greece to purchase art objects. Included are replicas of the *Venus de Milos*, the most famous statue in the Paris Louvre; *Mourning Athena*, a replica of a piece from the Acropolis in Athens; and an exact copy of the *Temple of Hera*, situated at Olympia near the stadium where the ancient Olympic Games took place. Jasmine Hill has the largest display of Japanese cherry trees south of Washington, D.C. Open Tuesday through Sunday, 9 a.m. to 5 p.m., during the months of March through November. Admission fee. Japanese cherry trees are in bloom in mid-March.

Leaving Jasmine Hill, return to Montgomery.

TOUR 13
Eufaula and the Wiregrass

From Montgomery

Union Springs

Clayton

Eufaula

Abbeville

Columbia

Headland

Dothan

Ozark

Fort Rucker

Enterprise

Troy

Return to Montgomery

antebellum mansions

nuclear plant

peanut experiment station

pioneer exhibits

U.S. Army Aviation Museum

tenant houses

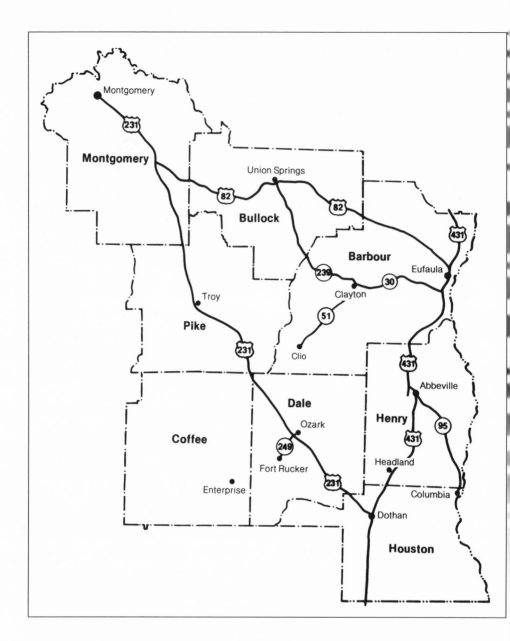

The Wiregrass

Southeastern Alabama was once Creek Territory. After the Upper Creeks, or Red Sticks, lost the Battle of Horseshoe Bend, their leaders ceded a large portion of central Alabama, including the present Wiregrass area, to

the United States. Still Creeks retained more than five million acres on the eastern edge of central Alabama. They had made the mistake, however, of granting to the American government the right to maintain a horse path, known as Federal Road, through this territory. Hordes of pioneers poured along this crude roadway toward south-western Alabama. American militia and supply wagons traversed the branch Pensacola Road from Fort Mitchell to Pensacola. White settlers began to encroach on the remaining Indian lands.

Creek leaders, under pressure, signed a treaty in 1832 ceding their eastern lands as a tribe but providing that any Creeks who wished to remain would be allowed to settle on individual homesteads. But unscrupulous land agents and white squatters swindled many Creeks out of their holdings. Angry Indians staged a brief uprising in 1836 but they and their leaders were soon rounded up, marched to Montgomery, put aboard steamboats, and shipped to Oklahoma. More than 23,000 Creeks had lived in Alabama in 1832. Most eventually immigrated to Oklahoma.

When the Creeks left, pioneers took over. Highland Scots, bearing names such as McRae, McDonald, and McSwean, settled along the Pea River in a community known as "Little Scotland." Among them, perhaps, was an ancestor of former Governor George C. Wallace, born in Clio near the banks of the Pea. Such pioneers found the most fertile portions of Alabama already taken. They wrestled with infertile red soil covered by grass so tough that they christened it "wiregrass."

Because slaves were few and cotton sparse, there was some lack of zeal for the Confederate cause in the Wire-grass region. Desertions from Confederate units were reported in Henry, Dale, Coffee, and Covington counties. Alfred Holley, a prosperous Covington farmer and Alabama legislator, strongly opposed secession, helped Union prisoners escape, and traded with Federal forces at Pensacola.

After the war, many small farmers in the Wiregrass and other areas of Alabama had no money to buy seed, fertilizer, or other needs. Because almost no banks were operating, merchants began to lend farmers these supplies in return for a share of the future crop. Because these "advancing merchants," as they were called, took such huge risk, they charged high interest rates (sometimes 50 to 75 percent). When drought killed their cotton and when cotton prices dropped to four cents a pound, many farmers were forced to give up their land to settle their debts. Thus merchants became landowners and numerous farmers became sharecroppers or tenants, working someone else's land for a percentage of the crop. Tenant shacks still dot the countryside of southeastern Alabama.

Poverty and struggle in the Wiregrass are poignantly illustrated by the pioneer artifacts at West-Mize Museum in Clayton and Pike Pioneer Museum at Troy. In 1914 boll weevils destroyed most of the cotton crop of this region, forcing farmers to turn to other products such as peanuts, watermelons, potatoes, livestock, and cattle. Agricultural diversification, industry, and military installations such as Fort Rucker have brought a measure of prosperity to Alabama's Wiregrass area.

suggestions for background reading

Clayton, Victoria V. *White and Black Under the Old Regime*. Young Churchman Co., 1899. Reprint. Freeport, N.Y.: Books for Libraries Press, 1970. (Locale: Eufaula)

Eufaula Heritage Association. *Historic Eufaula: A Treasury of Southern Architecture, 1827–1910*. Eufaula: 1972.

Frady, Marshall. *Wallace*. New York: New American Library, 1976.

Fretwell, Mark. *This So Remote Frontier: The Chattahoochee Country of Alabama and Georgia*. Eufaula: Historic Chattahoochee Commission, 1980.

Jeane, D. Gregory, ed. *The Architectural Legacy of the Lower Chattahoochee Valley in Alabama and Georgia*. University: University of Alabama Press, 1978.

Rogers, William Warren. *The One-Gallused Rebellion: Agrarianism in Alabama, 1865–1896*. Baton Rouge: Louisiana State University Press, 1970.

Willoughby, Lynn. *Fair to Middlin': The Antebellum Cotton Trade of the Apalachicola/Chattahoochee River Valley*. Tuscaloosa: University of Alabama Press, 1993.

Leaving Montgomery, take U.S. 231 south to U.S. 82. Turn east to Union Springs.

Union Springs

Shortly after the end of the Civil War, Union Springs became the county seat and thus the social and commercial hub of Bullock County. Its main street has not been rendered obsolete by competition from shopping malls nor has its late nineteenth-century appearance and character been altered in an effort to create a mall-like downtown. **Bullock County Courthouse Historic District**, on the National Register, comprises a three-block stretch of Prairie Street, including forty-seven commercial, civic, and church structures. Focal point of the district is Alabama's only **Second Empire courthouse** (c. 1871). Other structures of interest include a three-story Victorian Gothic **jail** with turrets; **Baptist Church** (1860); **Trinity Episcopal Church** (1909); **City Hall** (1889), formerly a Masonic lodge; and **First National Bank**, originally an opera house. Nearby, late-nineteenth-century residential neighborhoods are also intact. Championship bird dog trials take place each February at Sedgefield Plantation nearby.

Leaving Union Springs, take Alabama 239 south to Clayton.

Clayton

This small community, seat of Barbour County, produced two nationally known political figures. Henry D. Clayton, member of Congress 1896–1914, was the author of the Clayton Anti-Trust Act of 1913, which greatly strengthened the antitrust laws of the nation. George C. Wallace, born in nearby Clio, practiced law in Clayton until elected to the Alabama legislature in 1947 and governor of Alabama in 1962.

Clayton also contains Alabama's only example of the "octagon fad" of architecture. Like covered bridges, octagon houses now are rare. They were inspired by the book *A Home for All* by Orsen Squire Fowler, published in 1848. The style follows the plan of an eight-sided figure and is usually one or two stories in height. The roof is flat or low, often topped by a belvedere or cupola. Surrounded by a verandah or featuring only a porch to the front door, the octagon is either plain or embellished with Greek Revival, Italianate, or Gothic Revival details.

Octagon House (c. 1861), 103 North Midway, is the only known octagonal structure in Alabama built during this fad. Plans probably came from *A Home for All*. Inside rectangular-shaped rooms were arranged around a square staircase in the center, creating eight small corner rooms, four on each of the two floors. On the National Register, Clayton's Octagon House is open during the Clayton Tour of Homes each May.

Also on the National Register are the **Henry D. Clayton House** (c. 1850), a Greek Revival cottage near the southern city limits of Clayton, and the **Miller-Martin Townhouse** (c. 1859), Louisville Avenue, a handsome antebellum townhouse with Gothic Revival influences.

Davis-Wallace Home, 309 Eufaula Avenue, where George and Lurleen Wallace lived in Clayton, contains documents, memorabilia, and pictures of both governors and is open during the Clayton Tour of Homes.

West-Mize Museum, just south of North Midway Street, consists of eight structures and numerous artifacts of farm life. In the farm shed are a 1942 peanut picker, a boll weevil catcher, and numerous implements. The main museum houses hundreds of items such as an Indian carriage, a bootlegger's still, a two-horse wagon, old barber and dentist chairs, and a 1942 truck used to haul German prisoners of war to work on Barbour County farms during World War II. On the museum grounds are an old well, windmill, gristmill, log cabin, blacksmith shop, smokehouse, an iron jail (called "the cooler"), and cane mill. (Each November sugar cane is ground into syrup here.) Open Sunday, 2 to 5 p.m. Small admission fee.

Whiskey Bottle Tombstone (c. 1863), Clayton Baptist Church Cemetery, North Midway Street, has replicas of whiskey bottles as the headstone and footmarker for the grave of W. T. Mullen, a notorious drinker who died in 1863.

Clio

Those interested in the rise of George C. Wallace from the rural South to national political prominence may wish to make the fifteen-mile trip from Clayton to Wallace's birthplace, Clio.

Take Alabama 51 south.

Old Barbour County High School (c. 1910), where Wallace was a student, is now closed. Local citizens have converted it to a Wallace museum, containing photographs and personal memorabilia. Open weekdays, 8 a.m. to 3 p.m. No admission charge.

Leaving Clio, return to Clayton. Take Alabama 30 east to U.S. 431 and proceed north to Eufaula.

Shorter Mansion, Eufaula

Eufaula

On the northern edge of the Wiregrass, Eufaula has a heritage quite unlike that of poverty-stricken small farmers. Originally known as Irwinton for an early settler, the town's name was changed in 1843 to Eufaula for a branch of the Creek Confederacy that had lived in this region. Eufaula prospered as a shipping point to the north and east for cotton produced in the fertile Black Belt. In the late 1830s, 5,000 bales of cotton a year were shipped from here by steamboat and barges to New York, Liverpool, and other markets. Closely tied to cotton production and trade, Eufaula was a stronghold of southern sentiment during the turbulent 1850s as Americans disputed over the issue of slavery in U.S. territories. One wealthy Eufaula slaveowner, Major Jefferson Buford, organized a group of 250 Alabamians to move to Kansas to provide votes for a proslavery government there. Soon they were involved in a bloody civil war ("Bleeding Kansas") between advocates of slavery and those who opposed it. Eventually some, including Buford, returned to Alabama.

After the Civil War, another member of Eufaula's planter class led another futile venture. Reuben F. Kolb, a descendant of prominent Barbour County families, returned from Confederate service to find the plantation system in chaos. Convinced that the end of slavery meant the end of cotton production, Kolb experimented with vegetables and watermelons. Kolb became state commissioner of agriculture in the late 1880s and traveled over the country promoting immigration and investment in Alabama. Three times Kolb ran for governor during the last decade of the nineteenth century as the state's leading spokesman for Populist ideas. Denied the Democratic nomination, Kolb and his followers formed a party known as Jeffersonian Democrats. But Kolb was defeated in each of his tries for the governorship because Democrats manipulated black

The Tavern, Eufaula

votes, primarily in the Black Belt. Historians generally agree that Kolb would have been elected in an honest count.

Barbour County, however, does claim Alabama governors John G. Shorter (1861–63), William D. Jelks (1901–07), Chauncey Sparks (1943–47), George C. Wallace (1963–67, 1971–79, 1983–87), and Lurleen Burns Wallace (1967–68).

Untouched by the Civil War, Eufaula retains most of its antebellum mansions. It is often compared with Natchez, Mississippi, another river port, in the richness of its architectural heritage. An annual pilgrimage of antebellum homes takes place each April.

Those interested in antebellum mansions may begin their tour at the **Shorter Mansion** (c. 1906), 340 North Eufaula Avenue, owned by the Eufaula Heritage Association, where driving tour maps may be obtained. Shorter Mansion originally was owned by a cotton planter and his wife, who was heiress of a tonic business. Started in the mid-1800s, the house was enlarged in 1906 to its present dimensions. It is an exceptional example of Neoclassical Revival. Open Monday through Saturday, 10 a.m. to 4 p.m.; Sunday, 1 to 4 p.m. Small admission fee.

Among the many National Register sites in Eufaula are **The Tavern** (c. 1836), 105 Riverside Drive, which was the first permanent structure in Irwinton and which has served as an inn, residence, and Confederate hospital; **Bray-Barron House** (c. mid-nineteenth century), 413 North Eufaula Avenue, one-story Greek Revival; **Cato House** (c. 1858), 823 West Barbour Street, owned by Lewis L. Cato, an ardent secessionist, and scene of a great celebration when Alabama left the Union; **Fendall Hall** (c. 1858), 917 West Barbour Street, two-story Italianate with cupola and hand-painted interior, was restored as a

Fendall Hall

house museum by the Alabama Historical Commission. Open Monday, Thursday, and Saturday, 10 a.m. to 4 p.m. by appointment with the Barbour County R.S.V.P. and during Spring Pilgrimage. Telephone (334) 687-6055 or (334) 687-8469. Small admission charge.

Also on the National Register are: **Kendall Manor** (c. 1862), 534 West Broad Street, two-story with belvedere and three-sided verandah (now a bed and breakfast); **McNab Bank Building** (c. 1850), 201 East Broad Street, one of the first free banks chartered after the collapse of the Alabama state banking system, now restored as offices; **Sheppard Cottage** (c. 1837), 504 East Barbour Street, Southern adaptation of a raised Cape Cod cottage; **Hart House** (c. 1850), 211 North Eufaula Avenue, now the office of the Historic Chattahoochee Commission, which publishes tour guides to the region, (open Monday through Friday during business hours); **Drewry-Mitchell-Moorer House** (c. 1867), 640 North Eufaula Avenue, two-story Italianate with elaborate porch columns; **St. Luke's African Methodist Episcopal Church** (c. 1840), 234 South Van Buren Avenue, frame with Doric columns.

Still other National Register sites in Eufaula are: **Sparks-Flewellen House** (c. 1857), 257 Broad Street, one-story frame Greek Revival once the home of Reuben F. Kolb and of Governor Chauncey Sparks; **Wellborn House** (c. 1837), Front Street, Greek Revival mansion; and the **Seth Lore Historic District** (c. 1834–1911), containing seventy-five Greek Revival, Italianate, and Victorian homes, two churches, and many commercial buildings.

Eufaula National Wildlife Refuge (c. 1964), established in cooperation with the U.S. Army Corps of Engineers, consisting of 11,160 acres in Alabama and 3,231 acres in Georgia, was created to provide a feeding and resting habitat for waterfowl migrating from Canada to South America. Large tracts are planted in grain sorghum, Japanese millet, and corn for use during the winter by the large populations of waterfowl that visit the refuge. A peak population of 40,000 ducks representing sixteen species has been reached. The goose population is also on the rise with four different species present. Common egrets, great blue herons, cattle egrets, ring-billed gulls, common snipes, mourning doves and bobwhites, as well as numerous songbirds, use the refuge.

Sightseeing, nature observation, and photography are encouraged. An auto tour route is marked, and picnicking is permitted. Open during daylight hours seven days a week.

Accommodations: Lakepoint Resort State Park, seven miles north of Eufaula, offers cottages, a campground, and resort inn. Eufaula has comfortable motels.

Leaving the Eufaula area, follow U.S. 431 south toward Abbeville.

Abbeville

Abbeville is one of the oldest settlements in eastern Alabama. Before Alabama became a state in 1819, an Indian trading post thrived at the old hamlet of Franklin near here. Abbeville derived its name from the Indian words *yatta abba*, meaning dogwood grove. Among its historic structures are **Kennedy House** (c. 1870), 300 Kirkland Street, on the National Register, a late Creole-style cottage unusual for this area (see *Baldwin County*), now the Chamber of Commerce, and **Kennedy-Stokes-Messick House** (c. mid-nineteenth century, Columbia Road, cottage-style plantation house.

Accommodations: Blue Springs State Park, seventeen miles west of Abbeville on Alabama 10, has a modern campground and a swimming pool fed by an underground spring.

Leaving Abbeville, take Alabama 95 south to Columbia.

Columbia

Columbia Jailhouse (c. late nineteenth century), North Street, once contained three rooms, two of which were cells.

The wooden structure has walls eight to ten inches thick. In addition, the walls are covered with closely

exhibit, Farley Nuclear Plant

spaced iron spikes to deter attempts to escape by sawing through the walls. The building has neither chimneys nor fireplaces.

This jailhouse is a significant example of common service building architecture. Now a museum, it is open Sunday afternoons. No admission charge.

Five miles south of Columbia on Alabama 95 is the Joseph M. Farley Nuclear Plant.

Joseph Farley Nuclear Plant

Begun in 1977, this Alabama Power facility contains a **Visitors Center** with exhibits explaining how an atom splits and how a nuclear reactor works, as well as the history of man's efforts to harness the forces of nature to produce energy. Open Monday through Friday, 9 a.m. to 4 p.m.; Sunday, 2 to 5 p.m., June through August. Closed Saturday. No admission charge. Telephone: (334) 899-5108.

Leaving Columbia, take Houston County 22 west to Headland.

195

Auburn University Peanut Experiment Station

The world's largest peanut experiment station (sixty acres) is located on U.S. 431 in Headland. All of Alabama's peanut research and fieldwork is conducted here. Research plots are easily available by car following an auto tour guide available at the office. Visitors welcome. Open daily except Sundays.

Continue south on U.S. 431 to Dothan.

Dothan

The major metropolis of southeastern Alabama, Dothan mushroomed after the Civil War from a small rural settlement into a railroad and lumbering center. Development of commercial fertilizers made it possible to convert infertile, cutover pine land into profitable farms yielding peanuts, cotton, corn, potatoes, and watermelons. Dothan celebrates one of its major crops with an annual Peanut Festival in October.

Dothan Landmarks Center for Natural Science and History, (located on U.S. 431 approximately three miles north of Ross Clark Circle) is an 1890s living history farm. The farm, with the **Waddell Farmhouse** (c. late nineteenth century) as its centerpiece, includes a smokehouse, cane mill, syrup shed, windmill and livestock. Other points of interest include a Vic-

torian gazebo, a one-room schoolhouse, a turn-of-the-century church, plus nature trails, wildlife exhibits, interpretive center and planetarium. Open Monday through Saturday, 9 a.m. to 5 p.m.; Sunday, noon to 6 p.m. Small admission fee.

Other sites of historic interest in Dothan include the **Opera House** (c. 1915), 103 North St. Andrews Street, Neoclassical Revival structure originally built as a city auditorium, and the **Federal Building and U.S. Courthouse** (c. 1911), 100 West Troy Street, considered a fine example of high-quality governmental architecture at the turn of the century. Both are on the National Register. **Cherry Street African Methodist Episcopal Church** (c. 1908), a Gothic structure, is the oldest church of that denomination in Alabama. Tours may be arranged by calling (334) 793-9664.

Leaving Dothan, take U.S. 231 north to Ozark.

Ozark

From U.S. 231, turn west on Alabama 249.

Just a few hundred yards on the right stands **Clay Bank Log Church** (c. 1830), a typical one-story pioneer

Clay Bank Log Church, Ozark

196

U.S. Army Aviation Museum exhibit

house of worship. Open daily. No admission fee. Clay Bank Jamboree, an annual event, is held in late September or early October.

Continue on Alabama 249 four miles to **Fort Rucker.**

This U.S. Aviation Training School and Center has more than 14,000 military and civilian personnel.

U.S. Army Aviation Museum houses a collection of ninety aircraft and the world's largest collection of helicopters. Exhibits are laid out in chronological sequence with a brief prologue of army air observation beginning with the Civil War balloon and leading to the 1941 tests of Piper Cub aircraft. The main emphasis is on mid- and late-twentieth century army aviation, showing the development of the light airplane and helicopter through World War II, the Korean War, and Vietnam. Among aircraft on exhibit are the presidential helicopter used by President Dwight D. Eisenhower and the Constellation aircraft used by General of the Army Douglas MacArthur during the Korean War. The museum includes the Army Avia-

tion Hall of Fame, honoring twenty-eight military and civilian persons who have made outstanding contributions to U.S. Army aviation over the past forty years. Open daily, 9 a.m. to 4 p.m. No admission charge. Photography encouraged.

Continue through Fort Rucker to Enterprise.

Enterprise

Once the heart of a cotton-growing area, Enterprise now has a diversified economy including Fort Rucker, a number of small factories, livestock and poultry production, timber, and peanuts. Farmers of this area switched from an almost exclusive emphasis on cotton to peanut growing just before World War I. The catalyst for their switch was a pest known as the boll weevil, which entered Alabama from Texas in the early 1900s and began destroying cotton crops. In tribute to the bug that forced them to grow peanuts, corn, potatoes, sugarcane, and hay, and to produce cattle and hogs, citizens of Enterprise in 1918 erected a monument topped by a large, black boll weevil on the main street of their town. Inscribed on the base are these words: "In profound appreciation of the boll weevil and what it has done as the herald of prosperity, this monument was erected by the citizens of Enterprise, Coffee County, Alabama."

Leaving Enterprise, return through Fort Rucker to U.S. 231. Turn north to Troy.

Troy

Pike Pioneer Museum, on U.S. 231 north of Troy, contains Alabama's major collection of pioneer memorabilia. Local citizens built this collection, which opened in 1971.

Except for the most fortunate, many pioneer citizens of Pike County and other areas of Alabama lived in dilapidated, unpainted frame or log houses. Such structures, leaning out of plumb on rock or wood pillars, were usually unceiled, unscreened, and covered with wood shingle roofs. When cold winds blew through cracks in the floors and walls, members of the family huddled around the fire for warmth.

The **two-pen** (two-room) **dogtrot log house**, restored at Pike Pioneer Museum, is typical of many antebellum homes in Alabama (see *Bessemer*). The dogtrot separates two rooms. A small lean-to kitchen stands in the rear. Careful research has gone into selecting the handmade farmhouse antiques with which the house is furnished. Note the old style of rope bed used by most early Alabama settlers.

The small board and batten **tenant house** is basically a one-room struc-

Tenant House, Pike Museum (photo from kitchen)

Tenant House, Pike Museum

ture, fifteen by sixteen feet, with a fireplace. Behind the main room is a lean-to kitchen and eating space. The porch was added at a later date. The small house typifies the dwellings of tenant farmers in southeast Alabama from the 1870s until around 1930. Outbuildings and structures include a typical rail fence, an old windmill, an authentic privy, and a replica of an old open well.

The **Old Chancey-Adams Store** (c. 1920) was moved from the Orion community and was equipped and stocked as a typical country store with authentic counters, shelves, drink box, checkerboard, stove, spool case, cash drawer, and signs. Inside is an old rural post office moved from Letohatchee. Country stores often served as post offices with the storekeeper

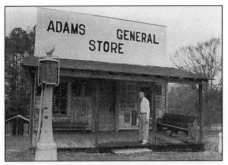

Adams General Store, Pike Museum

old logging locomotive, Pike Museum (drawing)

doubling as postmaster, dispatching and receiving mail, selling stamps, and reading and writing letters for those who could not do so. Outside are a hand-operated gasoline pump and a hitching rail. The rail, moved from the Troy post office, has hitching rings for four horses, spaced so as to accommodate buggies or road carts as well.

Old country stores were gathering places to discuss weather, news, and the latest farming methods. They were important socially, politically, and economically.

The **Agricultural Building** displays antique farm implements. An entire wall is lined with plows of every variety, all mule-powered. Special exhibits include a blacksmith shop, carpentry shop, wagons, buggies, and a carriage. A horse-drawn hearse (containing a casket) and a genuine moonshine still are features of this collection.

The **Household Building** displays articles in common use in pioneer homes, such as hand-pegged pie safes and clothing. An old overhead loom is used to produce handwoven goods.

Open weekdays, 10 a.m. to 5 p.m.;

Sunday, 1 to 5 p.m. Small admission fee. Telephone (334) 566-3597.

In Troy are **Troy State University**, founded in 1887 as Troy State Normal School, and **College Street Historic District**, an area of eighteen residential structures reflecting the lifestyle of prominent and prosperous citizens of Troy during the late nineteenth century. On the National Register, this street contains excellent examples of the Queen Anne and Revival styles. The old **Three Notch Road**, blazed in 1824 as a military pathway between Fort Mitchell and Fort Barancas at Pensacola, passed through Troy on what is now Alabama 21. This road also was used during the final campaign against the Creeks in 1836.

Leaving Troy, continue north on U.S. 231 toward Montgomery.

On both sides of the highway are a number of old tenant houses, some refurnished and modernized but others empty and dilapidated. Most have tin roofs and sagging porches and are unpainted. Some were built in the popular saddlebag style, with a central chimney serving rooms on either side.

Fort Morgan Archways (p. 212)

TOUR 14
Baldwin
County

Mobile Delta

Fort Mims site

Blakeley

Daphne

Montrose

Fairhope

Point Clear

Malbis

Bon Secour

Fort Morgan

Creek War sites

Civil War sites

utopian communities

Creole cottages

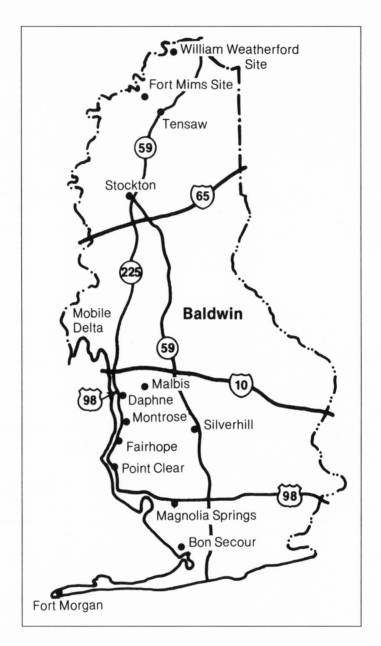

William Weatherford Site

Fort Mims Site

Tensaw

59

Stockton

65

225

Mobile Delta

Baldwin

59

Malbis

10

98

Daphne

Montrose

Silverhill

Fairhope

Point Clear

98

Magnolia Springs

Bon Secour

Fort Morgan

A glance at a map of the United States shows that Alabama has retained less of its natural coastline than any other seaboard state. The Florida panhandle between the Perdido and Apalachicola rivers is the natural extension of Alabama. But in a long pro-

cess of international wars and treaties, followed by a series of fruitless negotiations with Florida, Alabama lost most of what should have been its seacoast. Final negotiations to annex the panhandle from the state of Florida broke down after the Civil War. One reason was that Mobile shipping interests feared competition if the port of Pensacola were to become part of Alabama.

Alabama's seventy-mile coast lies mostly within one county that is larger than Rhode Island and only slightly smaller than Delaware. Once covered by forest, Baldwin County was stripped of timber by lumber companies. After the Civil War, groups of migrants, attracted by the mild climate and the natural fertility of this land, moved to Baldwin County, forming communities of Italians, Greeks, Germans, Poles, Czechs, Slovaks, French Canadians, American Quakers, and Hooker Mennonites.

Among Baldwin County's agricultural enterprises today are soybeans, potatoes, pecans (severely damaged in 1979 by Hurricane Frederic), livestock, truck crops, and gladioli. Commercial fishing is a major source of income for many residents. In northern Baldwin County, lumbering is a major enterprise.

Hurricane Frederic brought tourism to a virtual standstill, wiping out hundreds of beach homes, businesses, and motels in Gulf Shores. However, that area has been rebuilt and business is booming.

Accommodations: Gulf State Park at Gulf Shores offers campgrounds, cottages, and motel units. There are comfortable motels throughout the county and in nearby Mobile.

Coming from Montgomery, leave Interstate 65 at the Alabama 225 exit. Turn north toward Stockton.

Mobile Delta

The second largest river delta in the United States (after the Mississippi Delta), Mobile Delta has been designated by Congress as a National Natural Landmark because it contains rare and endangered plants, a cypress forest, and ancient swamps. Weeks Bay National Estuarine Research Reserve, "the place where rivers meet the sea," is one of seventeen designated reserves in fourteen states and Puerto Rico. Collectively, the reserves protect nearly 300,000 acres of estuarine waters, marshes, shorelines, and adjacent uplands for research and education. Telephone (334) 928-9792. Eight rivers come together to form this delta and flow into Mobile Bay. For a glimpse of the swamps, follow any side road west to the edge of the delta.

Stockton

The area that is now the town of Stockton was once part of a vast plantation belonging to Major Robert Farmar, commander of the British regiments at Mobile from 1763 to 1765, who acquired this site around 1772. The naturalist William Bartram visited the Farmar plantation. Stockton was originally located on the banks of the Tensaw River but moved to its present site a few years later to escape yellow fever.

Bartram's book *Travels of William Bartram* contains this description: "August 5th [1778] set off from Mobile up the river in a trading boat, and was landed at Taensa bluff, the seat of Major Farmar, to make good my engagements, in consequence of an invitation from that worthy gentleman to spend some days in his family: here I obtained the use of a light canoe to continue my voyage up the river. The settlement of Taensa is on the site of an ancient town of a tribe of Indians of that name, which is apparent from many artificial mounds of earth and other ruins. Besides Mr. Farmar's dwellings, there are many others inhabited by French families, who are chiefly his tenants. It is a most delightful situation, commanding a spacious prospect up and down the river, and the low lands of his extensive plantations on the opposite shore. In my excursions about this place, I observed many curious vegetable productions, particularly a species of Myrica (*Myrica inodora*): this very beautiful evergreen shrub, which the French inhabitants call the Wax tree, grows in wet sandy ground about the edges of swamps; it rises erect nine or ten feet, dividing itself into a multitude of nearly erect branches, which are garnished with many shining deep green entire leaves of a lanceolate figure; the branches produce abundance of large round berries, nearly the size of bird cherries, which are covered with a scale or coat of white wax; no part of this plant possesses any degree of fragrance. It is in high estimation with the inhabitants for the production of wax for candles, for which purpose it answers equally well with beeswax, or preferably, as it is harder and more lasting in burning."

In the swamps seven miles west of Stockton, the **Bottle Creek Indian Mounds** constitute the largest temple mound complex in southern Alabama. A large village of Mississippian people occupied this area from approximately A.D. 1200 to 1600. The 157-acre Bottle Creek site was given to the Alabama Historical Commission in 1992, so the land and Indian mounds on it can be studied by archaeologists. The mounds are accessible only by boat.

From Stockton, follow Alabama 59 north to Tensaw.

Tensaw

Tensaw is an Anglicized form of Tensas (or Taensa), the name of a group of Indians who came to this area after being driven from Louisiana by the Chickasaws. These Indians occupied a site called Tensaw Bluff, later acquired by Major Robert Farmar, near present Stockton. After the Tensaw Region became British territory in 1763, a trickle of colonists settled here. Most traveled from the Carolinas, but others came from as far away as New England, the Caribbean, and the British Isles. During the American Revolution a number of American Loyalists (also called *Tories*) who sympathized with England fled from other colonies to settle here and in the lower Tombigbee Valley. Mobile and its surrounding areas were captured by Spain in 1780. Encouraged by the Spanish, more Americans settled in the Tensaw area, including large numbers of men who traded with Indians, as well as wealthier settlers who operated cotton plantations and shipped their cotton through Spanish Mobile. During the War of 1812, the Mobile district was seized from the Spanish by an American force and eventually became part of the new state of Alabama.

More than two hundred years after the first settlers came to the Tensaw region, this area is still sparsely populated. Lumber, turpentine, and naval stores are major products today.

At Tensaw, turn west on Baldwin County 80 and proceed three and one-half miles to the Fort Mims site.

suggestions for background reading

Foscue, Virginia O. *Place Names in Alabama.* Tuscaloosa, University of Alabama Press, 1989.

Halbert, H. S., and T. H. Ball. *The Creek War of 1813 and 1814.* N.p. 1895. Reprint, edited by Frank L. Owsley, Jr. Tuscaloosa: University of Alabama Press, 1969. Reprint (paper) 1995.

Thompson, Lynn Hastie. *William Weatherford: His Country and His People.* Bay Minette: Lavender Publishing Company, 1991.

Fort Mims Site

The first fighting of the Creek War broke out on Burnt Corn Creek along the present border between Escambia and Conecuh counties in July 1813. Eighty Creeks, on their way home from Pensacola with arms and ammunition obtained from Spain, were ambushed by 180 American militiamen. But the Creeks counterattacked and forced the Americans to retreat.

Although the Red Sticks won this initial skirmish, they were infuriated by the surprise attack. Swearing revenge, they gathered a war party of 750 Creeks. In the meantime, scattered settlers who lived in the fork of the Alabama and Tombigbee rivers gathered for protection at several stockades, including the home of Samuel Mims, a wealthy trader. About 300 people, including settlers, many mixed bloods, black slaves, and friendly Indians, were guarded here by 120 militiamen.

Their commander, Major Daniel Beasley, refusing to believe reports that warriors in war paint were nearby, allowed the wooden gates of Fort Mims to stand partially open. As drums sounded the call to the noonday meal, hundreds of Creeks, led by William Weatherford, stormed the fort. Major Beasley, attempting to close the gate, was clubbed to death. Settlers and soldiers tried to find shelter in houses and behind fences, but the angry

Creeks, caught up in the fever of killing, shot, clubbed, and burned to death more than 250 soldiers and settlers, women and children as well as men. It is said that Weatherford attempted without success to curb his infuriated followers and that he left the scene when he was unable to halt the slaughter. News of the Battle of Fort Mims spread quickly through the frontier. Whites, enraged at the slaughter of women and children, echoed the battle cry, "Remember Fort Mims!" American militia from Mississippi, Georgia, and Tennessee began to move into Alabama to aid the settlers and exact revenge upon the Red Sticks. The skirmish at Burnt Corn Creek, followed by the slaughter at Fort Mims, widened what had been a civil war between Upper and Lower Creeks over the issue of cooperation with whites into a war between the Creek Nation and the United States (see *Horseshoe Bend National Military Park*).

Visitors to this isolated spot may find it difficult to believe that one of the bloodiest conflicts ever between Indians and whites took place in this lonely glade of moss-hung trees. A stone marker, walkways, and signs remind visitors of the events that took place here in August 1813. For information contact the Alabama Historical Commission.

Leaving Fort Mims, return to Alabama 59. Continue north to the Little River community. Turn west on Baldwin County 80 toward Dixie Landing. In two and one-half miles, turn left onto a dirt road. Proceed two miles to Tate Chapel. Follow the road in front of this church a few hundred yards to the right to Weatherford's grave.

Grave of William Weatherford

William Weatherford ("Red Eagle") was the son of a Creek princess and a Scottish trader. Through his mother, Sehoy, he was related to the famous McGillivray family, one of whose members, Alexander McGillivray, had been the most important leader of Alabama Indians at the time of the American Revolution. As a mixed-blood, Weatherford was torn by his loyalties to both whites and Creeks, but when the Creek War broke out in 1813 he reluctantly joined the Red Stick (war) faction and became known as Red Eagle, a major leader of the militant Creeks. After Andrew Jackson crushed the Red Sticks at the Battle of Horseshoe Bend, William Weatherford rode into Fort Jackson alone to surrender to

Grave of William Weatherford

the American general and to plead for food for starving Indian women and children. Jackson, impressed by Weatherford's courage, refused to imprison him and eventually allowed him to return to his land along the banks of the Alabama River in Baldwin County. Here Weatherford lived peacefully until his death in 1824.

His grave and that of his mother, Sehoy, a princess of the Wind Clan, are side by side in a quiet family cemetery.

Return via Alabama 59 to Alabama 225. Just before Alabama 225 intersects Interstate 10 it will pass the site of Blakeley on the west.

Historic Blakeley State Park

A Connecticut shipper, Josiah Blakeley, founded a port here after the War of 1812. His intention was to outdo Mobile as a shipping point for cotton, lumber, and locally distilled whiskey. Built in Federal-style architecture, Blakeley resembled a New England seaport. Briefly the town enjoyed a land boom and a bustling business at its port. But yellow fever, inflated land speculation, and silt in its harbor ended Blakeley's boom period. By 1836 it was a ghost town.

Confederates built earthworks here in 1865 to protect their artillery positions on the Tensaw River. Spanish Fort and Blakeley were fortified in a two-mile defense line to protect Mobile from land assault from the east. In March 1865, Union General E. R. S. Canby led 32,000 troops against Spanish Fort and Blakeley. Outnumbered eight to one, Confederates held out for twelve days before surrendering. Union troops seized Mobile on April 12, 1865.

The park has interesting nature trails, a boardwalk with two observation decks along the Tensaw River, and primitive campsites. The Blakeley Historic Foundation hopes to construct replicas of some of the wharfs and buildings of old Blakeley. The site is the largest National Register site east of the Mississippi River. Fort Blakeley Battle Festival is held in early April with a reenactment of the last major battle of the Civil War on the site where it was originally fought April 9, 1865. For information, call (334) 626-0798.

Spanish Fort

In the mid-eighteenth century, a trading post here supplied Indians and explorers following the old Spanish Trail (now U.S. 90) to Pensacola. During the American Revolution, the Spanish built a fort here that was considered practically impregnable. In January 1781, Spanish defenders of this fort managed to repel a British attack force. Both sides suffered heavy loss of life.

For a good view of Mobile Bay, turn west off Alabama 225 to the overlook just before Interstate 10.

Mobile Bay

On an early Spanish map, this huge bell-shaped bay was called *Mar Pequena*, meaning Little Sea. The bay first appeared on a map by the famous European mapmaker Martin Waldseemüller in 1507. However, some historians believe that other Europeans knew of the bay centuries earlier. Despite the fact that scholars have found no evidence to support it, a legend persists that Prince Madoc of Wales led an expedition to this area in 1170.

Thirty-six miles long and varying in width from eight to eighteen miles, the bay has belonged at various periods of history to France, England, Spain, the Confederacy, and the United States. Before the Civil War hundreds of paddlewheel steamers brought cotton and passengers from central Alabama down to the bay to be transferred to sailing ships bound for the East Coast, Europe, and other far-off places.

Today Mobile Bay is the destination of ships from around the world, bringing bananas, bauxite, iron ore, and other products to the Alabama State Docks and returning with shiploads of Alabama coal, timber, soybeans, grain, and oil.

For directions to the following communities, see local signs or consult a map.

Daphne

Daphne was the landing point for steam ferryboats that crossed Mobile Bay before the building of a bridge. Italians hoping to grow grapes for wine established a colony here in 1888 but Prohibition forced them to turn to other crops. Two churches are of interest.

Little Daphne Baptist Church (c. 1867) was built after Major Lewis Starke deeded two acres to his former slaves and their heirs for this purpose. One member of this congregation, Russell Dick, once owned all of downtown Daphne. His mother, Lucy, had come to Mobile on the last voyage of the slave ship *Clotilde* in 1859.

Daphne Methodist Church (c. 1858), severely damaged by Hurricane Frederic in 1979, was constructed of heart pine logs and handmade pegs. It has a slave gallery. To enhance its tone, the church bell was lined with a band of silver dollars where the clapper strikes.

Bayside Academy (c. mid-1800s), a frame building, has served as a hotel and Jesuit school and is now a private school.

Montrose

Écor Rouge (red bluff) at Montrose is the highest point on the seacoast from Maine to Mexico. The red clay bluff is plainly visible from Interstate 10. This site was marked on Spanish maps of the 1500s and named Écor Rouge by the French in the 1700s. In 1771 the British established a camp here in the hope that soldiers from Fort Charlotte in Mobile might escape yellow fever during the summers. One British governor recommended that a new town be built in this higher and more healthful site to replace low-lying Mobile. Clay from this bluff was used to make bricks and pottery.

Montrose Historic District, Main and Second streets, is on the National Register because of its collection of Creole cottages showing Greek Revival influence. The Creole cottage style of architecture was an early house type in the region. It features a gable roof, steeply pitched to carry off tropical downpours, and a full-width recessed porch. Some Creole cottages have two front doors. Baldwin County contains numerous examples of Creole cottage architecture, both old and new.

Jubilee!

The cry of "Jubilee!" on the eastern shore of Mobile Bay means that a rare and remarkable event is taking place. Thousands of fish, crabs, and shrimp are moving into the shallow waters of the shoreline. Even though jubilees usually occur between midnight and dawn, crowds quickly gather to fill buckets, sacks, nets, and even wash tubs with fish and shellfish. Some jubilees yield mostly flounder. Others are made up primarily of shrimp or crabs.

So far as is known, this phenomenon takes place only on the eastern shore of Mobile Bay during the sum-

mer months. One theory is that jubilees are caused by a sudden merging of fresh and salt water. Another theory holds that heavy rains cause a change in water temperature.

Utopian Communities

Cheap land, mild climate, and a fertile soil attracted a number of immigrant groups to Baldwin County. Most groups were held together by their common language, religious faith, and customs, but two Baldwin County settlements were distinguished by unusual economic philosophies.

suggestions for background reading

Alyea, Paul E., and Blanche R. Alyea. *Fairhope, 1894–1954: The Story of a Single-Tax Colony.* University: University of Alabama Press, 1956.

Gaston, Paul M. *Man and Mission: E. D. Gaston and the Origins of the Fairhope Single Tax Colony.* Montgomery: Black Belt Press, 1993.

Malbis Plantation. *The Faith of Jason Malbis: Founder of Malbis Plantation.* Daphne: Privately published, 1972.

Malbis

Jason Malbis, a former monk, came to America from Greece in 1906 when he was thirty-seven years old. His dream was to build a community in which every member would work for the common good, sharing equally in the profits of their brotherhood.

To begin his experiment, Malbis purchased 100 acres of Baldwin

Malbis Greek Orthodox Church

County land for five dollars an acre. Three years later his community purchased an additional 600 acres. Eventually this property was incorporated as Malbis Plantation.

During the next thirty years, about 100 immigrants from Greece shared the communal life and profits of Malbis Plantation. Initially the community prospered from its harvests of potatoes. Gradually Jason Malbis expanded his enterprises to include a canning plant, bakery, resin products, an ice plant, nursery, dairy, restaurant, bank, and motel. At the time of his death in 1942, Malbis apparently had achieved his dream of a prosperous communal development.

In 1965 a handsome Byzantine-style **Greek Orthodox Church** was dedicated by the Malbis community to the memory of its founder, who is buried in its mausoleum. Marble was brought from quarries in Greece to construct the elaborate structure, which resembles a church in Athens. Its large dome is centered by a large fresco depicting God with outstretched arms. Carved wooden figures were im-

ported from Greece and delicate mosaics were imported from Italy.

Although its enterprises prospered, Malbis's community steadily dwindled. He and his followers did not believe in marriage; male and female members lived in separate dormitory-style buildings. Few immigrants came from the old country to join them.

A few members of the community, most of them elderly, still live at Malbis Plantation. Most of their enterprises have been sold or discontinued. Suburbs and interstate highways have encroached on what was once isolated farmland. Soon only their remarkable church will remain to testify to the vision of Jason Malbis.

Malbis Greek Orthodox Church is open daily. Donations accepted.

Fairhope

Unlike Malbis Plantation, Fairhope was not a communal enterprise in the sense of sharing profits from labor. Its original settlers did, however, believe that land should be socialized because its supply was fixed by nature. In 1893 a group of followers of Henry George, the single-tax philosopher, migrated from Iowa to Baldwin County to found Fairhope.

The Fairhope Single Tax Corporation, incorporated in 1904, leased its lands in return for a rent ("single tax") based on the valuation of the land, which was reassessed annually. These rents went to pay all county, state, and local taxes and to improve community services such as streets, parks, a library, water system, and electric plant.

Another unusual feature of the Fairhope colony was the **Marietta Johnson School of Organic Education**, an early experiment in progressive education by a Minnesota schoolteacher. Founded in the early twentieth century, the school practiced the concept that young people should not be restricted by the pressure of grades but should be free to express their creativity.

The school still practices the concepts of its founder, and the corporation continues to follow the theory of Henry George by leasing its land for a single tax.

Silverhill

During the hard economic times of the 1890s a group of Scandinavians decided to leave Chicago and return to the land. They founded Silverhill.

Magnolia Springs

This picturesque village along the banks of the Magnolia River, originally a summer colony, now has a number of year-round residents.

Point Clear

Well-to-do southerners have come to this area of the eastern shore since the 1830s. Before the Civil War, planters and other gentility from Alabama, Mississippi, Louisiana, and Georgia brought their families to Point Clear each summer to swim, sail, and court.

The advent of war brought this idyllic life to a standstill. As one young man wrote his sweetheart in 1861: "Dearest, I fear I shall not see you at Point Clear this summer. I am leaving for Vicksburg." The old Point Clear Hotel became a Confederate hospital.

After the Battle of Mobile Bay in 1864, Admiral David Farragut's fleet operated in the bay and shelled Point Clear, leaving a cannonball hole in a wall of the Gunnison House (c. 1830), now demolished, near the Grand Hotel, a present-day resort on the site of the original hotel. The hole was covered by a brass plate inscribed: "Compliments of Admiral Farragut." After the war Gunnison House became a casino for a time. Cotton crops and sometimes plantations changed hands at its gaming tables.

Bon Secour

Ruins of a building made of tabby (oyster shells and water) and probably built by French or Spanish explorers in the early 1700s have been found near this fishing village. During the Civil War a Confederate camp and salt works here were destroyed by Union troops. Today Bon Secour (meaning "safe harbor") is home for a fleet of fishing boats and a major shrimp and oyster business.

Bon Secour National Wildlife Refuge

Some 10,000 acres of barrier islands on the Fort Morgan peninsula and on Little Dauphin Island across the bay have been designated as a wildlife refuge to help preserve the spawning grounds for Alabama's fishing industry and to serve as home for 100 resident species of birds and various other species of animals as well as a resting place for migratory birds.

Fort Morgan

During the War of 1812 between the United States and England, a small sand and wooden fort was built at Mobile Point on the eastern shore of Mobile Bay. Named for its commander, Fort Bowyer had a garrison of 161 men charged by General Andrew Jackson with defending this crucial point from British attack.

In September 1814, 150 Royal British Marines and 200 Creek Indians attacked Fort Bowyer from the beach as four British warships sailed into the bay to surround the point. The small American garrison managed to repulse these larger enemy forces, thereby gaining a victory, saving Mobile, and changing the British plan of attack against New Orleans.

The British fleet of twenty-eight ships returned in February 1815 after the British defeat at the Battle of New Orleans, surrounded the fort, and forced its defenders to surrender. However, the treaty ending the war had already been signed, so Mobile Point was returned to the United States. Frail Fort Bowyer was destroyed by a storm in the 1820s.

In the meantime, Congress, realizing the need for stronger fortifications along this coastline, had authorized construction of the present fort. One of the finest examples of brick architecture in America, Fort Morgan was designed by Simone Bernard, a French engineer and former aide-de-camp to Napoleon. His designs conformed to the theory of Sebastien le Prestre, marquis de Vauban, fortification engineer who revolutionized fort construction in France during the reign of Louis XIV. The five-pointed-star fort with its arches within arches was built by white and black craftsmen between 1819 and 1834. It was named for General Daniel Morgan, a hero of the American Revolution.

Fort Morgan, entrance

Fort Morgan

In 1837, 3,000 Creek Indians were brought down the Alabama River from Montgomery to Fort Morgan where they were incarcerated for several months before being put aboard boats for their forced journey westward to Oklahoma.

Seven days after Alabama seceded from the Union, Governor Andrew B. Moore ordered the Alabama militia to seize Fort Morgan and Fort Gaines. Fort Morgan remained part of the republic of Alabama for five weeks before becoming part of the Confederate States of America.

Fort Morgan, a crucial fortification during the Civil War, was the next-to-last Confederate seacoast fort to fall to the Union. In the Battle of Mobile Bay, August 5, 1864, guns from the fort inflicted serious damage on Admiral David Farragut's fleet of fourteen wooden ships and four ironclads.

At the end of this engagement Admiral Franklin Buchanan, commander of the Confederate navy, surrendered to the Union fleet. Federal troops then began to move on Fort Morgan. More than 3,000 shots were fired at the fort before Confederates raised the flag of surrender. On August 23, 1864, Fort Morgan was again part of the United States.

Before and during the Spanish-American War of 1898, coastal defense batteries were constructed near the fort, as well as wooden barracks, officers' homes, a hospital, and other buildings. During World War I, Fort Morgan was a training base for artillery corpsmen but was abandoned as a training base at the end of that war.

The site was transferred in 1927 to the state of Alabama. During the 1930s, Works Progress Administration employees helped clear the area for a state park. During World War II, the Navy, Coast Guard, and Coastal Artillery again came to Fort Morgan to guard this point from German submarine attack. Horses and jeeps were used to patrol the beach from Fort Morgan to Alabama Point. At the close of World War II, the reservation was returned to the state of Alabama.

Fort Morgan, a National Historic Landmark operated by the Alabama Historical Commission, is open daily 8 a.m. to sunset. Admission charge.

The Park **Museum**, open daily 9 a.m. to 5 p.m., contains exhibits depicting the history of the fort and the surrounding area. No admission charge. Telephone (334) 540-7125.

U.S.S. *Tecumseh*

One of four Union ironclad monitors, the *Tecumseh* struck a marine mine during the Battle of Mobile Bay and sank. The monitor, in an excellent state of preservation, lies under thirty feet of water in Mobile Bay north of Fort Morgan. The federal government and the Smithsonian Institution have considered raising the *Tecumseh* but have decided to wait until improved methods are developed for preserving a metal vessel that has been underwater more than a century. The *Tecumseh* is on the National Register.

Lighthouses

Sand Island Lighthouse (c. 1873), a 132-foot conical masonry lighthouse three miles south of Mobile Point, is on the National Register. This light is no longer in operation.

Mobile Point Light (c. 1870s), an iron-lattice tower lighthouse was removed from its original site and replaced by an automated light tower. The tower was restored in 1992 and relocated near the museum at Fort Morgan.

TOUR 15

In and around Mobile

Alabama's seaport

World War II battleship

Creole cottages

iron lacework

reconstructed fort

fishing fleet

31° parallel

Alabama's territorial capital

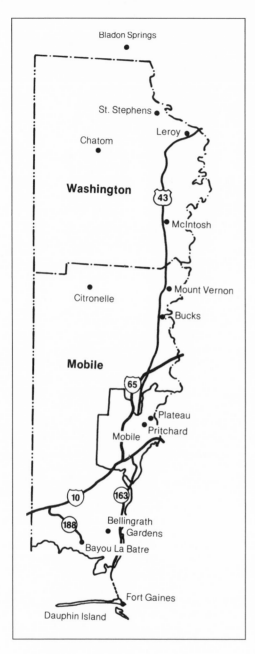

Although Mobile Bay was on a world map as early as 1507 and three Spanish expeditions entered its waters during the sixteenth century, a permanent colony was not established at this site until 1711. Discouraged by the floods that plagued his original settlement located thirty miles to the north, Jean Baptiste Le Moyne, Sieur de Bienville, moved his French colony downriver to the area where reconstructed Fort Condé stands today.

Until 1720 Mobile held the title of capital of the vast French holdings known as Louisiana, extending from the Gulf of Mexico into Canada and westward to the Rocky Mountains. In that year, however, the French moved their capital to New Orleans.

During Mobile's long, war-torn history, five flags have flown over the city. It was ceded by France to England in 1763, remaining in British hands until captured by Spanish forces in 1780. Mobile remained Spanish territory until captured again in 1813 by American troops. When Alabama was admitted to the Union in 1819, Mobile was its largest urban and trading center. During the antebellum period, its port was a busy scene of exchange between steamboats from interior Alabama and ocean-going vessels from around the world, with cotton and lumber its major commodities. At the outbreak of the Civil War, Mobile remained a major port of the Confederacy despite the Union blockade. Finally, on August 5,

Mobile is Alabama's oldest city, predating Huntsville by almost a century. Except for the Spanish settlements of St. Augustine and Pensacola, Florida, Mobile is the oldest Latin town east of Mexico.

1864, Admiral David Farragut and his fleet defeated Confederate vessels in the famous Battle of Mobile Bay, thereby closing one of the Confederacy's last outlets to the sea. Nine months later the city itself fell to Union forces. Shortly after the end of the war, a huge warehouse filled with ammunition exploded north of downtown Mobile on the river, laying waste much of the old city.

Mobile remained Alabama's largest city until superseded in 1900 by the new industrial center of Birmingham. Gradually its port facilities were developed and modernized. Industries also sought out Mobile. Today it is a center for the manufacture of wood pulp and paper products, rayon fibers, naval stores, clothing, furniture, and chemicals, as well as steel fabricating, shipbuilding, and foundries.

Despite modernization, however, Mobile retains in its Mardi Gras, architecture, street names, and blithe spirit much of its old French and Spanish heritage.

suggestions for background reading

Amos, Harriet E. *Cotton City: Urban Development in Antebellum Mobile*. Tuscaloosa: University of Alabama Press, 1985.

Boykin, Edward Carrington. *Ghost Ship of the Confederacy: The Story of the* Alabama *and Her Captain, Raphael Semmes*. New York: Funk and Wagnalls, 1957.

Bradlow, Edna. *Here Comes the* Alabama: *The Career of a Confederate Raider*. Birmingham: Southern University Press, 1968.

Craighead, Erwin. *Mobile: Fact and Tradition*. Mobile: Powers Printing Co., 1930.

Crouse, Nellis M. *Lemoyne d'Iberville: Soldier of New France*. Ithaca, N.Y.: Cornell University Press, 1954.

Daniels, George H., ed. *Gulf City Cook Book*. Compiled by The Ladies of the St. Francis Street Methodist Episcopal Church, 1856. Reprint. Tuscaloosa: University of Alabama Press, 1990.

Delaney, Caldwell. *The Story of Mobile*. Mobile: Gill Press, 1953.

Gould Elizabeth Barrett. *From Fort to Port: An Architectural History of Mobile, Alabama, 1711–1918*. Tuscaloosa: University of Alabama Press, 1988.

Hamilton, Peter J. *Colonial Mobile*. Boston: Houghton Mifflin Co., 1887. Reprint. Mobile: First National Bank, 1952.

Higginbotham, Jay. *Old Mobile: Fort Louis de la Louisiana, 1702–1711*. Museum of the City of Mobile, 1977. Reprint. Tuscaloosa: University of Alabama Press, 1991.

Holmes, Jack D. L. *Gayoso: The Life of a Spanish Governor in the Mississippi Valley*. Baton Rouge: Louisiana State University Press, 1965.

Holt, Thad, Jr., ed. *Diary of Miss Mary Waring of Mobile During the Final Days of the War Between the States*. Chicago: Wyvern Press, 1964.

McLaurin, Melton, and Michael Thomason. *Mobile: The Life and Times of a Great Southern City*. Woodland Hills, Calif.: Windsor Publications, 1981.

McWilliams, Richebourg Gaillard, trans. and ed. *Fleur de Lys and Calumet, Being the Penicaut Narrative of French Adventure in Louisiana*. 1953. Reprint. Tuscaloosa: University of Alabama Press, 1988.

McWilliams, Richebourg Gaillard, translator and ed. *Iberville's Gulf Journals*. Tuscaloosa: University of Alabama Press, 1991.

Summersell, Charles G. *Mobile: History of a Seaport Town*. University: University of Alabama Press, 1949.

Mardi Gras

For ten days each February citizens of Mobile celebrate Mardi Gras, an an-

Mardi Gras, Mobile

nual festival of revelry preceding the start of the Lenten season. Mobile claims that its Mardi Gras tradition is the oldest in North America, predating that of its longtime rival New Orleans. It dates back to New Year's Eve, 1830, when a lighthearted Mobilian led fellow carousers to raid a hardware store, steal a supply of cowbells, and proceed to awaken the entire city.

Masks and costumes were added to the celebration, then carts and wagons, as members of the "Cowbellion de Rakin Society" danced, feasted, and paraded each New Year's Eve. Other "mystic societies" formed to join in the revels. Parades began to focus around themes of ancient gods and goddesses.

In 1842 a society known as the Strikers was organized by young men who could not get into the Cowbellions. This group now is the oldest American mystic society. During the Civil War, Mardi Gras was suspended, but in 1866 another happy-go-lucky Mobilian, Joe Cain, dressed as an Indian and paraded through the streets in a charcoal wagon urging his fellow

citizens to resume their joyous festival. In 1869 Mardi Gras, transferred to the period prior to the Lenten season, resumed at full scale. In 1872 the tradition of good King Felix, who rules over Mobile during the celebration, was begun.

Modern Mobile's many mystic societies fill the days prior to Lent with sixteen parades and numerous balls. Two parades still preserve the tradition of having floats drawn by costumed mules. Visitors are invited to attend the Krewe de Bienville Ball. The celebration climaxes on Mardi Gras Day, the final festive Tuesday before Ash Wednesday and the traditional fast of Lent.

HARBOR AREA

U.S.S. Alabama

Battleship U.S.S. *Alabama* was launched in Portsmouth, Virginia, in 1942. During World War II the ship convoyed shipping to Murmansk, Russia, and took part in the Norway invasion feint against the Nazis before being dispatched to join American

U.S.S. *Alabama*

strike forces in the Pacific theater. Its 2,500-man crew took part in battle action throughout 1944 and the first half of 1945, earning battle stars for the Marshalls, Hollandia, Marianas, Carolines, Philippines, far-ranging Pacific raids, Okinawa, Leyte, and Japan. At the close of the war, the 35,000-ton *Alabama* led the U.S. fleet into Tokyo Bay. After the battleship was decommissioned, Alabamians contributed to a campaign to tow her from Seattle, Washington, to Mobile. The U.S.S. *Alabama* became a state shrine in 1965.

Alabama State Docks

Also on display in Battleship Park on Battleship Parkway are the U.S.S. *Drum*, a World War II submarine, and several World War II fighter planes, including an Air Corps P-51 Mustang and a Marine Corsair.

Open daily 8 a.m. to sunset except Christmas. Admission charge. Audio guide tapes available.

Alabama State Docks

Early Spanish explorers of the Mobile area were quick to see the advantages of sheltering their ships in this ample bay. Admiral Alonso Alvarez de Pinéda entered Mobile Bay with four ships in 1519, remaining for forty days to repair his vessels. In 1558 another Spaniard, Guido de las Bazares, with three ships under his command, explored the bay and sent back a glow-ing report on this harbor and environs. However, the expedition of Don Tristan de Luna the following year had the misfortune of arriving in Mobile Bay during hurricane season. Many of Luna's followers were killed and most of his ships and cargoes destroyed by a tremendous tropical storm.

At the start of the eighteenth century, the French Canadian Le Moyne brothers, Iberville and Bienville, established a colony and seaport in the Mobile area. They located their port on Dauphin Island so that large ocean-going ships could unload. During the French, British, and Spanish domination of this region, cargoes of pelts, furs, tallow, and wax were transported down Alabama rivers to Mobile, reloaded on shallow-draft barges, and transported down the bay to ocean-going vessels anchored at its mouth.

In the early nineteenth century,

219

paddlewheel steamboats began to transport cotton down Alabama rivers to Mobile's wharves. By the late 1850s, after its ship channel was improved with federal aid, Mobile ranked second only to New Orleans as a great cotton port. Lumber from the virgin timberlands of south Alabama also passed through the port of Mobile. Great clipper ships, schooners, brigs, and barkentines bustled in and out of the bay.

During the Civil War, Mobile was an important Confederate port. Blockade runners managed to slip past a Union patrol to bring in badly needed medicines, munitions, and other supplies. But Admiral David Farragut's victory in the Battle of Mobile Bay closed this Confederate outlet to the sea.

Although the first ocean-going steamship arrived at this port in 1880, Mobile did not achieve adequate port facilities until a State Docks Commission was established in the 1920s. General William Sibert, a native Alabamian and one of the builders of the Panama Canal, came out of retirement to plan and build the Alabama State Docks. The first vessel to use this new facility arrived in 1927.

Today the docks handle not only ocean-going vessels from many nations but also barges from fourteen inland ports on Alabama's river systems. Modern cranes, cargo berths, and warehouses have been added to these facilities. Alabama coal, oil, soybeans,

and grain pass through the docks en route to overseas customers. Bananas, iron ore, bauxite, and numerous other products of foreign nations are unloaded at Mobile. With the opening of the Tennessee Tombigbee Waterway in the 1980s, traffic through the port of Mobile has produced additional activity.

Guided bus and harbor tours of the state docks may be arranged through the Alabama State Docks public affairs department. Telephone (334) 441–7001.

HISTORIC DISTRICTS

Information, brochures and maps detailing Mobile's historic districts, buildings, cemeteries, and museums are available at Fort Condé Welcome Center, 150 South Royal, Mobile, AL 36602. Telephone 1-800-666-6282 or (334) 434-7304.

Church Street East Historic District

South of the main downtown business area, this district includes some seventy structures, including townhouses of the 1850s and 1860s. Many have been adapted for use as offices, apartments, museums, and shops. The original site of the small village of Mobile, erected in 1711 by French settlers under Bienville, lies within a portion of this historic district.

Its historic sites include the following:

Government Street Sites

Statue of Admiral Raphael Semmes, foot of Government Street, commemorates the feats of the Confederate naval hero who commanded the raider *Alabama*, which sank fifty-seven Union vessels and captured many more before being sunk in the English channel by the Union ship *Kearsarge*. **LaClede Hotel** (c. 1855), 150 Government Street, has a cast iron gallery over the sidewalk. **Government Street Presbyterian Church** (c. 1836), 300 Government Street, is Greek Revival with Ionic columns and is on the National Register.

Bernstein House (1872), 355 Government Street, Italianate structure formerly the home of a Mobile mayor, houses the **Museum of the City of Mobile**. Displays include original portraits of explorers and colonizers, furniture, silver, arms, ship models, costumes, maps, and historical documents. Open Tuesday through Saturday, 10 a.m. to 5 p.m.; Sunday, 1 to 5 p.m. No admission charge. Telephone (334) 434-7569.

Spanish Plaza, in the 400 block of Government Street, commemorates the Spanish period of Mobile history between 1780 and 1813. **Barton Academy** (c. 1836), 504 Government Street, the first public school in Alabama, is on the National Register. **Gilmore-Gaines-Quigley House**, 751 Government Street, Italianate with cast iron verandah, formerly the home of descendants of the prominent Gaines family, now is used as offices for the Mobile Jaycees. **Admiral Semmes Home** (c. 1859), 802 Government Street, bought by public subscription and presented to the naval hero in 1871, now is owned by the First Baptist Church.

Conti Street Sites

Bishop Portier House (c. 1834), 307 Conti Street, Creole cottage with dormer windows, was the residence of the first bishop of Mobile and later of Father Abram Ryan, poet-priest of the Confederacy. It is on the National Register. At the corner of Conti and

Fort Condé, view from cannon post

221

Claiborne streets is the **Cathedral-Basilica of the Immaculate Conception** (c. 1835–49), three-story brick with twin towers, one of Alabama's earliest churches and one of fewer than thirty churches in the nation designated as a minor basilica (a designation signifying antiquity, dignity, and historical significance). It is on the National Register. Go inside to view the stained-glass windows.

Horst-Guste House (c. 1867), 407 Conti Street, two-story Italianate with ironwork fence, built by an early mayor of Mobile, is on the National Register.

Fort Condé Area

City Hall–City Market (c. 1858), 111 South Royal Street, two-story with octagonal cupola, was originally a market for vendors of fish, meat, and vegetables. It is a National Historic Landmark. **Reconstructed Fort Condé**, on Royal Street diagonally across from City Hall, is a partial reconstruction of a brick fort built by the French between 1724 and 1735. It was a bicentennial project of the city of Mobile and is now the city's welcome center. Open daily 9 a.m. to 5 p.m. No admission charge.

Fort Condé–Charlotte House (c. 1822-24), 104 Theatre Street, Mobile's first city jail, was later used as a residence and is now a house museum. On the National Register, it is fur-

nished to depict periods of Mobile history under five flags. A walled Spanish garden is in the rear. Note the unusual combination of Tuscan columns on the first floor with Corinthian columns on the second. Open Tuesday through Saturday, 10 a.m. to 4 p.m. Admission charge.

Claiborne Street–Church Street Area

Waring Quarters (c. 1851), 108 South Claiborne Street, a two-story brick dependency originally a laundry and servants' quarters for a Government Street mansion since demolished, now is used as offices. **Waring "Texas"** (c. 1840), 110 South Claiborne Street, originally a "garçonniere" or dwelling place for the sons of the Waring household, was called a "Texas" because it was separate from the main house as Texas was once separate from the United States.

Patio Gallery (c. 1850), 201 South Claiborne Street, a mid-nineteenth-century structure relocated from its original site, is now a shop. **Phoenix Fire Museum** (1859), 203 South Claiborne Street, houses exhibits on the history of volunteer firefighting in early Mobile as well as later firefighting equipment. Open Tuesday through Saturday, 10 a.m. to 5 p.m.; Sunday, 1 to 5 p.m. No admission charge. Nearby is a **mule-drawn trolley car**, one of the few remaining examples of this

Phoenix Fire Museum

Richards-DAR House

form of public transportation. **Twin Italianate houses** (c. 1862), 357–359 Church Street, have been adapted for use as a small inn. Note patio.

Downtown

Bienville Square (c. 1830s) was created by the city as a public area in the center of Mobile. In 1866 it was dedicated to Jean Baptiste Le Moyne, Sieur de Bienville, founder of Mobile. A stone marker commemorates Bienville's brother Iberville. Shaded by live oaks, the park remains a restful spot in the midst of a busy modern city.

De Tonti Square

Located north of the downtown business district, this was Mobile's most fashionable townhouse section between 1840 and 1900 when many cotton merchants built residences in this area. The square is named for Henri De Tonti, an early explorer known to Indians as "the man with the Iron Hand" because he had lost a hand

in battle and replaced it with an iron hand. De Tonti died in the yellow fever epidemic of 1704 at Twenty-Seven Mile Bluff, the original site of Mobile.

The nine-block area lends itself easily to a walking tour. Its fifty-two structures include Creole cottages, Federal houses, Greek Revival, Italianate, and Victorian dwellings. Some are private residences; others have been adapted as offices.

Richards-DAR House (c. 1860), 256 North Joachim Street, Italianate with elaborate iron grillwork, was built by a riverboat captain who later became a food importer. Now a house museum and on the National Register, Richards-DAR House is open Tuesday through Saturday, 10 a.m. to 4 p.m.; Sunday, 1 to 4 p.m. Admission charge. (Note Neoclassic figurines of the four seasons in the design of the iron lacework.)

Carlen House (c. 1842), 54 Carlen Street at Willcox on the campus of Murphy High School, is a fine example of the Creole cottage as adapted from

Carlen House

Oakleigh

the French colonial form to early American use. The only such house publicly preserved and maintained in Mobile, Carlen House has been restored as a house museum by the Mobile Museum Board. Its furnishings typify a house of the antebellum period. Open Tuesday through Saturday, 10 a.m. to 5 p.m.; Sunday, 1 to 5 p.m. No admission charge.

Oakleigh Garden Historic District

Located west of downtown Mobile, this nineteenth-century residential area includes more than 500 historic buildings, including Gulf Coast and Victorian cottages and Italianate townhouses, most of which have been restored and still are used as private residences. Its most widely known structure is **Oakleigh** (c. 1833), 350 Oakleigh Place, a Greek Revival raised cottage built in the once-popular T-shape to seek cross-ventilation. Note outside cantilevered staircase and windows, convertible to doors, which

open onto the upstairs balconies. On the National Register, Oakleigh is a house museum of the Early Victorian, Empire, and Regency periods. It contains a portrait by Thomas Sully of Octavia Walton LeVert, Mobile's famous antebellum hostess. Open Monday through Saturday, 10 a.m. to 4 p.m.; Sunday, 2 to 4 p.m. Admission charge. Special event: Candlelight Christmas at Oakleigh, each December.

Spring Hill Historic District

Fleeing epidemics of yellow fever that once plagued Mobile, hundreds of early residents built summer retreats on this wooded rise seven miles from the bay. Another group of refugees, French aristocrats who had supported Napoleon Bonaparte, settled at Spring Hill after the failure of their wine-growing venture at Demopolis (see *Demopolis*).

Eventually Spring Hill developed into a permanent subdivision, centered around Spring Hill College, one of Alabama's earliest colleges, started in 1830 by Michael Portier, first Roman Catholic bishop of Mobile. Wealthy cotton merchants built many handsome mansions here during the prosperous 1850s. These homes reflect Creole, Greek Revival, and Federal styles of architecture.

Spring Hill's most significant historic site is **Spring Hill College** (c. 1830), 4307 Old Shell Road, operated by Jesuits. Note especially the **Avenue of Oaks** leading to **Stewartfield** (c. 1845), frame cottage with circular ballroom at rear, once the home of a wealthy cotton merchant; **Quadrangle** (c. 1866–1909), on the National Register; **St. Joseph's Chapel** (c. 1906), Gothic style; and **Sodality Chapel** (c. 1850), one-story frame structure of heart pine. Nearby is another interesting church, **St. Paul's Episcopal Chapel** (c. 1859), 4051 Old Shell Road, a one-story frame with cupola. An outstanding example of a private residence built by a well-to-do cotton factor (merchant) is **Carolina Hall** (c. 1843), 7 Yester Place, with

St. Joseph's Chapel

matching porticos and handsome decorative plaster work. (Difficult to find but worth the effort.) It is listed on the National Register.

Three historic structures from downtown Mobile have been relocated on the campus of the University of South Alabama, 307 University Boulevard, to form a **Museum Gallery Complex**. They are the **Toulmin House** (1828), the last surviving example of an early plantation Creole home in the Mobile environs, with long frame first story raised high above a brick ground story and a

Stewartfield, Mobile

Toulmin House

225

Seamen's Bethel

"galerie" running the full length of the facade (now used as offices); the **Seamen's Bethel** (place of worship; 1860), Gothic Revival masonry structure with heavily bracketed overhanging cornices, pointed sections of windows and doors, and small, six-part rose window; and the **Isaac Marx Townhouse** (c. 1870), Italianate combined with Federal, built at a cost of $10,000, which classed it as expensive in that era.

Mobile Museum of Art, 4850 Museum Drive in Langan Park, houses paintings, prints, contemporary crafts, silver, porcelain, quilts, African art, furniture, duck decoys, Boehm birds, sculpture, and lithographs depicting sports in art. Of special interest to historians is its collection of seventeenth- and eighteenth-century southern furnishings, including a variety of chairs, a huntboard (c. 1800) from the Georgia Piedmont, dower chests, and a rare Federal-period card table. Open Tuesday through Sunday, 10 a.m. to 5 p.m. No admission charge. The museum now has a satellite gallery at 300 Dau-

phin Street in downtown Mobile. Open Monday through Friday, 8:30 a.m. to 4:30 p.m. Telephone (334) 343-2667.

Other Mobile Sites

Among Mobile's other National Register sites are **City Hospital** (c. 1833–36), 850 St. Anthony Street, three-story masonry with Doric columns, one of the South's oldest hospitals, now restored for offices; **Bragg-Mitchell House**, 1906 Spring Hill Avenue, two-story Greek Revival T-shaped house with slender columns and iron lace balcony, one of Mobile's four house museums. Open Monday through Friday, 10 a.m. to 4 p.m.; Sunday 1 to 4 p.m. Small admission charge. It is also the site of **The Exploreum Museum of Discovery** dedicated to hands-on science learning. In addition to permanent exhibits, it offers traveling exhibits. Call (334) 476-6873 for schedule. Open Tuesday through Friday 9 a.m. to 5 p.m.; Saturday and Sunday, 1 to 5 p.m.;

Bragg-Mitchell Mansion, Mobile

and **Georgia Cottage** (c. 1845), one-story frame raised cottage, once the home of the widely known nineteenth-century writer Augusta Evans Wilson, author of *Beulah*, a novel that elicited widespread sympathy for the Confederate cause, and *St. Elmo*, a best-seller after the Civil War and the inspiration for two silent films.

SOUTH OF MOBILE

Take Interstate 10 south to Grand Bay exit. Follow Alabama 188 to Bayou La Batre.

Bayou La Batre

The village of Bayou La Batre, only a few miles from the Gulf of Mexico, is home port for a fleet of wooden hull boats and steel hull trawlers that ply nearby waters in search of oysters, crabs, shrimp, and a wide variety of fish. The Bayou La Batre area is also the largest producer of fishing and work boats in the world. Many boats are used locally but hundreds are shipped to countries around the world.

Blessing of the Fleet at Bayou La Batre

Fishermen here pause each year on the last Sunday in July for the annual blessing of their boats, a colorful event. Owners bedeck their vessels with pennants and flags. Some captains invite visitors aboard to ride in the annual boat parade that follows the fleet-blessing Mass. Thousands of spectators throng to this moss-hung bayou to watch the boat parade and enjoy seafood dinners. Although a religious event, the fleet blessing takes on the festive aura of a summer Mardi Gras.

Leaving Bayou La Batre, continue east on Alabama 188 to Alabama 163. Turn south toward Cedar Point and Dauphin Island.

Dauphin Island

Ancient Indian mounds give mute testimony that this island was inhabited in prehistoric times.

The French Canadian Le Moyne brothers, Iberville and Bienville, exploring here in 1699, found so many skulls and bones bleaching by the sun that they named this "Massacre Island." Later the French renamed this island "Dauphine" for the wife of an heir to the throne of France. Gradually the "e" was dropped. (*Dauphin* is the French term for the son of a king who will one day be king himself.)

On the western end of this fifteen-mile-long island Bienville built Port Dauphin as a trading point with the Spanish at Pensacola as well as for fur

227

trading with Indians who lived along the Alabama and Tombigbee rivers. A log fort was erected to protect the houses of settlers. Port Dauphin's ship channel became heavily clogged with sand as a result of a severe hurricane in 1717. Thereafter the port dwindled in importance, although the French kept a garrison there until 1742.

In 1821 work was begun on a fort at the eastern end of Dauphin Island. President James Monroe recommended construction of a fort on the island after British forces launched an attack on Fort Morgan from this site during the War of 1812. Fort Gaines and Fort Morgan were seized by Alabama troops at the start of the Civil War. Both became Confederate strongholds and links in the defense ring surrounding the port of Mobile. Cannon from these forts bombarded Admiral David Farragut's vessels during the Battle of Mobile Bay in 1864, but both forts were later captured by Federal troops.

Hurricane Frederic of 1979 severely damaged homes and resorts on Dauphin island, sweeping away the bridge that connected the island with the mainland. A new bridge was completed in 1982 connecting the island with the mainland. Also, a scenic toll vehicle/passenger vessel, the Mobile Bay Ferry, connects Dauphin Island and Fort Morgan. For schedule, call 1-800-634-4027.

Fort Gaines, on the ramparts

Fort Gaines, on the National Register, is open daily 9 a.m. to 5 p.m. Small admission charge. At its entrance may be seen the huge anchor and chain from Admiral Farragut's flagship at the Battle of Mobile Bay, the U.S.S. *Hartford*.

Fort Gaines is named for Edmund Pendleton Gaines, who captured the fugitive Aaron Burr in 1807 near Fort Stoddert in southwest Alabama (see *Fort Stoddert Site*). The fort houses a museum containing Confederate relics.

Indian mounds, although not excavated, may be glimpsed by proceeding on Bienville Drive to Iberville Drive, then turning left on Iberville Drive for three-tenths of a mile.

Leaving the Dauphin Island area, continue north on Alabama 163. Watch for signs to Bellingrath Gardens.

Bellingrath Gardens

Although not a historic site, this former private estate, now open to the public, is famed for its gardens filled with the flowers (including azaleas, roses, chrysanthemums, poinsettias, and camellias), shrubs, and trees of the South.

Located on a bluff overlooking the Isle-aux-Olies River, the gardens are a bird sanctuary. Flamingos, ducks, turkeys, geese, as well as squirrels and deer make their homes here. Bellingrath House, also open for tours, contains old English silver and a large collection of china and rare porcelain. The world's largest public exhibit of porcelain sculptures by Edward Marshall Boehm is displayed in the visitors' lounge.

The gardens are open dawn to dusk every day. Home tours begin at 8 a.m. and end at 5 p.m. There are separate admission charges for the gardens and house.

Leaving Bellingrath Gardens, continue north on Mobile County 59 to Interstate 10 and return to Mobile.

NORTH OF MOBILE

The town of **Prichard** just outside Mobile is Alabama's largest predominantly black town. North of Mobile are many historic sites, although little evidence remains today of the significant events that took place near what is now U.S. Highway 43.

Travelers on this sparsely settled road should be aware, however, that they are passing through an area rich in early Alabama history.

suggestions for background reading

Abernethy, Thomas P. *The Burr Conspiracy.* New York: Oxford University Press, 1954.

Ball, T. H. *A Glance into the Great Southeast, or Clarke County, Alabama, and Its Surroundings from 1540 to 1877.* Grove Hill: 1879. Reprint. [Grove Hill]: Clarke County Historical Society, 1973.

Brantley, William H. *Three Capitals: A Book About the First Three Capitals of Alabama, St. Stephens, Huntsville, and Cahawba.* Boston: Merrymount Press, 1947.

Matte, Jacqueline A. *The History of Washington County: First County in Alabama.* Chatom: Washington County Historical Society, 1982.

Plateau

The last illegal slave ship from Africa to arrive in Alabama was the *Clotilde*, which dropped anchor in Mobile Bay in 1859 on the eve of the Civil War. Its owner was unable to sell most of the slaves in his cargo. When hostilities broke out, many of these Africans settled in what came to be called Africa Town, now Plateau. Africatown Folk Festival is held by their descendants as a commemoration during Black History Month (February).

Ellicott's Line

During the American Revolution, Spanish forces sympathetic to the American cause seized Mobile from England. In the Treaty of Paris of 1783 that ended the American Revolution, Spain received what was then called East and West Florida, including Mobile.

The Ellicott Stone

with the crude skills of his day, were remarkably accurate. The Ellicott Stone stands today only 500 feet south of the true 31° parallel. It is on the National Register.

About one-half mile east of U.S. 43, at Bucks, the stone is one of the few landmarks in Alabama dated before 1800.

The boundary between Spanish West Florida and the Mississippi Territory of the new United States was fixed by a treaty in 1795 as the 31st parallel. Spain and the United States appointed a joint boundary commission to locate the parallel.

Andrew Ellicott, an experienced American surveyor, headed a party of Spanish and American soldiers that hacked its way through the wilderness from Natchez, Mississippi, taking sightings from the stars to determine the boundary line. Ellicott's men notched trees and built small mounds of earth to mark the 31st parallel.

When the party reached an area about twenty miles north of Mobile, Ellicott made twenty-four different observations on the stars before fixing 31° north. He marked the spot with a large sandstone boulder, inscribed on one side in English and on the other in Spanish. Ellicott's calculations, made

Fort Louis de la Mobile

The site of the first French town in the Gulf of Mexico region, built in 1702, was Twenty-Seven-Mile Bluff on the banks of the Mobile River near what is now Mount Vernon. This settlement was named Fort Louis de la Mobile for the king of France, Louis XIV, and for the Maubilian Indians who had a large settlement nearby.

Old Mobile, laid out like a modern city, contained a log fort, a number of Creole houses, a church, and various shops and warehouses. The main occupation of its settlers was trading for furs and skins with the Indians. To this colony in 1704 came the so-called *cassette* girls, twenty-three young women dispatched from France to become

Fort Louis de la Mobile (artist's concept)

wives of settlers, each bringing her small trunk or *cassette*.

Eight years after the founding of Fort Louis, a huge flood rose above these high bluffs and drowned crops for miles around. Bienville decided to move his settlement closer to Port Dauphin on Dauphin Island. In 1711, settlers loaded their household goods on rafts and canoes and moved down the river to the present site of Mobile, leaving their original town to be swallowed up by the forests and swamps.

The site is on the National Register. Intensive archaeological work is being done at the site.

Fort Stoddert Site

Fort Stoddert, a crude frontier fort, was built in 1799 to protect the earliest American settlers who lived along the Tombigbee River and to guard the boundary between the United States and Spain. For a time Fort Stoddert was the southernmost port in the United States. The earliest known newspaper in Alabama, the *Centinel*, first was issued here in 1811. A branch of the old Federal Road passed through the area, bringing many travelers and settlers.

In 1807 a famous fugitive, former vice-president Aaron Burr, was captured near here by the commander of Fort Stoddert, Lieutenant Edmund Pendleton Gaines. Burr had fled to the wilderness following a duel in 1804 in which he had killed Alexander Hamilton. He later was accused of treasonous intent to set up a separate nation.

Alerted by Nicholas Perkins of Wakefield, Gaines arrested Burr near a ferry near the site of the present McIntosh Methodist Church on the road to Spanish West Florida. Burr was held at Fort Stoddert several weeks before being escorted via horseback to trial at Richmond, Virginia. Chief Justice John Marshall, who presided at Burr's trial, ruled that he was not guilty of treason.

At the start of the Creek War of 1813–14, General F. L. Claiborne and 700 men made their headquarters at Fort Stoddert to help defend this area as well as Mobile from possible Indian attack. From 1887 to 1894 some Apache Indians, along with their famous leader Geronimo, were held in an army barracks at Mount Vernon, now the site of Searcy Hospital.

The site of Fort Stoddert, on the National Register, is four miles east of Mount Vernon on the Mobile River. Ask directions locally.

Choctaws

Located between the small towns of Mount Vernon to the south, Citronelle to the west, and McIntosh to the north, live the descendants of Choctaw Indians who remained in this lonely woodland area after most members of their nation had moved west. While Article 14 of the 1830 Treaty of

Dancing Rabbit Creek provided reservations for Choctaws who wanted to stay in their homeland east of the Mississippi River, only sixty-nine were allowed to sign. The others were to be removed in divisions. Promises broken by the government and hardships and diseases encountered during the first migration west discouraged others from making the trek. The majority of Choctaws were left to fend for themselves, landless in Alabama, Mississippi and Louisiana. The federal government continued to attempt to move them west until the Civil War, when all removal activity ceased. The Choctaws who live in Mobile and Washington counties (MOWA) were never removed. About 4,000 individuals continue to live in the same area along the Mobile-Washington county line.

In 1979 the Alabama legislature officially recognized the MOWA Choctaws, as did a U.S. Senate committee in 1991. Governed by a constitution and by-laws, they are currently seeking federal recognition as a tribe by the Bureau of Indian Affairs. Their tribal complex, consisting of offices, school, health clinic, ball field and alligator farm, is the hub for activities on the 300-acre reservation. The tribe celebrates its culture and heritage annually on the third weekend in June. To get to the reservation, follow the sign located on Highway 43 north, at Red Fox Road between Mount Vernon and Calvert. For information, call (334) 829-5500.

Washington County

Alabama's first county was established in 1800 and was named for George Washington. Washington County, then part of the Mississippi Territory, stretched from the 31° parallel on the south to 32° 28' on the north, and from the Pearl River on the west to the Chattahoochee on the east. Although this vast county encompassed 26,000 square miles, it was sparsely populated in 1800. The census of that year revealed only 733 whites and 517 blacks. Some of its original settlers were French people who had moved inland from Mobile before 1763. Others were loyalists during the American Revolution who fled from rebellious colonies to relatively tranquil British West Florida. Some inhabitants were fugitives who sought haven in this wild territory.

Alabama's oldest county has been subdivided through the years. Sixteen Mississippi counties and twenty-nine Alabama counties were formed, in whole or in part, from lands framed by Washington County's original boundaries.

Nanna Hubba Bluff
(Blue Ford Landing)

On the west bank of the Tombigbee River near its confluence with the Alabama River at the Washington-Mobile county line, several sites contain evidence of habitation by prehistoric and historic Indians. Nanna Hubba Bluff is on the National Register.

McIntosh

McIntosh Methodist Church (c. 1860), one of Alabama's few remaining log churches, is a one-story, single-pen structure with gabled wooden shingle roof. It contains its original pews and pulpit and is on the National Register.

Turn east on Washington 35 to **McIntosh Bluff** on the banks of the Tombigbee River. This was the site of the ancient capital of the Tohomee Indians. Later it became the earliest American settlement north of the 31st parallel in present-day Alabama and the first seat of both Washington and Baldwin counties.

Near Sunflower on U.S. 43 north of McIntosh is **Wakefield** (c. 1804), the site where the fugitive Aaron Burr was spotted and also an early county seat. Also at Sunflower alongside U.S. 43 is the **Williams-Turner House** (c. 1871), a simple plantation home.

Two miles north of Sunflower on U.S. 43 is a highway rest area containing a historic marker with the names of many early settlers of the Tombigbee settlements, sometimes known prior to the American Revolution as "the fourteenth colony."

Post Office at Leroy

Two miles north of Wagarville, U.S. 43 crosses historic **Bassett's Creek**, named for Thomas Bassett, who received a land grant from King George III of England in 1775 and who was killed by Indians in 1781 on the creek that bears his name.

At **Leroy** is a **post office** (c. 1896) that, except for the Mooresville post office in north Alabama, is probably the only currently active post office established in Alabama before 1900. It is in its original building and contains the original call windows.

Turn west on Washington County 34 at Leroy to St. Stephens.

Note old **Washington County Courthouse** (c. 1853), now a masonic lodge, and **St. Stephens Methodist Church** (c. 1857).

Old Washington County courthouse

233

Nearby is the site of old **St. Stephens** (c. 1804), capital of the Alabama Territory in 1817. The Spanish erected a fort near Hobuckintopu Bluff on the Tombigbee in 1789 as a trading post with the Indians and for protection of the settlers against the British. When Andrew Ellicott established the 31st parallel, however, the Spanish discovered to their dismay that their fort lay on the American side of the border. In 1799, Spain ceded authority over the fort to the United States.

Although it was located on a river rather than on the Gulf of Mexico, St. Stephens was the southernmost port in the United States until Fort Stoddert was constructed farther downstream. St. Stephens grew in the early 1800s to include a post office, school, land office, and the headquarters of the government's Indian agent, George Strother Gaines. Eventually the Federal Road reached this western outpost.

When Alabama became a territory in 1817, Congress designated St. Stephens as the capital. The Alabama house of representatives, with thirteen members, and senate, with one member, met here. When Alabama became a state in 1819, the capital was moved, first to Huntsville, then to Cahaba. Gradually the site of Alabama's territorial capital was destroyed by the quarrying of limestone. Forest has now reclaimed old St. Stephens.

Take Washington County 28 south from St. Stephens to Alabama 56 west to Chatom.

Chatom

The **Washington County Museum**, in the County Courthouse at Chatom, contains a twenty-one-foot-long dugout canoe found on the banks of the Tombigbee in 1974. The canoe was dated by scientists as having been constructed in the mid-fourteenth century.

From Chatom, take Washington County 31 north to Bladon Springs.

Bladon Springs

Alabama's most important antebellum spa, often called "the Saratoga of the South," was here. The famous Mobile social leader Octavia Walton LeVert wrote in 1847 that Bladon Springs resembled the famed spas of Germany. Guests came by steamboat up the Tombigbee or by carriage to stay at summer cottages or in the 200-room Bladon Springs Hotel. After the war, the spa continued to attract patrons from Mobile, New Orleans, and other cities until more sophisticated resorts lured them away. Abandoned around the time of World War I, the hotel later burned in 1938. **Bladon Springs Methodist Church** (c. 1847), frame with belfry, was built by the master carpenter from New England who built the hotel. **Bladon Springs State Park**, centered around four mineral springs of the old resort, offers daytime picnic facilities.

Leaving Bladon Springs, return to Mobile or join Tour 11 at Demopolis.

Glossary of Architectural Terms *

Architrave: The lowermost section of a classical entablature.

Artifact: A physical product of a culture.

Baluster: A rectangular or turned upright used to support a handrail.

Balustrade: A row of balusters topped by a rail.

Beaux-Arts Classicism: A late nineteenth- and early twentieth-century classical style that features coupled columns and symmetrical facades.

Belvedere: Generally a structure or deck built on a roof to afford a view.

Board and batten: Wood construction in which a vertical strip covers the joint between the boards.

Capital: The top part of a column, post, or pier.

Cast iron: Iron that has been cast in a mold.

Circa (c.): "Approximately"; used in this text to mean a range of ten years.

Classical: Referring to the architecture of ancient Greece or Rome or any of the later styles derived from these sources.

Corbel: A series of short projections built outward from the surface of a wall to support a projecting element such as the eaves of a roof.

Corinthian column: A classical column that is characterized by a capital ornamented with acanthus leaves.

Cornice: The uppermost projecting feature of a wall or entablature.

Creole cottage: A cottage based on an early house type of the Gulf Coast region. The most notable features of this house type are a gable roof and full-width recessed porch on the long side of the structure.

* Courtesy of the Alabama Historical Commission

Cupola: Generally any small structure rising from the main roof of a building; specifically a small dome on a circular or polygonal base.

Dentils: A series of small rectangular blocks used as ornaments beneath the cornice of a classical entablature.

Doric column: A classical column characterized by a fluted shaft and a simple capital consisting of a curved molding beneath a square block.

Dormer window: A window that projects from a roof.

Double portico or **double verandah:** A portico or verandah with two levels or floors.

Eclectic: Composed of elements drawn from various styles.

Entablature: In classical architecture, the horizontal part supported by columns or pilasters and divided into three parts—the architrave, frieze, and cornice.

Facade: Usually the front of a building, but sometimes other sides given special architectural treatment.

Fanlight: A fan-shaped window over a door or window.

Federal: Pertains to buildings constructed during the Federal period (1790–1830). Simple, rectangular structures with delicate woodwork are generally classified as being in this style.

Fresco: A mural painted on fresh plaster.

Frieze: The part of an entablature found between the architrave and cornice.

Froed: Made with a froe, a wedge-shaped tool for splitting wood into shingles.

Georgian: The style of the American colonies on the East Coast until about 1790. Late examples without Federal refinements are called *Georgian retardere*.

Gothic Revival: The mid-nineteenth-century revival of the pointed-arch medieval style. Pointed arches, ornate bargeboards, steep roofs, and battlements are evidence of Gothic influence.

Greek Revival: The early- and mid-nineteenth-century revival of the architecture of ancient Greece. The use of Greek details and symmetrical forms are characteristic of this style. Buildings that feature Roman details or a mixture of Greek and Roman often are called Greek Revival.

Hipped roof: A roof having a sloping plane on each of the four sides.

Ionic column: A classical column characterized by a capital with violutes (a spiral scroll).

Italianate: A term for buildings based on the architectural forms and details of the country villas and Renaissance palaces of Italy. A bracketed cornice is the common feature of the variations that include Renaissance Revival and Italian Villa.

Lancet: A narrow pointed arch or window.

Lights: Window panes.

Lintel: A horizontal beam or member supported at both ends and carrying a weight.

Louver: One of a series of horizontal slats fixed in an opening to allow the flow of air but not sun or rain.

Neoclassical Revival: A turn-of-the-century revival of the Greek and Roman styles.

Palladian window: A three-part window that has an arched central portion flanked by shorter flat-topped windows.

Pediment: In classical architecture, a triangular space formed by the slope of a gabled roof on the top and a horizontal element beneath.

Pen: A log or frame room of a traditional or folk building.

Pier: An upright structure of masonry that serves as a support for beams or arches.

Pilaster: A flat representation of a column attached directly to a wall.

Porte cochere: A shelter for a vehicle outside an entrance doorway.

Raised cottage: A cottage that has its main entrance on the second floor.

Richardsonian Romanesque: A round-arched style based on the work of nineteenth-century architect H. H. Richardson. Its distinguishing features are heavily rusticated stonework and contrasting stone lintels and arches.

Romanesque Revival: A mid-nineteenth-century revival of the round-arched medieval style. Round arches and arcaded corbel tables are indicative of the style.

Saddlebag: A traditional house type, now rare, that has two separate rooms joined by a central chimney.

Shotgun: A traditional folk house consisting of rooms in a straight line.

Sidelight: A narrow light on either side of a door or window.

Stucco: A mixture of portland cement, lime, and sand that is used as a wall finish.

Terra cotta: Fired clay used as ornament or tiles.

Transom: Horizontal glassed area above a window or door.

Turret: A small corbeled tower at the corner of the building.

Tuscan column: A simplified doric column.

Verandah: A long, roofed space supported by posts, columns, or arches that crosses the front or sides of a building.

Victorian: A general term applied to the several asymmetrical, eclectic styles of the late nineteenth century. *Queen Anne*, *Shingle*, *Eastlake*, and *Second Empire* are distinguishable variations.

Wrought iron: Iron decoration that has been worked by hand.

Magnolia Grove, Greensboro (p. 165)

Appendixes

Appendix 1.
House Museums

Mobile Area

Bellingrath House, Theodore, 229
Bragg-Mitchell Mansion (c. 1855), Mobile, 226
Carlen House (Creole Cottage, c. 1842), Mobile, 223
Fort Condé–Charlotte House (Greek Revival Townhouse, c. 1822–24), Mobile, 222
Oakleigh (Greek Revival Raised Cottage, c. 1833), Mobile, 224
Richards-DAR House (Italianate Townhouse, c. 1860), Mobile, 223

Black Belt and Wiregrass

Bluff Hall (Federal and Greek Revival, c. 1832), Demopolis, 159
Fendall Hall (Italianate, c. 1854), Eufaula,193
Gaineswood (Greek Revival, 1821–50s), Demopolis, 158
Grey Columns (Greek Revival, c. 1857), Tuskegee, 176
Hart House (Greek Revival, c. 1850), Eufaula, 194
Kirkwood (Greek Revival, c. 1857–60), Eutaw, open by appointment, 164
Magnolia Grove (Greek Revival, c. 1840), Greensboro, 165
The Oaks (Brick Cottage, c. 1899), Tuskegee, 177
Shorter Mansion (Neoclassical Revival, c. 1906), Eufaula, 193
Spring Villa (Gothic Revival, c. 1850), Opelika, 181
Sturdivant Hall (Greek Revival, c. 1853), Selma, 154
Wellborn House (Greek Revival, c. 1837), Eufaula, 194

Montgomery

First White House of the Confederacy (Italianate Townhouse, c. 1835), 133

Governor's Mansion (Neoclassical Revival, c. 1907), 135

Murphy House (Greek Revival, c. 1851), 131

Rice-Semple-Haardt House (Greek Revival with Victorian Gothic, c. 1855), 133

Scott and Zelda Fitzgerald Museum, 135–36

Teague House (Greek Revival, c. 1848), 135

Old Alabama Town, Montgomery, 130

Davis-Cook House (Greek Revival and Italianate, c. 1857), 130

DeWolf-Cooper Cottage (Gothic Revival Clapboard Cottage, c. 1856), 130

Dogtrot House (Antebellum), 130

Lucas Tavern (Stagecoach Tavern, early 1800s), 130

Ordeman-Shaw House (Italianate Townhouse, c. 1848), 130

Mayor Reese House (Greek Revival Cottage, c. mid-1850s), 130

Central Alabama

Arlington (Greek Revival, c. 1822), Birmingham, 75

Battle-Friedman House (Greek Revival, c. 1835), Tuscaloosa, 99

Buena Vista Mansion (Greek Revival, c. 1821), Prattville, 61

Faith Manor (Georgian, 1833), near Talladega, open by appointment, 116

Gorgas House (Low Country Raised Cottage, c. 1829), Tuscaloosa, 96

King House (Federal, c. 1823), Montevallo, open on special occasions, 104

Looney House (Two-Story Double Dogtrot, c. 1820), near Ashville, 41

McAdory House (One-Story Dogtrot, c. 1840), Bessemer, 92

McGuire-Strickland House (Wood-frame raised cottage, c. 1820), Tuscaloosa, 98

Mildred Warner House (Log Cabin to Georgian, 1822), Tuscaloosa, 99

Old Tavern (Stagecoach Inn, c. 1827), Tuscaloosa, 98

Owen House (Two-Story Dogtrot, c. 1833), Bessemer, 92

Sadler House (Two-Story Dogtrot, c. 1817), near Bessemer, 92

Tanglewood (Small Plantation Home, 1859), near Havana, open by appointment, 102

North Alabama

Cullman House (Swiss Victorian, replica), Cullman, 57

Daniel Murphree Cabin (Single-Pen Log Cabin, 1816), 52

Donnell House (Greek Revival, 1840s), Athens, 55

Ivy Green, birthplace of Helen Keller (Two-Story Frame Cottage, c. 1820), Tuscumbia, 33

W. C. Handy House (Log Cabin, c. 1845), Florence, 29

Wheeler House (Two-Story Frame House, c. 1880), Wheeler, open by arrangement, 24

Weeden House (Federal Townhouse, c. 1819), Huntsville, 12

Appendix 2. Museums

General

Alabama Department of Archives and History, Montgomery, 133

Native American

Birmingham Museum of Art, Birmingham, 74

Fort Toulouse, Wetumpka, 185

Hall of History Museum, Bessemer, 92

Horseshoe Bend National Military Park, Dadeville, 113

Indian Mound Museum, Florence, 27

Moundville Archaeological Park, Moundville, 102

Old Dallas County Courthouse (Smitherman Building), Selma, 153

Russell Cave National Monument, near Bridgeport, 5

West Point Dam, near Opelika, 183
Wheeler Dam, Courtland, 25
Wilson Dam, Florence–Muscle Shoals, 27

Pioneer Life

Burritt Museum, Huntsville, 14
Hall of History Museum, Bessemer, 92
Noccalula Falls Park, Gadsden, 42
Pike Pioneer Museum, Troy, 198
Pope's Tavern, Florence, 27
Tannehill Historical State Park, near Birmingham, 93
West-Mize Museum, Clayton, 191

Public Figures

Alabama Jazz Hall of Fame, Birmingham, 71
Alabama Military Hall of Honor, Marion, 168
Alabama Newspaper Hall of Fame, Auburn, 179
Alabama Sports Hall of Fame, Birmingham, 75
Alabama Women's Hall of Fame, Marion, 168
Civil Rights Memorial, Montgomery, 134
George C. and Lurleen B. Wallace Museum (Old Barbour County High School), Clio, 192
George Washington Carver Museum, Tuskegee, 176
Helen Keller Museum, Tuscumbia, 115
Hugo Black Room, Tuscaloosa, 98
W. C. Handy Museum, Florence, 29

Medicine

Doctor's Office, Old Alabama Town, Montgomery, 130
Dr. J. C. Francis Medical Museum, Jacksonville, 124
Reynolds Historical Library, Birmingham, 76

Appendix 3.
Covered Bridges

Blount County: **Easley**, 51; **Horton Mill**, 52; **Swann**, 51
Calhoun County: **Coldwater**, 125

Cullman County: **Clarkson** (Legg), 56
Etowah County: **Gilliland**, 42
Lee County: **Salem-Shotwell**, 182
Madison County: **Cambron**, 15
Sumter County: **Alamuchee**, 161
Talladega County: **Kymulga**, 109; **Waldo**, 117

Appendix 4.
Historical Festivals

Blessing of the Fleet (last Sunday in July), Bayou La Batre, 227
Candlelight Christmas (December), Oakleigh, in Mobile, 224
Christmas-on-the River (first Saturday in December), Demopolis, 158
Fall Festival (fall) Looney House, near Ashville, 41
First Monday (first Sunday and Monday of each month), Scottsboro, 7
Kentuck Festival (October), Northport, 100
Mardi Gras (Tuesday before Ash Wednesday), Mobile, 217
MOWA Band of Choctaw Indians Pow Wow (June), Mount Vernon, 232
Riverfront Market and Tale Tellin' Festival (October), Selma, 155
Sorghum Festival (late September or early October), Waldo, near Talladega, 116
Thanksgiving Day Homecoming of the Poarch Band of Creeks (Thanksgiving Day), Poarch, near Atmore, 65

Appendix 5.
Historical Dramatic Productions

Alabama Shakespeare Festival (year-round), Montgomery, 136
The Miracle Worker, Helen Keller and Anne Sullivan (June–July), Tuscumbia, 34
Looney's Tavern (year-round), Winston County, 86

Appendix 6.
Home Tours
and Pilgrimages

Pilgrimages are offered in Alabama almost year-round. For more information, call 1-800-ALABAMA and request a Calendar of Events.

March

Mobile
Selma

April

Athens
Eufaula
Huntsville
Opelika
Talladega
Tuscaloosa

May

Cullman
Monroeville
Mooresville
Prattville
Union Springs

June

Montgomery

October

Eutaw

Noccalula Falls, Gadsden (p. 42)

Credits

The authors express their appreciation to the following for photographs used in this book:

Aaron White Photography, Monroeville
Abbeville Chamber of Commerce
Alabama Bureau of Tourism and Travel
Alabama Mountain Lakes Tourist Association, Mooresville
Alabama State Docks, Mobile
Auburn/Opelika Convention and Visitors Bureau
Auburn University
Birmingham Museum of Art
Birmingham Public Library-Archives
Bragg-Mitchell Mansion, Mobile
Decatur Convention & Visitors Bureau
DeKalb County Tourist Association, Fort Payne
Dothan Area Convention & Visitors Bureau
Eufaula/Barbour County Tourism Council
Huntsville/Madison County Convention & Visitors Bureau
Ivy Green, Tuscumbia
Landmarks Foundation of Montgomery
Mobile Area Chamber of Commerce
Mobile City Museum
Montgomery Chamber of Commerce Convention & Visitor Development
Natural Bridge of Alabama
Theodore B. Pearson, Leroy
Perry County Historical and Preservation Society
Tuskegee University
Trinity Episcopal Church, Demopolis
The University of Alabama, Hoole Special Collections Library
University of Montevallo
University of South Alabama

Ivy Green, Tuscumbia (p. 34)

Index

Alison, Samuel, 145
American Missionary Association, 114
Anniston, 120
Anniston Museum of Natural History, 122
Apache, 231
Appalachian Trail, 120
Arbacoochee, 118, 119
Archaeology: Bottle Creek Indian Mounds, 204; Indian Mound Museum, Florence, 27; LaGrange Bluff Shelter, 35; Limestone Creek Indian Mound, 64; Moundville, 101; Quad Site, 21; Russell Cave, 5; Stanfield-Worley Bluff Shelter, 31
Arcola, 158
Ardmore, 54
Arlington, 75
Army Aviation Hall of Fame, 197
Arrington, Richard, Jr., 69
Ashland, 118
Ashville, 41
Athens, 19, 27, 54
Athens College, 55
Atlatl, 5
Atmore, 65
Auburn, 178, 183
Auburn Depot, 179
Auburn University, 178
Auburn University at Montgomery, 136
Auburn University Chapel, 178
Auburn University Historic District, 178
Auburn University Peanut Experiment Station, 196
Autauga County: Buena Vista, 60; Prattville, 60
Ave Maria Grotto, 58
Avondale Mills, 111

Bagby, Arthur Pendleton, 99, 147
Baker, James, 109
Baldwin, Joseph G., 162
Baldwin County, 203, 207, 233; Daphne, 208; Fairhope, 210; Fort Morgan, 212; Montrose, 208; Point Clear, 211; Spanish Fort, 207; Stockton, 203; Tensaw, 204; Weeks Bay National Estuarine Research Reserve, 203
Bankhead, John H., Jr., 85

Bankhead, John H., Sr., 84
Bankhead, Tallulah, 84
Bankhead, William B., 84
Bankhead National Forest, 85, 86, 87; Ranger Station, 86
Barbour County, 193; Clayton, 190; Clio, 189; Eufaula, 192; Eufaula National Wildlife Refuge, 194
Barker Slave quarters, 151
Barton Academy, 221
Bartram, William, 61, 178, 183, 203
Bartram Trail, 61, 178
Bassett, Thomas, 233
Bassett's Creek, 233
Battelle, 40, 44
Battery Hill, 4
Battle, Alfred, 99
Battle of Day's Gap, 57
Battle of Hog's Mountain, 57
Battle of Horseshoe Bend, 107, 128
Battle of Maubila, 95, 170
Battle of Mobile Bay, 211, 213, 214, 217, 220, 228
Battle of Selma, 152, 155
Battle of Talladega, 114
Battle of the Holy Ground, 62, 63, 171
Battleship Park, 219
Bayou La Batre, 227
Bazares, Guido de las, 219
Beasley, Daniel, 205
Beaty, Robert, 55
Bee, Bernard E., 168
Bee Branch, 87
Beechwood, 144
Belle Mina, 12, 18
Belle Mina village, 18
Bellefonte, 3
Bellefonte Nuclear Plant, 6
Bellingrath Gardens, 228
Bell Tavern, 150
Benedictine monks, 58
Bernard, Simone, 212
Bessemer, 92
Bessemer, Henry, 92
Bethel Associate Reformed Presbyterian Church, 146
Bevill State Community College, 84

248

256

Murphy, Edgar Gardner, 131, 182
Muscle Shoals, 2, 19, 26, 32
Museums: Aero Replica Fighter, Guntersville, 8; Alabama Department of Archives and History, 133; Alabama Mining, Dora, 83; Alabama Museum of Natural History, 97; Aliceville Museum and Cultural Arts Center, 162; Anniston Museum of Natural History, 122; Birmingham Museum of Art, 74; Blount County Memorial, 52; Burritt, Huntsville, 14; Carver, Tuskegee, 176; Columbia Jailhouse, 195; Confederate Memorial, 60; Discovery Place, Birmingham, 78; Dr. J. C. Francis Medical, 124; Edith Nourse Rogers, 123; Exploreum Museum of Discovery, Mobile, 226; Fort Gaines, 228; Fort Morgan, 214; George C. Wallace, Clio, 192; Hall of History, Bessemer, 92; Horseshoe Bend National Military Park Museum, 113; Huntsville Museum of Art, 14; Indian Mound, Florence, 27; Iron and Steel, Tannehill State Park, 94; Kentuck, Northport, 100; L. & N. Depot, Selma, 153; Magnolia Grove, Greensboro, 165; Military Police Corps, 123; Mobile Museum of Art, 226; Monroe County Courthouse, 63; Montgomery Museum of Fine Arts, 137; Moundville Archaeological, 102; Museum Gallery Complex, Mobile, 225; Museum of the City of Mobile, 221; National Voting Rights, Selma, 153; North Alabama Railroad, 32; Old Dallas County Courthouse, Selma, 153; State Bank Building, Decatur, 20; Ordeman-Shaw House, Montgomery, 130; Paul W. Bryant, Tuscaloosa, 98; Phoenix Fire, Mobile, 222; Pike Pioneer, 198; Red Mountain, 77; Scott and Zelda Fitzgerald, Montgomery, 135; Scottsboro/Jackson County Heritage Center, 7; Stevenson Depot, 6; Susan K. Vaughn, Florence, 28; U.S. Army Aviation, Fort Rucker, 197; W. C. Handy House, Florence, 29; Washington County, 234; West-Mize, Clayton, 191. *See also* Appendix 1: House Museums, 239–40

Muskogees, 106

Nanipacana, 63
Nanna Hubba Bluff, 232
NASA's Marshall Space Flight Center, 13, 16, 54
Natchez Trace, 30
National Air and Space Museum, 16
National Fertilizer Development Center, 32
National forests: Bankhead, 85, 86; Talladega, 119; Tuskegee, 178
National Geographic Society, 5
National Historic Landmark: Fort Morgan, 214
National Voting Rights Museum, 153
Natural Bridge, 85
Newbern, 166
Newbern Baptist, 166
Newbern Presbyterian Church, 166
New South, 40, 68, 120, 182
Noble, John Ward, 122
Noble, Samuel, 46
Noble family, 120
Noccalula Falls, 42
Normal, 15
North Alabama Railroad Museum, 32
Northport, 100
Northport District, 100
North River Historic Area, 94
Nuclear plants, 55, 195; Bellefonte, 3, 6; Brown's Ferry, 3

Oak Grove Methodist Church, 62
Oak Hill, 146
Oak Hill Cemetery, 74
Oakleigh, 224
Oakleigh Garden Historic District, 224
Octagon House, 191
Odum Scout Trail, 117
Ohio River, 3
Old Alabama Town, 130
Old Brick Church, Mooresville, 18
Old Brick Presbyterian Church, Leighton, 35
Old Cahawba Archaeological Interpretive Park, 150
Old Center Church, 94
Old Dallas County Courthouse, 153
Old Decatur Historic District, 19

Waldo Historic District, 116
Waldseemüller, Martin, 208
Walker College, 84
Walker County, 83; Jasper, 84
Wallace, George C., 129, 189, 190, 191, 193
Wallace, Lurleen, 191, 193
Wallsboro, 184
Ward, George B., 80
War of 1812, 62, 205, 228
Warrior Coal Field, 84
Warrior River, 84
Washington, Booker T., 114, 144, 174
Washington, George, 107, 109, 232
Washington County, 140, 178, 232; Chatom, 234; Leroy, 233; McIntosh, 233; Nanna Hubba Bluff, 232; St. Stephens, 234
Washington County Courthouse, 234
Washington County Museum, 234
Water Avenue Historic District, 153
Waugh, 130
Wawmanona Indian Mound, 27
Weatherford, William (Red Eagle), 171, 185, 205; grave, 206
Weeden, Howard, 12, 15
Weeden House, 12
Weeks Bay National Estuarine Research Reserve, 203
Weiss Lake, 46
Wesleyan Hall, 29
Western of Alabama Railroad, 180
West-Mize Museum, 191
West Point Dam, 183
West Point Lake, 183
Wetumpka, 112, 184–85
Wheeler, 24
Wheeler, Joseph, 24, 25
Wheeler Dam, 25
Wheeler National Wildlife Refuge, 21
Wheeler State Park, 26, 27
White, Asa, 163
White, Martha Todd, 154

White, Stanford, 4
White Plains, 124
Whitfield, Nathan Bryan, 158
Widow's Creek steam plant, 3
Wilcox County, 141; Camden, 146; Furman, 145; Gee's Bend, 148; Oak Hill, 146
Wilcox Female Institute, 146, 147
William Bartram Arboretum, 185
Wills Town, 42
Wilson, Augusta Evans, 227
Wilson, James H., 27, 103, 104, 129, 135, 152, 184
Wilson Dam, 3, 25, 27, 32
Wilson Lake, 26
Wilson's raiders, 171
Wind Clan, 207
Wind Creek State Park, 113
Winston, William Overton, 44
Winston County, 85; Bankhead National Forest, 86; Double Springs, 86; Natural Bridge, 85
Winston Place, 44
Winterboro, 110
Wiregrass, 188
Wisdom, John, 48
Women's Army Corps Center, 123
Woods, Alva, 96
Woodstock Iron Company, 120
Woodward, Thomas S., 62
World War I, 8, 26, 213
World War II, 69, 213, 218
Wright, Frank Lloyd, 29
Wright, I. W., 109
Wright, Wilbur, 129
Wynton M. Blount Cultural Park, 136

Yancey, William Lowndes, 128, 130, 135, 185
Yellow fever, 150, 223, 224
Yonge, William Penn, 182
Young, Andrew, 167

About the Authors

Virginia Van der Veer Hamilton is Professor of History Emerita, The University of Alabama at Birmingham, where she served also as head of the department. She received bachelor's and master's degrees from Birmingham-Southern College and a doctorate from The University of Alabama. She is a widely published expert on the history of Alabama. Her publications include *Hugo Black: The Alabama Years* (1972), *Alabama: A History* (1977), *Hugo Black and the Bill of Rights* (editor, 1978), *Your Alabama* (1980), *The Story of Alabama* (1980), *Lister Hill: Statesman from the South* (1987), and *Looking for Clark Gable and Other 20th-Century Pursuits: Collected Writings* (1996).

Jacqueline A. Matte began teaching in 1972 at Mountain Brook Junior High School. She taught Alabama history at the ninth grade level for 23 years and served as department head from 1979 to 1991. Her degrees include Bachelor of Science in Business Administration from Samford University; Master of Arts in History, Master of Arts in Secondary Education, and Certificate of Advanced Studies in Education from The University of Alabama at Birmingham. She wrote the teacher's guide and workbook for *The Story of Alabama* by Virginia Van der Veer Hamilton. Her publications include *The History of Washington County: The First County in Alabama* (1982). In 1991 she received a Teacher-Scholar Award from the National Endowment for the Humanities for a year of independent study. Her study that year of southeastern Indians was published in *Social Education*, the National Council for the Social Studies professional journal.